MICHAEL JACKSON

MICHAEL JACKSON THE ICON

Jos Borsboom

Copyright © 2011 by Jos Borsboom

All rights reserved under Title 17, U.S. Code, International and Pan-American Copyright Conventions. No part of this work, whether in printed or digital form, may be reproduced or transmitted in any form or by any means, electronic or mechanical, including (but not limited to) photocopying, scanning, recording, live performance or broadcast, or duplication by any information storage or retrieval system without prior written permission from the author(s) and publisher(s), except for the inclusion of brief quotations with attribution in a review or report. To request permissions, please visit the michael-jackson.mobi website.

Front cover and back cover designed by Jos Borsboom. Photography by Jos Borsboom, Copyright © 2011. One or more fonts used in the cover and/or interior designs are specifically licensed by and customized for the exclusive use of the publisher, and may not be reproduced elsewhere in any form without prior written permission.

This is a work of opinion. All characters, events, products, corporations, institutions, and/or entities of any kind in this book are depicted strictly as a personal recollection of the author. There is no intend to establish events, dates, times or actions of individuals as a basis of fact. The author makes no claim that may be construed an allegation of guilt or innocence, or liability of any kind. The author accepts no responsibility for conclusions reached by readers of this book. If you do not agree with these terms in advance, you may return this book to the author for a full refund. For more information about the author, please visit the website: josborsboom.com.

- Second Edition -

ISBN 978-1-4475-1692-7

This book is dedicated to Michael Jackson's
fans, friends and family.

*"Our spotlight was always
on Michael Jackson."*

Michael Jackson:

*"I'm never pleased with anything,
I'm a perfectionist, it's part of who I am."*

Michael Jackson:

"Thank you all my friends and fans for your love and support. You've given me so much, it allowed me to take some of that love and pass it on to those people whose problems in this world need and deserve our help. A perfect example is the recent U.N. announcement that 1 to 3 million lives could be saved if Third World children were given a vitamin A pill three times a year. Cost per child is just six cents, that's all. So we must join together in healing the world so we can share this beautiful planet in joy and love. I love you very much."

Preface

Michael's tragic death shocked the world for weeks. The King of Pop tried to hide his addiction to painkillers for years. A doctor, who visited his trashed hotel suite in The Mirage in Las Vegas said: "It is Elvis all over again." His sudden death still remains a mystery. Michael told close friends: "If I don't tour, they'll kill me." His slender but exhausted body finally collapsed after grueling rehearsals for his comeback shows. The pop star said he was being pushed by people into a corner and he had an irrational fear that he would die or be killed if he didn't perform in London. Michael kept saying that he had to do the concerts because he owed too much money. Tarak Ben Ammar claimed his friend Michael had previously been a victim of 'charlatan doctors'. At the time of his death Michael Jackson was almost bankrupt and living on friends' generosity and bank handouts. Michael's sister La Toya announced: "I am going to get down to the bottom of this. I am not going to stop until I find out who is responsible. Why did they keep the family away? It's not about money. I want justice for Michael. I won't rest until I find out what, and who, killed my brother."

Table of Contents

INTRODUCTION..1

A STAR WAS BORN...............................7

THE SUCCESS...21

THE FAME..71

KIDS & ALLEGATIONS.......................101

THIS IS IT...165

THE MEMORIAL..................................257

ACKNOWLEDGMENTS.......................365

ABOUT THE AUTHOR.........................367

Introduction

The King of Pop made his debut as a singer as a young child and became arguably one of the most popular recording artists and entertainer of all time. Michael Jackson was lauded, in recent years more often ridiculed and spent what should have been the best years of his life in the spotlights, beloved by millions of fans but feeling haunted and confused. Michael Jackson had millions of fans who adored him but he couldn't enjoy the stardom.

Michael's tragic and sudden death on June 25, 2009, shocked the world for weeks. Michael was planning the biggest concert tour the world had ever seen. In this first book about his passing, the author describes in detail how the mysterious death of Michael Jackson could be explained.

Michael's death came less than a month before the start of a scheduled series of so-called comeback concerts. Michael was scheduled to perform 50 sold-out concerts at London's O2 Arena, from July 13 to March 6, 2010. For the first time ever family members and relatives of Michael spoke up, friends shared their private information and so many others expressed their grief and sadness.

Michael Jackson will be forever immortalized for his global fame, his chart-topping success, his fluid groundbreaking multi-dance moves, his outstanding stage presence, his world-famous and record breaking videos, *and* his devotion to help others. Beyond the many lies, the tragedies, the controversies and the reams of his documented eccentricities, Michael Jackson was a multi-talented entertainer. He broke down many musical and cultural barriers his entire life. His 1982 album *Thriller* smashed records. It was number 1 for 37 weeks and at its peak sold more then a million copies a week worldwide. Michael Jackson turned into a global singing sensation destined to win 13 Grammies and sell over 750 million records. He was an ultimate fashion icon, known for his leather (military) jackets, his gloves, his white socks and black fedora. Michael build mountains of barriers around himself but broke as much -unbreakable- barriers for thousands of others. He was a towering figure in entertainment and a role model for many children.

Michael Jackson was something special. He was shocked and surprised by all the attention in his life. He often wondered why *he* was born to be *the* Michael Jackson. Michael's death came unexpected for many people, others had feared his death for years. These people have seen the famous pop star becoming more and more self-destructive. Among them myself. Michael couldn't find any help but many people were available to help him.

Throughout the years I must have received more then a dozen emails from Uri Geller. Uri became a friend like no other. I admire him, respect him and feel loved by him. Uri Geller is a wonderful and caring person. Throughout all these years we talked over the telephone or send each other emails about mainly one subject, Michael Jackson. We both were worried and we both had the same fear. Uri wanted to take care of Michael in a positive way. After a while Uri felt he made a terrible "mistake". As from what I understood of Uri Geller, Michael never saw the material of the film *Living With Michael Jackson* before it was broadcast. Uri told me over the telephone: "He didn't care."

What started as a good idea -by me- in 2002, "making a film about the more then 10 years that Michael was a well praised and acknowledged humanitarian," became a disaster and Michael's fear. Instead of calling Michael, Uri Geller called journalist Martin Bashir. Michael Jackson became a broken man.

Michael raised millions for charity, charmed world leaders and made noble contributions to society. He became, the last months of his life, a physical and financial wreck and had the fragile demeanor of a man several years older. He had on a few occasions been confined to a wheelchair and was unable to work for weeks. The last months of his life, he was almost certainly incapable of singing and dancing and said he was forced into the fatal London concert run.

After writing this book, and after reading statements, announcements, interviews, and all kind of articles, it was easy to understand that Michael has been praised, but also has been well ignored and misunderstood. It is heartbreaking and sad to believe that even Michael could have been 'saved' or 'rescued'. It is unbelievable that no other reporter or journalist ever knocked on Michael's door with a similar idea. I believe that is still a shame.

In 2006, I talked with Lieutenant-Colonel Alida Bosshardt, fondly referred to as "The Major", about Michael and his struggles. In The Netherlands, Alida Bosshardt was one of its most beloved citizens and its most famous Salvationist. She spent a lifetime serving the poor and needy in in the name of GOD, and was lauded for her care of Jewish children during the Nazi occupation of the Netherlands during World War II. She is also remembered for her work to help prostitutes in Amsterdam's red light district.

"Major Bosshardt" died on June 25, 2007, at 14.42 p.m., almost exactly 2 years before Michael at the age of 94. She believed Michael became the victim of *bad* press. She told me, she "would always call up a journalist after every interview." She would tell the reporter if he did a good job or not. When she didn't like the article, she "would ask for another interview." Alida Bosshardt knew the press could destroy a career. "Michael did wonderful things," she told me. "Look at how he dances, look what he established in his life. Hear his music! It is sad to see Michael is so misunderstood by the press." About the documentary of Michael in 2003, she said: "I believe it was a great idea of Michael to put the boy on television. It is difficult to know exactly what happened but in my opinion Michael should have not been too shy, but instead he should have talked to the press."

When I started this book, I have been asked by a young man, age 15, if I could find out if Michael really touched 'boys' in an inappropriate manner. He said he never believed that story. The question came a few days after Michael's death and shocked me. I believed still many questions regarding Michael Jackson had never been answered, well documented or shown to millions of fans out there. I hope this book will answer a few questions.

I have been asked if the book would contain information about the dangers of drugs. Dr. Klein's stories are worthwhile reading. Other people were interested in facts instead of gossips and lies. This book shows a part of Michael's life. It is important to know that Michael has never been convicted of any crime. He was, all his life, a free man. To answer the question of the young man, who never could see a life performance of the world's biggest pop star, I can only say this: "Read the book and decide for yourself."

For me it was always clear that Michael 'never ever' behaved in any inappropriate manner towards children. At least no hard evidence has been found, ever. Michael simply couldn't take the risk to get in trouble, and he wasn't interested in children in that kind of sense. He simply wasn't interested in sex, that much at all. When it came to his own sexuality, Michael remained shy, and did not like to talk about it in public.

This book is written out of respect for Michael Jackson. I admired him as much as probably anybody else did. Our King of Pop Michael Jackson was a perfectionist and was never satisfied with his success. Michael Jackson will never be forgotten. Our memories of him will always stay with us, through his music, his films and his videos. Michael will always remain in our hearts.

May we learn from his life and his tragic death. May we have learned from Michael how to communicate with each other, regardless of his or her background, race or status. May this book be a lesson for it.

Jos Borsboom

Chapter 1
A Star Was Born

Michael Joseph Jackson was born on August 29, 1958. He died in the early afternoon of June 25, 2009, in Los Angeles, after a cardiac arrest. The world was in shock and millions of fans around the world mourned. His sister claimed Michael was murdered and also Michael's father believed it was foul play. "Michael was murdered," La Toya, 53, told London's Daily Mail, "And we don't think just one person was involved. Rather, it was a conspiracy of people. I feel it was all about money. Michael was worth well over a billion in music publishing assets and somebody killed him for that. He was worth more dead than alive." Joe Jackson suspected his son's death may not have been an accident at all. "I just couldn't believe what was happening to Michael. I do believe it was foul play. I do believe that. Yes," he told ABC. La Toya said that Michael was convinced that if he didn't perform in London he would die soon. Michael had told his family, 'They will kill me', but no one ever really understood who he was talking about. "He seemed paranoid."

June, 25, 2009, was a day, most people will never forget. It was the day the world's most famous personality died suddenly and unexpected. Some people were so shocked, they couldn't stop crying for days. Others were said to be "as shocked as on 9/11". According to Britain's The Sun, Michael desperately needed the estimated $85 million (£52 million) he was set to make from the shows he planned in London in July, 2009. "He had plunged into debt despite being worth $570 million (£347 million) in his heyday. At the time of his death he was almost bankrupt, living on friends' generosity and bank handouts," the magazine stated. The Sun: "Michael hoped the *This Is It* gigs would revive his flagging career and boost his tarnished image." The Jackson family's lawyer Brian Oxman blamed Michael's inner circle for pushing him too hard. "This was something I feared and something which I warned about. I suspect that the death of Michael Jackson is only the beginning of the legal battles over not only his property but also his children," he said hours after Michael's death.

Michael was beloved all around the world. Millions of people admired Michael Jackson in one way or another. We should not forget Michael was given conscious sedation per his own request for many years. His problems with drugs started already more then 20 years ago. Michael was using a drug, Propofol, to help him fall asleep. Propofol (Diprivan) is extremely addictive and lights up in the addiction center in the same place as alcohol, morphine and nicotine. Michael Jackson was an addict for years. Michael drunk alcohol and stuffed himself with prescription drugs. According to an article in The Sun, written by Nick Parker and Steve Kennedy, a source close to Michael said: "There were serious concerns for his mental health near the end, so much so that he was seeing a psychiatrist. He said he was being pushed into a corner and had an irrational fear that he would die or be killed if he didn't perform in London. He kept saying that he had to do the concerts because he owed too much money. But all the time he was saying these things, his body was starting to shut down as he became more and more dependent on drugs."

The declining revenues from worldwide record sales had seriously affected his income the last years. The veteran TV reporter Diane Dimond told reporters: "He's mortgaged everything he owns, and his wealth was always exaggerated anyway. Every penny of income is needed to service income payments on loans." Michael's remaining assets were more or less his own back catalog. Michael's typical day involved rising at lunchtime or later and knocking several back painkillers from different pillboxes. He watched Disney films and other cartoons and was drinking bottle after bottle of expensive wine. A source said: "The man has been flat-broke for most of the past decade."

The last years Michael almost didn't want to eat. Doctors were prescribing him medications such as Demerol, Propofol (Diprivan), Diazepam (Valium), Tamsulosin (Flomax), Lorazepam (Ativan), Temazepam (Restoril), Clonazepam (Klonopin), Trazodone (Desyrl), Tizanidine (Zanaflex), Propofol (Diprivan), Lidocaine (Xylocaine), Midazolam (Versed) and Flumanezil (Anexate). Michael's family members and news reports have documented that Michael had used the aliases of Jack London, Mike Jackson, Mick Jackson, Frank Tyson, and Mic Jackson to get prescription drugs. Michael would also had prescriptions written in the name of members of his entourage. An unknown female caller provided the names, Omar Arnold, Fernand Diaz, Peter Madonie and even Josephine Baker as names Michael would use when seeing his dear friend and doctor Dr. Klein. Michael started to use his first prescription drugs after a serious accident in 1984.

He told people he had so much pain, that he became addicted to painkillers.

Michael Jackson was not only an American icon, a musician, singer, songwriter, producer, dancer, choreographer, actor, fashion-icon, and certainly one of the most commercially successful entertainers of all time. He was not only a prominent figure in popular culture for four decades with estimated record sales of over 750 million records worldwide. Michael Jackson was also a praised humanitarian and a respected philanthropist. Throughout his career he donated millions of dollars to various charities and he raised money by his own Heal the World Foundation. Michael Jackson was probably the most misunderstood celebrity. He was always surprised and disturbed by paparazzi attention. Michael believed in Jehovah and genuinely wanted to help people. There were reports of Michael ringing doorbells as part of his Jehovah's Witness faith. Michael Jackson really cared about people and he didn't want anything back. When he joined USA for Africa in 1985, "a major moment in world music that showed we can change the world" and co-wrote the song *We Are the World,* he was already a world famous pop star. The idea of creating a group of people, to raise money was something Michael Jackson loved. Michael tried to change the world in his way and did all he could do to *Make the World a Better Place, For You And For Me, And the Entire Human Race.*

In many ways Michael has changed the world forever. Michael became one of a handful of artists to be inducted twice into the *Rock and Roll Hall of Fame.* The Guinness Book of World Records recognized Michael as the *Most Successful Entertainer of All Time* and he received the American Music Award's *Artist of the Century Award.*

Michael, the seventh child of the Jackson family always liked to perform. He performed in front of classmates during a Christmas recital at the age of five. Michael and his brother Marlon joined the Jackson Brothers in 1964. In 1966, when Michael was only 8, he joined his brothers in the band his father put together. He started singing lead with brother Jermaine. It was obvious Michael had a great voice and he loved to dance. Michael made his debut on the professional music scene in 1968 as a real member of The Jackson 5. Thanks to their squeaky-clean image, the Jackson 5 became teen idols, unusual for a group of African-American youngsters. Michael's face appeared already on the covers of teen magazines and the band even became the subject of an animated Saturday-morning TV show, another first for an African-American group. Michael told at an early age: "Whatever I sing, that is what I really mean, when I am singing a song. I don't sing if I don't mean it."

The Jackson 5 recorded several songs for the local record label Steeltown in 1967, including *Big Boy*. Rolling Stone magazine described Michael as "a prodigy" with "overwhelming musical gifts." They noticed that Michael quickly emerged as the main draw and lead singer. The Jackson 5 signed with Motown Records in 1968. A chart record was set when its first four singles of the new album, *I Want You Back*, *ABC*, *The Love You Save*, and *I'll Be There* peaked soon at number 1 on the Billboard Hot 100. In the beginning of the Jackson 5, Motown's public relations team claimed that Michael was nine years old, to make him appear more accessible and more cute.

In 1961 Diana Ross auditioned for and signed eventually with Motown Records. Motown CEO Berry Gordy made Diana the lead singer of the group The Supremes. Berry believed the group could cross over to the pop charts with Diana's vocal quality. Diana was the focal point of the group and began by the summer of 1969 with the recording of her first solo tracks. In November of the same year, three years after the first rumors started, Billboard magazine confirmed Ross's exit from the group. Television specials TCB (1968) and G.I.T. on Broadway (1969) were putting Diana Ross in the spotlight. Motown released Diana's second album *Everything Is Everything* in 1971 followed by *Surrender,* which included the pop hit, *Remember Me*. In the same year Diana hosted her first solo TV special, Diana!, featuring guest appearances by Danny Thomas, The Jackson 5 and Bill Cosby. It was Diana Ross who introduced the newest act from Motown, The Jackson 5, to national audiences. Diana Ross became a close friend of Michael Jackson. She co-starred years later with Michael in the 1978 film version of the Broadway musical, The Wiz, a remake of The Wizard of Oz. Michael publicly stated in the '80s he had a crush on Diana and told people many times he wanted to marry her. But Diana was like a mom for Michael. She learned him how to stay out of trouble and she helped him with his homework when they were together backstage. Diana was an example for Michael. He thought she was the ultimate female pop singer.

Diana Ross became immensely popular and has recorded more then 60 studio albums. Since the beginning of her career she has sold more than 100 million records. Billboard magazine named Diana in 1976 the *Female Entertainer of the Century*. The Guinness Book Of World Records declared Diana Ross in 1993 the *Most Successful Female Music Artist* in history with a total of eighteen American number 1 singles: twelve as lead singer of The Supremes and six as a solo artist. Diana was however later equaled by Mariah Carey. Diana was the first female solo artist to score six number-ones. She is in the top five among solo female artists with the most number 1s on the Hot 100. Diana is one of the few recording artists to have two stars on the Hollywood Walk of Fame.

Michael started a solo career in 1971. His voice descended between 1971 and 1975 from boy soprano to androgynous high tenor. He said about growing up and his father's wish to be as perfect as possible as a singer: "I wish I could just understand my father. He was very strict, very hard. Just his look would scare me."

Starting in 1972, Michael released 4 solo studio albums with Motown. Among these albums were *Got to Be There* and *Ben*, including the successful singles *Got to Be There* (number 4 in 1971), *Rockin' Robin* (number 2, 1972) a remake of Bobby Day, and *Ben* (number 1, 1972). *Rockin' Robin* was originally written by Bobby Day and it was his only hit single. *Rockin' Robin* and *Over And Over* was a monster double-sided hit, the A-side reaching number 1 R&B, for 3 weeks, and number 2 Billboard Pop Hot 100 in late summer 1958, and the flipside making it to number 41 Hot 100 and a number 1 R&B "follow-along". These were his only R&B charters under his own name. The song *Rockin' Robin* was covered in 1964 by The Hollies on their first album, and it would be revived by teenaged Michael Jackson in 1972 as a single again. It was his second single release on Motown. Michael's solo albums were released as part of the Jackson 5 franchise. The same year Michael took his own version to number 2 on the U.S. pop singles chart. The group had enviable afros, a little boy with a beautiful voice and slick choreography.

Music & Me, Michael's third solo album was released on April 13, 1973. Singles from the album were in the 70s, *With a Child's Heart*, *Morning*

Glow, Music and Me, and in the early 80s, *Happy* (released in the United Kingdom only). The producer was Hal Davis, Michael's favorite producer at that time. Michael was heavily influenced by label mates Stevie Wonder and Marvin Gaye and wanted to include his own songs on the album, but he wasn't allowed to. The promotion on this album however was limited, mainly because Michael was on a world tour with his brothers as a member of The Jackson 5. It was at that time, in early 1973, that Michael adopted a 'vocal hiccup'. It can be seen in full force in the *Shake Your Body (Down to the Ground)* promotional video. The purpose of it was to help promote Michael's emotions, sadness, fear or excitement. The cover, *With a Child's Heart*, from Stevie Wonder was released as a single in the United States, where it reached number 14 on the Billboard R&B Singles chart and number 50 on the Billboard Pop Singles chart. The singles *Music and Me* and *Morning Glow* were released as singles in the United Kingdom, and *Too Young*, was only released as a single in Italy. The song *Happy* was released in Australia and *Doggin' Around* was a limited-release single , only in the Netherlands. It took Michael two years to work on a follow-up album which was *Forever, Michael*. *Music and Me*, the album released in the beginning of 1973 is often confused with a compilation album of the same name by Motown Records released in the early 90's. This compilation contained all the music from the album, with the exception of *Doggin' Around*. The complication included songs from previous albums, *Got to Be There*, *Ben*, and *Forever, Michael*. Singles from the album were *Rockin' Robin*, *Johnny Raven*, *Shoo-Be-Doo-Be-Doo-Da-Day*, *Happy*, *Too Young*, *Up Again*, *With a Child's Heart*, *Ain't No Sunshine*, *Euphoria*, *Morning Glow*, *Music and Me*, *All The Things You*

Are (Listed as *All The Things You Are, Are Mine*), *Cinderella Stay Awhile* and *We've Got Forever.*

The Jackson Brothers scored several top 40 hits, including the top 5 disco single *Dancing Machine* and the top 20 hit *I Am Love*. The group had great succes in the many years with Motown, but the strict refusal to allow creative control or input by the Jacksons, did band members complaining after a while. They decided to leave Motown in 1975. Their last album was *Moving Violation*. In the summer of 1975, Michael and his brothers signed a new contract with CBS Records. The group joined in June the Philadelphia International Records division, later Epic Records, and renaming themselves The Jacksons. The Jacksons made two good albums, *The Jacksons* and *Going Places,* but these albums were not big sellers.

Throughout 1974 and 1975, Michael recorded his fourth album: *Forever, Michael* and released within 3 months after it's album release on January 16, 1975, three singles, *We're Almost There*, *Just a Little Bit of You*, and *One Day in Your Life*. The album was released by the Motown label in 1975, and was produced by Edward Holland, Jr., Brian Holland and Hal Davis. It was reissued in 2009 as part of the 3-disc compilation *Hello World: The Motown Solo Collection*. It was Michael's final album released with Motown before he and his brothers left for CBS Records in 1976. Michael, only sixteen-year-old, adopted a smooth soul sound that he would continue to develop on his records for Sony's Epic Records. Michael returned with his hits to the top 40.

Michael returned to the group for an album *Destiny*, and accompanying tour. Finally the group was given "creative freedom". Nobody was surprised that the Jacksons were able to create such memorable dance grooves. It's the first

Jacksons album which marked the true ability to work together as a group. The *Destiny* tour was the hottest tour of the year, despite complaints about sales practices.

The album was one of the best of The Jacksons. The album included top songs like *Blame It On The Boogie, Push Me Away, Things I Do For You, Shake Your Body (Down To The Ground), That's What You Get (For Being Polite)*. Even though, according to some people, the previous albums had been disappointing, the album *Destiny* changed for good the general perception that The Jacksons couldn't land a hit album. *Blame It On The Boogie* established the return of The Jacksons to the top of the charts.

The group was able to create dreamy ballads, up-tempo songs, funky disco and pulsating dance tracks. The album's lead single, *Blame It On The Boogie*, was written by an English writer/performer, named Mick Jackson. He was an English writer and performer who had his own version of the song in the United Kingdom charts at the same time as the Jacksons. Jacksons' version was the more successful and is consequently the best known rendition of the song. Some songs from the album like *Blame It On The Boogie* and *Shake Your Body (Down To The Ground)* are considered Jacksons classics. This album is one step towards the maturity of the Jacksons' music. The album, filled with their trademark 'smooth harmonies', and Michael's distinctive vocals, hit number 11 on the billboard album charts (number 3 R&B) and was certified platinum. The albums *Destiny* and the following *Triumph* are still extremely good records, but were highly underrated. The Jacksons' *Triumph* (1980) sold a million copies and prompted a $5.5 million (£3.3 million) grossing tour. Already at this early stage, the brothers were exploring video. The short film that accompanied *Triumph's* title track was an imaginative, technically advanced film. Michael became more popular than the group as the 1980s began. When Michael turned 21 in August 1979, he fired his father Joseph as his manager and replaced him with John Branca.

Michael's first 'famous' album *Off the Wall* was his fifth studio album and was recorded from December 4, 1978 until June 3, 1979. The album, the first produced by Michael and Quincy Jones was released on August 10, 1979 with Epic Records. Michael and Quincy had become friends while working on the film The Wiz. *Off the Wall* included disco-pop, soul, funk, soft rock, jazz, pop ballads and was a commercial success, selling 20 million copies worldwide. It is certified for 7× Multi-Platinum in the United States. Michael became the first solo artist to have four singles from the same album peak inside the top 10 of the Billboard Hot 100. With *Off the Wall,* Michael won his first Grammy Award since the early 1970s. Songs on the album were: *Don't Stop 'Til You Get Enough, Rock with You, Workin' Day and Night, Get on the Floor, Off the Wall, Girlfriend* (written by Paul McCartney), *She's Out of My Life, I Can't Help It, It's the Falling in Love* (with Patti Austin) and *Burn This Disco Out* (by Temperton who also wrote *Thriller*). On October 16, 2001, a special edition reissue of *Off the Wall* was released by Sony Records. With the original album *Off the Wall,* Michael became the first solo artist to release 4 Top 10 hits from a single album. *Don't Stop Till You Get Enough* (number 1, 1979), *Rock with You* (number 1, 1979), *Off the Wall* (number 10, 1980), and *She's Out of My Life* (number 10, 1980).

Allmusic described Michael as a "blindingly gifted vocalist." Rolling Stone compared Michael's voice to the "breathless, dreamy stutter" voice of

Stevie Wonder. Rolling Stone wrote: "Jackson's feathery-timbered tenor is extraordinarily beautiful. It slides smoothly into a startling falsetto that's used very daringly." John Randall Taraborrelli, writer, journalist and biographer stated, "Fans and industry peers alike were left with their mouths agape when *Off the Wall* was issued to the public. Fans proclaimed that they hadn't heard him sing with such joy and abandon since the early Jackson 5 days."

Michael's father Joseph began in 1973 a secret affair with a young woman. She was 20 years younger than he was and the couple had a child in secret. When Joseph told his family in 1980 of the affair and child, Michael, felt so betrayed that he fell out with Joseph. Michael became deeply unhappy and said about it, "Even at home, I'm lonely. I sit in my room sometimes and cry. It's so hard to make friends. I sometimes walk around the neighborhood at night, just hoping to find someone to talk to. But I just end up coming home."

Michael changed the music business in 1980 by securing the highest royalty rate in the music industry: 37 percent of wholesale album profit. Michael's attorney John Branca noted that Michael would get approximately $2 (£1,2) for every album sold. According to Rolling Stone: "In 1982 Jackson and Jones collaborated on a storytelling record of Steven Spielberg's E.T.. The album, which was hastily withdrawn from the market due to a legal dispute, is now a prime Jackson collectible." That year, Diana Ross, one of Jackson's mentors, scored a number 10 hit with the Michael-written *Muscles*, named after one of his pet snakes. Michael had also begun an alliance with Paul McCartney, who had written *Girlfriend*, from *Off the Wall*. The two reconvened to co-write the duet *The Girl Is Mine*, the first duet off of *Thriller*.

Chapter 2
The Success

Thriller was Michael's sixth studio album. The album was released on November 30, 1982 by Epic Records. *Thriller* explored different styles of music genres like funk, disco, soul, soft rock, R&B, and pop. Recording sessions took place between April and November 1982 and many friends of Michael came to visit while he was recording the album. At Westlake Recording Studios in Los Angeles, California, Michael and Quincy had a production budget of $750,000 (£459,000). Four tracks were written by Michael. *The Girl is Mine* was the first single to be released. With the release of the second single *Billie Jean*, the album topped the charts all around the globe. In just over a year, *Thriller* became the best-selling album of all time. *Thriller* was the first album to have seven Billboard Hot 100 top 10 singles, including *Billie Jean*, *Beat It*, and *Wanna Be Startin' Somethin'*. At one point the album was selling a million copies a week worldwide. Michael also made record-breaking profits from *The Making of Michael Jackson's Thriller*, a documentary produced by John Landis, the director of the clip and Michael. *Thriller* remains the best-selling album of all time, with four others, *Off the Wall* (1979), *Bad* (1987), *Dangerous* (1991), and *HIStory* (1995), among the best selling.

Thriller has sold more then 110 million copies worldwide. *Thriller* won a record-breaking eight Grammy Awards at the Grammys in 1984. Rolling Stone's opinion about Michael's voice on *Thriller*: "Jackson was singing in a 'fully adult voice' that was tinged by 'sadness'." A special edition issue of *Thriller* was released in 2001, which contains additional audio interviews, a demo recording and the song *Someone In the Dark*. This song was a Grammy-winning track from the E.T. the Extra-Terrestrial storybook.

When the album was completed, both Quincy and Michael were unhappy with the result. They then remixed every song, spending a week on each. Quincy at first didn't like *Billie Jean*, but Michael liked the song a lot. Quincy didn't believe the song was strong enough for the album. Quincy Jones said he and Michael had just two months to record a follow-up album after *Off the Wall*. "I told Michael that we needed a black 'rock and roll' tune, a black *My Sharona*, and a begging tune for the album," Quincy said. "He came back with *Beat It* (Michael wrote it and even played the drums) and Rod (Temperton) came back with *The Lady in My Life*. Rod also brought in *Thriller* and Michael sang his heart out on it," he added.

Quincy is still amazed by the success of *Thriller*. He said; "At one point during the session the right speaker burst into flames, which none of us had ever seen before. How's that for a sign? All we were trying to do, was finishing the record. We had only three weeks. We had three studios going, and we just did it. We had no time to think or look back at the project, it had to be finished," Quincy said. *Thriller* was again reissued as *Thriller 25* in 2008, containing re-mixes that feature contemporary artists, a previously unreleased song and a DVD. The song *Thriller* was first called: *Starlight Love*. Quincy sang: "Starlight, Star Light

Love..." He continued: "We both weren't happy with that and we were going through [the song]. Michael sang the demo and we had fun with that, because we remixed it and used Pro Tools or something, to make it more out of tune. But *Thriller* was better, it had everything in it. This visual, it had a lot of room for a lot of drama."

On Rolling Stone magazine's 500 Greatest Albums of All Time list in 2003, *Thriller* ranked number 20. It was also listed by the National Association of Recording Merchandisers at number 3 in its Definitive 200 Albums of All Time. The Library of Congress to the National Recording Registry preserved it as it was deemed "culturally significant". The spoken portion on the single *Thriller* was written in a taxi on the way to the studio. Rod Temperton had brought in actor Vincent Price, who completed his part in just two takes. Sound effects such as creaking door, thunder, feet walking on wooden planks, winds and howling dogs made the record sound like a movie-track. The *Thriller* video was Michael's *spooky* one. Quincy said: "It was like a feature film. It went all over the world. No one had ever seen something like that before." Many years later Quincy said about Michael's music: "His music is still dominant. It's astounding."

Michael wanted a great director for the movie and asked John Landis to direct his movie. John moved to London after he worked for many years in the United States. He worked as an uncredited co-writer for the film The Spy Who Loved Me and returned to the United States. He made his feature debut as a director with *Schlock*. In 1977, John directed Kentucky Fried Movie a movie inspired by the satirical sketch comedy of shows like Monty Python, Free the Army, and Saturday Night Live. But he had bigger plans. In 1981, John wrote and directed An American

Werewolf in London, a project he wanted to do for many years. When John and his family lived in London they were approached by Michael. He called up in the middle of the night and asked John if he wanted to be the director of his new video. John heard Michael's new album but he did not know about *Thriller*. Michael told John that he loved the movie An American Werewolf in London and said he wanted to appear as a monster in his new video. John said, "OK, let's do it." He introduced Michael to Rick Baker. When Michael saw the work of *Monster Maker,* Rick Baker, he was impressed. Michael: "When I first walked in Rick's studio, it was like a museum of horror. I mean all these faces. I think he is an incredible artist." The movie *Thriller* changed the concept of music videos and has won many awards, including the *Video Vanguard Award* for *The Greatest Video in the History of the World.*

Michael performed live in March 1983, on the *Motown 25: Yesterday, Today, Forever* television special, with The Jackson 5. He also performed his own hit *Billie Jean*, wearing a distinctive sequined glove. That evening he debuted the -now- famous moonwalk, his signature dance move. The moonwalk, which former Soul Train dancer and Shalamar member, Jeffrey Daniel had taught him 3 years before was seen by 47 million viewers. The New York Times reporter Anna Kisselgoff said of the performance: "How does he do it? As a technician, he is a great illusionist, a genuine mime. His ability to keep one leg straight as he glides while the other bends and seems to walk requires perfect timing."

About that evening Michael wrote later in his book Moonwalk: "Right after Motown 25 my family read a lot of stuff in the press about my being "the new Sinatra" and as "exciting as Elvis" – that kind of thing. It was very nice to hear, but I knew the press could be so fickle. One week they love you, and the next week they act like you're rubbish. Later I gave the glittery black jacket I wore on Motown 25 to Sammy Davis as a present. He said he was going to do a takeoff of me on stage, and I said, "Here, you want to wear this when you do it?" He was so happy. I love Sammy. He's such a fine man and a real showman. One of the best. I had been wearing a single glove for years before Thriller. I felt that one glove was cool. Wearing two gloves seemed so ordinary, but a single glove was different and was definitely a look. But I've long believed that thinking too much about your look is one of the biggest mistakes you can make, because an artist should let his style evolve naturally, spontaneously. You can't think about these things; you have to feel your way into them."

Michael was doing promotion for his album. The Pepsi commercial accident, filmed in L.A.'s Shrine Auditorium on January 27, 1984, caused permanent disfigurement to Michael's scalp. In a detailed video, shown 25 years after the accident, the Pepsi commercial rehearsals appeared to move smoothly. The idea of the commercial was that Michael was going to emerge from a burst of flames in the back while his brothers were at the head of the stage. After Michael descended the stairs and began performing with his brothers the pyrotechnics exploded as planned. Things went horribly wrong on the sixth take of Michael's grand entrance before a life audience. A spark landed on Michael's head but he descended the stairs as normal. The fireworks erupted a few seconds too early, igniting Michael's head in flames. "Michael continued dancing for a few seconds because at first he was unaware of the fire," sources said. "The singer cries out for help from his brother Tito and then, in trying to put out the fire by pulling his jacket up over his head, falls to the floor. People with jackets and fire extinguishers descend on him, someone yells for a medic, and pandemonium breaks out among the youthful fans, many of whom are certain that Pepsi has somehow killed their idol. In fact the burns are minor. But in the first days after the accident, Pepsi and BBDO fear that the incident will force them to cancel the Jackson commercials." On his head appeared a bald red spot and Michael was immediately rushed to the nearest hospital. John Koten, Staff Reporter of The Wall Street Journal wrote on February 28, 1984, "One incident in particular causes a few chuckles at Coke. A group of Pepsi executives hear screams coming from the men's room and rush inside. There they find a panic-stricken Michael Jackson, who has just dropped his silver glove in the toilet. There is a flourish of activity as the glove is fished out, washed, blow-dried and returned to its owner." Further in the article we read about the editing of the commercial: "The process is complicated even more because lawyers associated with both Pepsi and the Jacksons have confiscated all but 27 feet of film from the last take, the one that the fire occurred. (No suits have been filed over the incident, however)."

Michael was prescribed several medications to relieve the second and third-degree burns on his scalp and body. The pills helped Michael tolerate multiple surgeries on the scorched spot on his head. Director of the commercial Bob Giraldi told Michael to delay his descent down the stairs in order to create a more dramatic effect. Michael wrote in his book Moonwalk: "[Giraldi] came up to me and said, 'Michael, you're going down too early. We want to see you up there, up on the stairs. When the lights come on, we want to reveal that you're there, so wait'." The fire safety inspector Don Donester said the decision went against the fire safety rules. Pepsi gave Michael a $1.5 million (£918,000) settlement. He donated the money to create the Michael Jackson Burn Center for Children at the Brotman Memorial Hospital in Culver City, California. A hyperbolic burn chamber was donated by Michael, and when he entered the chamber just to see how it felt he was photographed inside the chamber. He smiled to the photographer but did not know that the photo sparked rumors that, "Michael Jackson slept in an oxygen tank".

On May 14, 1984, at a ceremony in the White House, President Reagan presented Michael an award for special efforts. Michael was invited and honored for his participation in a national ad campaign against drunk driving. Ronald Reagan told the people that Michael was awarded for his support of charities that helped people overcome alcohol and drug abuse. Michael was standing next to the President's wife and first lady Nancy Reagan and waived to the audience.

The idea for *We Are the World*, a benefit single for African famine relief came from activist Harry Belafonte. Harry Belafonte contacted his fellow Ken Kragen who was an entertainment manager, and asked for singers Kenny Rogers and Lionel Richie. Harry Belafonte wanted to have a song recorded by the biggest artists in the music industry. He also wanted to have the proceeds donated to a new non-profit organization called United Support of Artists for Africa (USA for Africa). Stevie Wonder and Quincy Jones were asked and decided to work on the project. Lionel and Michael were asked to write the song. It was Lionel who decided to give Michael a call. Michael said immediately yes and offered to help writing the lyrics. Michael teamed with Lionel to write the fundraising song and decided to work in Michael's house for several months. In January 1985, just before the first recordings started, they finished the writing. The last recording session for the song which was produced by Quincy Jones and Michael Omartian was held on January 28, 1985 and the anthem was released, March 7, 1985, as the only single from the album *We Are the World*. The song entered the Billboard Hot 100 on March 23, 1985 at number 21 and won a *Grammy* for *Song of the Year* and *Record of the Year*. The single topped music charts throughout the world. It became the fastest-selling American pop single in history and was the first ever single to be certified multi-platinum. The song was honored numerous times, including three *Grammy Awards*, one *American Music Award*, a *People's Choice Award* and received a 4x certification by the Recording Industry Association of America. The anthem raised over $63 million (£38.5 million) for humanitarian aid in Africa and the United States and has sold over 20 million units. La Toya, Michael's sister, was at Michael's house when Michael and Lionel worked on the song. She revealed years later that Lionel only wrote a few lines for the track. She said that Michael wrote 99 percent of the lyrics, "but he's never felt it necessary to say that." Michael said about the writing: "I love working quickly. I went ahead without even Lionel knowing, I couldn't wait. I went in and came out the same night with the song completed—drums, piano, strings, and words to the chorus." The single became a number 1 hit in the United States on the R&B singles chart, the Hot Adult Contemporary Tracks chart and the Billboard Hot 100. *We Are the World* reached number 1 in Australia, Belgium, France, Italy, The Netherlands, New Zealand, Norway, South Africa, Sweden, Switzerland and the United Kingdom. The song had become the biggest single of the 1980s and was cited as the biggest selling single in both

United States and pop music history. Five of Michael's siblings, Jackie, La Toya, Randy, Marlon and Tito were in the studio to record the song. Michael's other family members were not invited and did not attend the recording. Prince, who was invited and would have had a part in which he and Michael sang to each other, did not attend the recording session either.

In the mid-1980s, Time described Michael Jackson as "the hottest single phenomenon since Elvis Presley." Time also marked Michael's influence as, "Star of records, radio, rock video. A one-man rescue team for the music business. A songwriter who sets the beat for a decade. A dancer with the fanciest feet on the street. A singer who cuts across all boundaries of taste and style and color too." Michael became a worldwide phenomenon, and his impact really began to be felt. The New York Times wrote that, "in the world of pop music, there is Michael Jackson and there is everybody else." He also became known as the man who liked to dance while recording his vocals in the studio. He said about it: "Consciousness expresses itself through creation. This world we live in is the dance of the creator. Dancers come and go in the twinkling of an eye but the dance lives on. On many occasion when I'm dancing, I've felt touched by something sacred. In those moments, I've felt my spirit soar and become one with everything that exists."

In 1985 Michael heard that ATV Music, a music publishing company owning thousands of music copyrights, including the Northern Songs catalog that contained the majority of the Lennon/McCartney compositions recorded by The Beatles, was put up for sale. Years before, Michael had learned from Paul McCartney that he made approximately $40 million (£24.4 million) a year from other people's songs. Paul told Michael he was not interested in buying the company because it was too expensive. Michael showed his interest in the catalog, beat the rest of the competition in negotiations that lasted 10 months, and purchased the catalog for $47.5 million (£29 million) Michael's personal life generated controversy. He changed his appearance with changes to the shape of his nose and to the color of his skin. Michael was diagnosed with Vitiligo and Lupus. The Vitiligo partially lightened his skin, and the Lupus was in remission. Both illnesses made him sensitive to sunlight and he decided to use creams to further bleach his skin tone. The structure of his face had also changed. Michael had undergone multiple nasal surgeries, a forehead lift, a cheekbone surgery and had a cleft put in his chin. From 1985 to 1990, Michael donated $500,000 (£306,000) to the United Negro College Fund, and all of the profits from his single *Man in the Mirror* went to charity.

Nearly five years after his previous studio album, *Thriller*, Michael launched in 1987 the album *Bad*. The song *Bad*, was the second of five Billboard Hot 100 number 1 hit singles from the album *Bad*. About the idea of *Bad*, Michael wrote in his book Moonwalk: "*Bad* is a song about the street. It's about this kid from a bad neighborhood who gets to go away to a private school. He comes back to the old neighborhood when he's on a break from school and the kids from the neighborhood start giving him trouble. He sings, 'I'm bad, you're bad, who's bad, who's the best?' He's saying when you're strong and good, then you're bad." Michael got the idea from a true story. He said: "This kid who was from the ghetto and he tried to make something of his life. He left all his friends behind and when he came back, his friends became so jealous of him they killed him. In the *Bad* music video, I don't die of course. But it was a true story.

He was a black kid like me, it's a sad story." The full 18-minute-long version of the video for *Bad* first appeared on the DVD version of *Video Greatest Hits - HIStory* in 2001 and was directed by Martin Scorsese.

The album which was again produced by Michael and Quincy Jones went on to sell over 30 million copies worldwide, and shipped eight million units in the United States alone. Michael adopted a street-tough image for the album's cover photo and was seen in the video as a guy who was wearing black leather jackets, black leather pants and black leather boots. It is the first, and currently only, album ever to feature five Billboard Hot 100 number 1 singles. It won two *Grammys*, one for *Best Music Video - Short Form* for *Leave Me Alone* and one for *Best Engineered Album - Non Classical*. It was also ranked number 202 in Rolling Stone magazine's 500 *Greatest Albums of All Time*. For the album Michael wrote sixty songs and recorded thirty. He wanted to use them all on a three-disc set but Quincy cut these down to a ten-track single LP. The single *Bad* was originally intended as a duet between Michael and singer Prince. But Prince turned down the project telling Quincy that the song was so great, it "would be a hit without (him) on it." The song *Bad* was often the closing act for concerts on the *Bad World Tour*, and less often in *Dangerous World Tour* concerts. Michael was so excited about his *Bad* tour, that he could hardly sleep. Quincy Jones said about his album *Bad*: "He sold 25 million copies of *Bad*. That's a lot of records. But Michael wanted to sell 100 million. In his bathroom he had written '100 million' on the mirror in lipstick. I said, 'Michael, nobody's going to convince me that 25 million is a bomb'. He was inventive and experimental. He'd try anything."

Michael also tried to fight his insomnia by dancing in special prepared hotel rooms for hours, his publicist Rob Goldstone said. The King of Pop had a dance floor installed in his hotel rooms during the *Bad* tour in the late '80s. Rob said: "At the end of a show it took him eight to ten hours to wind down. So he'd dance the entire time." He also told people Michael became hooked on sedatives and to relax he was reading kids' books. From July 1987 until October 1989, Michael released 10 singles from the album, *I Just Can't Stop Loving You*, *Bad*, *The Way You Make Me Feel*, *Man in the Mirror*, *Dirty Diana*, *Another Part of Me*, *Smooth Criminal*, *Leave Me Alone*, *Liberian Girl*, and *Speed Demon*. *Bad* became the first of Michael's albums to debut at number 1 on the Billboard 200 where it remained for the next six consecutive weeks. Rolling Stone Magazine believed that "even without a recording like *Billie Jean*, *Bad* was still a better record than *Thriller*."

Michael became the subject of increasingly sensational reports. When Michael bought a chimpanzee called Bubbles from a laboratory and brought him on his tour, reports claimed that this was a classic example of increasing detachment from reality. In reality Michael wanted to help the chimp. Michael also brought his snake Muscles along with him to his recording studio. Michael was upset about the negative press reports and told a reporter: "Why not just tell people I'm an alien from Mars. Tell them I eat live chickens and do a voodoo dance at midnight. They'll believe anything you say, because you're a reporter. But if I, Michael Jackson, were to say, "I'm an alien from Mars and I eat live chickens and do a voodoo dance at midnight," people would say, "Oh, man, that Michael Jackson is nuts. He's cracked up. You can't believe a damn word that comes out of his mouth."

In March 1988, Michael purchased land (2,700-acre) near Santa Ynez, California, about 100 Miles Northwest of Los Angeles. In the spring of 1988, Michael moved out of his home in Encino which he had shared with his parents for many years. He wanted to build his own ranch on Neverland at a cost of almost $20 million (£12.2 million). Michael hired a security staff of 40 people and started to install a movie theatre, Ferris wheels, and a menagerie on the property. He celebrated the purchase of his new house and threw a house warming bash.

Michael picked up two *Soul Train Music Awards* for *Bad* (Best Album, Male), and *The Way You Make Me Feel* (Best Single, Male). Neither he or his sister Janet, awarded for *Control* (Best Video), attended the award presentation.

On April 20, 1988, after four years in the works, *Moonwalk* was finally finished and released by DoubleDay and was edited by Jacqueline Onassis. The first manuscript of *Moonwalk* was put together by Robert Hillburn. But the publisher, DoubleDay refused it because it was lacking in juicy details. Stephen Davis was hired to help Michael put the book together. Michael drastically edited the manuscript and finally decided to write it himself with help from Shaye Ayreheart. *Moonwalk* had sold, within a few months after it was published, over 450,000 copies in fourteen countries.

Michael wrote: "One of the reasons that I haven't given interviews over the years is because I've been saving what I have to say for my book. Love, Michael." Michael described in the book his start with the Jackson 5, winning talent contests and singing with Motown. He described feeling proud and happy when *Thriller* became the biggest selling record in history. He wrote about what impact it made to his career, to win a record breaking eight *Grammy Awards*. Michael admitted having cosmetic surgery on his nose twice and having a cleft added to his chin. Other claims he had -extensive plastic surgery- were untrue.

He denied the charges that he had his skin lighted either by a skin peel, acid or other possible things. He described himself as being one of the loneliest people in the world and revealed details about his cold relationship with his father. He described being beaten after messing up at after school rehearsals. In People Magazine his father Joe denied the beatings Michael received and referred to them as "little spankings". But Marlon, Michael's brother, agreed they did get hit and a lot. Marlon: "My father is a person who loves to control your destiny. By him being your father, he feels he has the right to do that." Joe believed Michael made a mistake going solo. He felt, "that if the family performed together, the shows would be stronger then with just one member of the family involved."

Michael was characterized as "an unstoppable juggernaut, possessed of all the tools to dominate the charts seemingly at will: an instantly identifiable voice, eye-popping dance moves, stunning musical versatility and loads of sheer star power." Michael expressed his feelings about his dancing: "Silence is real dance. My dance is all motion without, all silence within. As much as I love to make music, it's the unheard music that never dies. And silence is my real dance, though it never moves."

After *Moonwalk* was published, the program Friday Night Videos was made up entirely of Michael Jackson's videos. The show included now classic videos for *Beat It*, the first video ever shown on Friday Night Videos, *Billie Jean* and the fourteen minute long video for *Thriller*.

Dirty Diana was a hit song by Michael, released in April 1988. It was the fifth and last number 1 hit on the Billboard Hot 100 from his 1987 album *Bad*. Billy Idol's former guitarist Steve Stevens was hired to back him on the track. Its video starts with a low guitar note and was shot in early 1988 in front of a live audience. Quincy Jones confirmed the song was not about Princess Diana but about groupies. Michael confirmed this also during a much-publicized interview with Barbara Walters. Michael, in the video, is ripping his shirt, ad-libbing, and he grabs his crotch. Michael and Princess Diana first met at his 1988 Wembley Stadium concert. But when she heard that Michael planned to drop the song *Dirty Diana* from his set out of respect to her, she asked him: "Please keep it in."

>Oh No . . .
>Oh No . . .
>Oh No . . .
>
>You'll Never Make Me Stay
>So Take Your Weight Off Of Me
>I Know Your Every Move
>So Won't You Just Let Me Be
>I've Been Here Times Before
>But I Was Too Blind To See
>That You Seduce Every Man
>This Time You Won't Seduce Me
>
>She's Saying That's Ok
>...

(© Lyrics by Michael Jackson *Dirty Diana* (1988), excerpt provided as citation.)

She informed him: "The song is actually one of my personal favorites." The concerts in the United Kingdom, were the most anticipated of the whole tour. Tickets for the initial 5 dates in July went on sale in January. More then 1.5 million people wanted to see the shows, enough to sell-out the 72,000 capacity venue 20 times. On July 16, Princess Diana and Prince Charles met Michael prior to his concert in which he donated $450,000 (£274,000) to the Prince's Trust and the Great Ormond Street Hospital.

Reynaud Jones and Robert Smith, both from Gary, Indiana, and Clifford Rubin, a man from Chigago, filed a $400 million (£245 million) lawsuit against Michael Jackson. They claimed Michael Jackson and Lionel Richie had stolen *We Are The World* from them. They also claimed that Michael had stolen *Thriller* from them. But *Thriller* was written by Rod Temperton.

On September 7, 1988, MTV presented its *Music Video Awards*. Michael had two nominations for Best Choreography for *The Way You Make Me Feel* and *Bad*. The MTV *Video Vanguard Award*, presented to an artist for career achievements in video, was given to Michael by Peter Gabriel. The award was presented to Michael live via satellite from London. Peter joked: "I sincerely hope this award will rescue this artist from obscurity and set him on the road to fame and fortune and it gives me great pleasure to give the *Video Vanguard Award* to Michael Jackson." Michael accepted the award by saying: "Thank You. Thank you very much." Seventeen years after Michael's first cartoon series aired, he agreed to lent his song *Beat It* to be used in another series of cartoons. The Flinstone Kids aired in September 1988. In the film Barney, Fred, Wilma and Betty work hard to earn enough money for tickets to a Michael Jackstone concert. They make it to the concert and see Michael Jackstone singing: "They told the girl. Why don't you step over here. You wanna be cool. Take a look in here. They wanna do drugs. And they're words are really clear. So beat it! You don't need it! (Say no!) You don't need friends. Doing things that are wrong. There's lots of kids like you. Who are cool and strong. I might be kinda tough. But you can move along. So Beat it! And say it ain't fair. Don't mean it. Don't need it. Just say no to drugs. Defeat it!"

Michael graced the covers of over hundreds magazines and was immense popular. Motown was aware of the *Michaelmania* and released through Silver Eagle Records, a three record set of old Motown hits of Michael and his brothers of the Jackson 5. Some never before released material was included with the hits from the Jackson 5 with Motown. The person who was in the television advertisement was probably not Michael Jackson. It is believed that a picture of the Michael Jackson impersonator is used as the album's cover too.

In 1988, Michael produced and launched his first feature film called *Michael Jackson: Moonwalker*. Instead of featuring one continuous narrative, the movie which contained more special effects then a Star Trek movie, is a collection of short films about Michael and his music. The project which was shot before, during and after the release of his *Bad* album, was paid by Michael and produced by Michael, his manager Frank Di Leo, Dennis E. Jones, Jerry Kramer and Will Vinton. The film, an idea of Michael, consists of a collage of short stories, music videos and concert footage. It was released theatrically in Europe and South America, but Warner Brothers canceled plans for a theatrical release in the United States for Christmas 1988. Just as Michael's *Bad World Tour* finished, Moonwalker was released on Home Video in the United States and Canada. By April 17, 1989, the video sold more than 800,000 copies in the United States. A live performance of *Man in the Mirror* acts as the opening music to the film and features a montage of clips of children from Africa including historical figures as John Lennon, Martin Luther King and Mahatma Gandhi. The 93 minutes movie was released on December 26, 1988 in the United Kingdom and on January 10, 1989 in the United States. "Moonwalker seems unsure of what it was supposed to be. At the center of the movie is the Smooth Criminal segment, a musical/dramatic piece full of dancing, schmaltzy kids, sci-fi effects and blazing machine guns," Variety reported. The film was directed by Colin Chilver. It has been released lately on both video and DVD. Moonwalker was also developed into an arcade video game by Sega with the help of Michael.

In January 1989, the *Say Yes To A Youngsters Future* program honored Michael in recognition of his efforts to encourage children to natural sciences and awarded him with the *National Urban Coalition Artist/Humanitarian Of The Year Award*. In March 1989, Michael received, at the Universal Amphitheatre in Universal City, California, the *Black Radio Special Award* for his humanitarian efforts.

Also in 1989, Michael announced a second set of commercials for Pepsi, and received an estimated $10-15 million, (£6 million-£9 million) the highest fee ever paid for a commercial endorsement. While announcing the deal with Pepsi, Michael received an award recognizing the record breaking fee. He accepted the award saying: "This is a great honor. Thank you Mr. Enrico, Pepsi associates, ladies and gentlemen. Thank you." Pepsi's investment in Michael paid off. Pepsi sales rose two hundred percent in Japan when Michael was on tour. During the tour in the United States sales rose three hundred percent. Michael became the first Westerner to appear in a television ad in the Soviet Union. Soviet officials asked specifically for Michael's commercials. Approximately 150 million people in the Soviet Union saw the Pepsi commercials. As part of the deal with Pepsi, they sponsored the *Bad World Tour*.

The Pepsi ads were the most popularly watched commercials. Michael seemed to have set precedents for other pop stars to follow, soon pop singer Madonna was hired to endorse Pepsi and George Michael signed with Diet Coke. Michael's annual earnings from album sales, endorsements, and concerts was estimated at $125 million (£76.3 million) for 1989 alone. In July 1989, a new California Raisin commercial was aired in theaters and later on television featuring the voice of Michael. Because of his exclusive contract with Pepsi he was not allowed to sing in any commercial. Michael received $25,000 (£15,000) fee for his contribution which he donated to charity. Elizabeth Taylor popularized Michael's self acclaimed title *The King of Pop* when she presented him with an *Artist of the Decade* award, proclaiming him *The True King of Pop, Rock and Soul*. She said in front of a huge audience: "Ladies and Gentlemen, the 1989 *Heritage Award* and the *Sammy Davis J. Award* recipient, and in my estimation, the *True King of Pop, Rock and Soul*, mister Michael Jackson." According to Nations Trails, "The *United States Heritage Award* was designed to give youth recognition for learning about the heritage of the United States of America, and being involved. By completing the *United States Heritage Award*, it is hoped greater understanding and pride of our nation will prevail. A medal and a patch can be awarded to all that successfully complete the award requirements. All requirements can be done with a unit, group, family, or individually. The *United States Heritage Award* has two different award levels: Silver award is for youth ages 6-10. Gold award is for youth aged 11-18. Adults can also earn the gold award if they complete the requirements and assist a youth in earning the *United States Heritage Award."* On September 22, 1989, The Capital Children's Museum awarded Michael with the *Best Of Washington 1989 Humanitarian Award* in recognition of his efforts to raise money for the museum and for his never-ending support of children. On November 13, 1989, the organization Wishes Granted helped 4-year-old Darian Pagan, who suffered from leukemia to meet Michael. Michael invited the little boy to a performance of Canadian acrobats and on January 6, 1990, Michael invited 82 abused and neglected children through Childhelp to his Neverland Ranch. There were games, a Barbeque and a movie show provided for them.

On February 3, 1990, Michael received a *Role Model Award* from Japan. Vanity Fair had cited singer Michael Jackson as the most popular artist in the history of show business. Michael cared much for children but also for animals. He had build his own zoo at his ranch in California. When he recorded in the studio, Michael brought his animals with him. He dressed up chimp Bubbles every morning, and learned him how to do the moonwalk. Bubbles even went with Michael on tour. Michael told a reporter why he was so fond of animals: "The same things that animals and children have, is that they don't judge you, they don't want anything from you." About his success he said: "I love what I do, and I would people to love what I do. To be loved. I simply want to be loved, were ever I go, all over the world. I love people of all races, from my heart, with true affect."

On April 5, 1990, during a ceremony, Michael was awarded as *Entertainer Of The*

Decade. He met President George Bush who explained Michael's humanitarian commitments to the press and honored him with the *Point Of Light* award. Michael received this award for his philanthropic activities. In July 1990, 45 children from the Project Dream Street, Los Angeles, for children with life-threatening illness were invited to Neverland Valley and on August 18, 1990, Michael invited 130 children of the YMCA summer program of Los Angeles and Santa Barbara to his Neverland Ranch.

Ryan Wayne White was an American teenager from Kokomo, Indiana, and became close friends with Michael, a few years before he died of AIDS. Michael felt sorry for the kid who was shunned after contracting AIDS through a blood transfusion. Ryan's mother was stunned at first when Michael contacted her and her son. She said that, "Michael was always 'amazed' with my son. And Ryan never wanted anybody to feel sorry for him. Ryan never talked about his illness, and Michael noticed that." When Ryan was only six days old, doctors diagnosed him with severe Hemophilia A. Hemophilia A is a hereditary blood coagulation disorder associated with the x chromosome which causes even minor injuries to result in severe bleeding. For treatment Ryan received transfusions of Factor VIII, a blood product created from pooled plasma of non-hemophiliacs. Ryan became extremely ill with pneumonia in December 1984 and on December 17, 1984, during a partial-lung removal procedure, he was also diagnosed with AIDS. Scientists had only found out earlier that year that HIV was the cause of AIDS. Doctors had told Ryan he only had six more months to live. Immediately after the diagnosis, Ryan wasn't able to return to school, but after a while he had begun to feel better.

In June 1985, Ryan wanted to return to school. A formal request, submitted on June 30, to permit re-admittance to school was denied by Western School Corporation superintendent James O. Smith. Parents and also teachers in Kokomo rallied against his attendance. After being expelled from school, Ryan became a national poster child for HIV/AIDS in the United States. Media coverage of his struggle to return to school made him into a national celebrity and spokesman for AIDS research and public education. Because AIDS was first diagnosed by people of the male homosexual community, it was a disease associated with them and not with young children. This perception shifted as Ryan and others with AIDS appeared in the media. Michael was among others to help him. President Ronald Reagan and Nancy Reagan, singers Elton John and John Cougar Mellencamp, actor Matt Frewer, diver Greg Louganis, Surgeon General Dr. C. Everett Koop, Basketball coach Bobby Knight and basketball player Kareem Abdul-Jabbar were all friends of Ryan. Ryan and his mother Jeanne White-Ginder both stayed at Michael's house in Neverland in 1989. Sometimes Ryan went alone to the ranch, but Ryan's mother had no reservations about letting her son stay with Michael in his house. "Michael didn't allow cameras on the property," she told a reporter once, "But we did manage to make photos together." She said Ryan seemed sometimes "more mature" around Michael and she knew Michael liked children, but in a good way. "Michael didn't care what color you were, what was your disease or what was your handicap. He just loved all the children regardless of their background," Jeanne told her friends. By the spring of 1990, Ryan's health was deteriorating rapidly. In his final public appearance where Ryan hosted an after-Oscars party with first lady Nancy Reagan and former president Ronald Reagan in California, he told the Reagans about his hopes of attending college and about his date to the prom.

Ryan lived five years longer than his doctors predicted and he died in April 1990, just before finishing high school. Over 1,500 people attended Ryan's funeral on April 11, a standing-room-only event held in Indianapolis. Ryan's pallbearers included Elton John, football star Howie Long and Phil Donahue. The funeral was also attended by First Lady Barbara Bush and Michael Jackson. AIDS activist Larry Kramer said about Ryan: "I think little Ryan White probably did more to change the face of this illness and to move people than anyone." Ryan's death inspired Elton John to create the Elton John AIDS Foundation. He also donated proceeds from *The Last Song* which appears on his album *The One* to a Ryan White fund at Riley Hospital. Michael Jackson dedicated the song *Gone Too Soon* from his *Dangerous* album to Ryan. Ryan's mother told The New York Times: "Ryan always said, 'I'm just like everyone else with AIDS, no matter how I got it.' And he would never have lived as long as he did without the gay community. The people we knew in New York made sure we knew about the latest treatments way before we would have known in Indiana. I hear mothers today say they're not gonna work with no gay community on anything. Well, if it comes to your son's life, you better start changing your heart and your attitude around." Michael gave Ryan his favorite car, a red Mustang, as a gift a year before he died. At Ryan's funeral Ryan's car was on display, and Michael started it and *Man in the Mirror* was playing. Jeanne: "You could see it in his eyes. He was smiling from ear to ear." Michael asked: "I was the last person that Ryan listened to?" The answer was yes because Ryan played *Man in the Mirror* over and over and over again.

A few days after the funeral, Michael called Jeanne to tell her he promised her son to be in his new video, but now Ryan was gone he could not do that. Michael explained to Ryan's mother he wanted to make a new video, featuring footage of Ryan. He told her: "The video would include his media attention as the face of the AIDS epidemic. I want to show his life growing up with the disease, and I also want to show his funeral." After Ryan's death, Jeanne said she and her family spent several vacations with Michael. She told that Neverland was "a place between Heaven and Earth." Jeanne: "A couple of years ago Michael called me and he said him and his mom had been talking and he said, 'I just thought I'd call you and tell you Happy Mother's Day.' And you know, people don't know those kinds of moments from Michael." Michael helped draw great public attention to HIV/AIDS, something that was controversial at the time. He publicly pleaded with the Clinton Administration to give more money to HIV/AIDS charities and research. On May 6, 1991, Michael was invited to the Jane Goodall Charity event. Michael supported her, an advocate of behavioral research concerning chimpanzees in Gombe, Nigeria for more than 30 years.

In March 1991, Michael renewed his contract with Sony for $65 million (£39.8 million). Again this was a record-breaking deal at the time, displacing Neil Diamond's renewal contract with Columbia Records. Michael released his eighth album *Dangerous* in 1991. As of 2008, *Dangerous* had shipped seven million copies in the United States and had sold over 32 million copies worldwide. The album is the most successful new jack swing album of all time. The New York Times noted that on some tracks, "Michael gulps for breath, his voice quivers with anxiety or drops to a desperate whisper, hissing through clenched teeth." The newspaper also wrote, "he had a wretched tone."

On July 26, 1991, Michael visited the Youth Sports & Art Foundation in Los Angeles. This Foundation supports families of gang members, and helps dealing with drug-abuse. Michael talked to the kids and presented them with a wide-screen TV set and a financial gift. In 1992 Michael founded the Heal the World Foundation. Michael invited underprivileged children to his ranch to enjoy theme park rides that he had built on the property. The foundation also helped children threatened by war and disease. Michael: "For me the form God takes is not the most important thing. What's most important is the essence. My songs and dances are outlines for Him to come in and fill." On May 1, President George Bush presented Michael with the *Point of Light* award for his continuing support of deprived children. Michael visited little Raynal Pope, who had been injured very badly by dogs and on June 3, 1992, the organization One To One, who is caring for better living conditions of young people, honored Michael with an award for his commitment to deprived youngsters. Michael made an announcement at a press conference in London about his Heal The World Foundation on June 23, 1992.

The *Dangerous World Tour* began on June 27, 1992, and finished on November 11, 1993. Michael and his team performed to 3.5 million people in 67 concerts. All profits from the concerts went to the Heal the World Foundation. On June 29, 1992, Michael visited the Sophia Children's Hospital in Rotterdam and presented a check for 100,000 pounds. Michael visited the Queen Elizabeth Children's Hospital in London on July 29,

1992. To surprise the children, he brought Mickey Mouse and Minnie Mouse from Euro-Disney to the hospital. On the evening of his second concert at Wembley Stadium, Michael presented Prince Charles with a check of 200,000 pounds for the Prince's Trust. 6 year old Nicholas Killen, who lost his eyesight caused by a life aiding cancer surgery, met Michael backstage in Leeds, England on August 16, 1992 and in September 1992, Michael donated 1 million pesetas to charity headed by the Queen of Spain. President Iliescu of Romania inaugurates a playground for 500 orphans which Michael had financed. Michael discussed his Heal The World Foundation on September 30, 1992. On November 24, 1992, at Kennedy Airport in New York, Michael supervised the loading of 43 tons of medication, blankets, and winter clothes destined for Sarajevo. The Heal The World Foundation collaborated with AmeriCares to bring resources totaling $2.1 million (£1.3 million) to Sarajevo. They were allocated under the supervision of the United Nations. During a press conference at the American Ambassy in Tokyo, on December 10, 1992, Michael was presented with a check for $100,000 (£61,000) for the Heal The World Foundation by Tour Sponsor Pepsi, and on December 26, 1992, during a broadcast request for donations to the United Negro College Fund, Michael declared: "Black Colleges and Universities are breeding some of the leading personalities of our time. They are on top in business, justice, science and technologies, politics and religion. I am proud, that the Michael Jackson Scholarship Program enabled more than 200 young men and women to get a qualified education." Michael was one of the stars to perform at the Presidential Inauguration of Bill Clinton, on January 19, 1993. Before he performed *Gone Too Soon*, he paid attention to the plights of the victims of AIDS and mentioned his friend Ryan White. At a press conference held at Century Plaza Hotel in Century City, Los Angeles, on January 26, 1993, Michael was presented with a $200,000 (£122,000) donation from the National Football League and the Sponsors of the Super Bowl. He received another $500,000 (£305,000) from the BEST Foundation for his Heal The World Foundation. At this occasion the foundation of 'Heal L.A.' was officially announced. Michael was presented with a $200,000 (£122,000) donation from the National Football League and the Sponsors of the Super Bowl on January 26, 1993. In association with Sega, Michael launched on February 1993, an initiative to distribute more than $108,000 (£66,000) of computer games and equipment to children's hospitals, children's homes, and children's charities throughout the United Kingdom.

Writer Tom Utley from Daily Telegraph called Michael an "extremely important figure in the history of popular culture" and a "genius." All these figures shouldn't really surprise people around the world. Michael's artistic and musical genius has been universally recognized. But, what maybe comes as a surprise is that Michael owns a patent. Michael's patent is on a method and means for creating anti-gravity illusion. In the video for *Smooth Criminal*, we see Michael and his dancers leaned forward, pausing slightly at a gravity-defying 45 degrees. One of the elements required to obtain a patent is that the invention must solve a technical problem. Michael's patent application stated that he had dance steps that would make it appear that a performer would lean forward beyond the center of gravity. Michael's trick can only be performed in his videos and not during a live performance on stage. Michael filed his patent in 1992, which means he has exclusive rights over this for 20 years, until 2012.

On February 10, 1993, Michael was special guest on the Oprah Winfrey Show. In the long expected interview with Oprah, Michael offered the world a glimpse into his gentle personality and his beautiful ranch near Santa Ynez. Millions of viewers were watching the show live. Michael candidly answered Oprah's unscreened questions. He told Oprah about his complicated relationship with his father and about his skin disease that was later named as Vitiligo. He said about his skin disorder and the changing color of his skin: "I am very proud of my culture and heritage and of being African American. Vitiligo is in my family, my father said it's on his side. I can't control it, I don't understand, I mean, it makes me very sad. I don't want to go into my medical history because that is private, but that's the situation here." Michael dispelled many rumors circulating about him, and explained about his childhood loneliness. In his first interview after 14 years he said: "I would do my schooling which was three hours with a tutor and right after that I would go to the recording studio and record, and I'd record for hours and hours until it was time to go to sleep. And I remember going to the record studio and there was a park across the street and I'd see all the children playing and I would cry because it would make me sad that I would have to work instead." He also said: "I was always most comfortable on stage. I am still most comfortable on stage, but once I got off stage, I am real sad...." Michael said about his father, "I love my father but I don't know him." Of his mother Michael stated: "My mother's wonderful. To me she's perfection." He choose his words very carefully aware that the tabloid media would twist everything he was saying.

Elizabeth Taylor briefly joined the interview. Liz called Michael, "generous to almost a fault of himself." Elizabeth had become a star at age nine and explained Oprah they became friends because they had their childhood experiences in common. Not understood by the press was Michael's story about something that had disturbed him for years. He'd gotten into a tank at a burn unit, which had been dedicated to him. Someone snapped a photo of Michael in the tank and spread the rumor that Michael slept in an oxygen tank. He couldn't believe that the press was still writing about his weird behavior. After the interview Michael drove Oprah around Neverland Park on a golf cart. Michael explained Oprah that he built Neverland to live out his childhood and to help heal terminally ill children. Michael said he sought to imitate Jesus, who said, "To be like children, to love children, to be as pure as children and make yourself as innocent." The TV show was watched by over 90 million viewers in the United States, one of the most watched TV shows ever. Michael's sister Janet, who became famous as a singer as well, said about Michael's disease: "Michael isn't the only one in the family to have Vitiligo. This doesn't mean that his sisters or brothers have to have it, it could have been a distant relative."

Karen Faye who was Michael's makeup artist for more then 20 years, said about Michael: "Michael is now almost completely devoid of color, his face was seriously uneven in color. He has a skin disease. It started happening relatively early, he even was trying to hide it from me. He'd always try to cover it with makeup. It's all over his body. In the beginning I tried to cover the light spots to match the darker part of his skin, but then it became so extensive that we had to go with the lighter part of his skin because his whole body was reacting. He'd have to be in complete full body makeup, every inch of his body." She wondered how many times we have seen Michael Jackson revealing his arms and legs? She said: "Rarely. If you compare the costumes of his *Victory Tour* to the *Triumph Tour*, then you'll see the difference in what he wore. Michael's face was seriously uneven in color. When you bleach your skin, you apply the bleaching agent evenly and it would not create spotting. Michael had no need to bleach his skin for aesthetic reasons. The argument that people present to me is that Michael wanted to appeal to a wider audience, so he bleached his skin. This is quite untrue."

Karen explained that after the success of *Thriller,* which was the biggest selling album in the world in 1984, Michael was already a global phenomenon. "There is no reason why he would need to appeal to a wider audience; because he already had the widest audience of any pop star or celebrity on the palmettos," she added. "Michael must have 30% - 50% Vitiligo on his body, and as he was always in the public eye, constantly being photographed, it would be quite embarrassing to show up to events and perform with spotted skin which shows two different colors. So he went through depigmentation therapy, because re-pigmentation was only become a more recent option for Vitiligo patients. There was not another option in the early 1990's for this disease. That's why we noticed that Michael gets lighter and lighter until he became literally white, around 1986," Karen Faye said.

Michael did not talk a lot with reporters but when he talked, he complained about the articles in the press. Once he said: "There is so much garbage, and so much trash, that is written about me. It is so untrue, and even complete lies." At that time Michael wrote about love: "Love is a funny thing to describe. It's so easy to feel and yet so slippery to talk about. It's like a bar of soap in the bathtub, you have it in your hand until you hold on too tight." About grabbing his crotch on the stage he said: "When I am doing a movie and I go 'Bang!' (to handle roughly) and I grab myself, it is the music that compels me to do it. It's not that I say, 'Grab down there', and it is not a great place... You don't think about it. Sometimes I look back at the footage and say, 'Did I do that?'"

The foundation of an independent film company was announced on March 1993. They produced family-oriented movies. A part of the earnings were going to the Heal The World Foundation. Within his 'Heal L.A.' tour, Michael visited the Watta Health Foundation, and two schools in Los Angeles South Central on April 26, 1993. Former President Jimmy Carter and Michael, who were chairmen of the 'Heal Our Children/Heal The World' initiative, were in Atlanta on May 5, 1993 to promote their 'Atlanta Project Immunization Drive'. Michael promoted the new DARE-program in June, 1993. The purpose of the program was to inform children about the dangers of drug abuse. Also in June 1993, 100 children from the Challengers Boys and Girls Club visited Neverland. Michael visited a hospital in Washington on June 18, 1993, and spent several hours with the young patients and played chess with some of them. In July 1993, Michael was honored with the *Scopus Award 1993* by the American Friends of Hebrew University, and in August 1993, *The Jack The Rapper Awards* were presented. Michael was honored with the *Our Children, Our Hope Of Tomorrow* award. Michael along with Pepsi-Cola Thailand, donated $40,000 (£24,000) in August 1993 to Crown Princess Maha Chakri Sirindhorn's charity, the Rural School Children and Youth Development Fund in support of school lunch programs in rural villages in

Thailand. Michael donated in conjunction with Pepsi-Cola International, new ambulances to the Contacts One Independent Living Center for Children in Moscow, Russia and the Hospital de Ninos Dr. Ricardo Gutierrez in Buenos Aires, Argentina, in August 1993.

In the summer of 1993, Michael was accused of child sexual abuse by a 13-year-old boy named Jordan Chandler and his father, Evan Chandler. Jordan told his father, who was a dentist, under the influence of sodium Amytal, a controversial sedative, that Michael Jackson had touched his penis. This was a year after Michael met the boy. Police in Los Angeles had refused to give details to the press. But it was clear that two of Michael's homes were searched at the weekend following allegations of child abuse. A police officer stated: "We are investigating allegations of child abuse made against singer Michael Jackson." Detectives who visited Neverland Ranch in Santa Barbara had interviewed the boy, the father and other youngsters including 12-year old actor Macaulay Culkin, star of the *Home Alone* films. Newspapers were using sensational headlines to draw in readers and viewers and was accepting confidential, leaked material from the police investigation in return for money paid. Newspapers and reporters showed mostly a lack of objectivity and were using headlines that strongly implied Michael's guilt. Anthony Pellicano, security adviser for Michael, has said the allegation is part of a $20 million (£12,2 million) extortion plot. He told: "Around 30 such blackmail attempts were made against Mr. Jackson each year." It was also reported that the father of one boy had alleged the singer for seducing the child and performed sex acts with him.

Michael was on tour in Thailand and issued a statement through his lawyer, Harold Weitzman.

"I am confident the police department will conduct a fair and thorough investigation and that the result will demonstrate that there was no wrong doing on my part," Mr. Weitzman read. Michael was never charged with a crime. But Michael was constantly subject to media scrutiny while the criminal investigation took place.

Many doctors were examined during the investigation. Interviews with different doctors made clear that Michael was using different kind of drugs. A Santa Barbara County Sheriff's deputy served a search warrant on Dr. Arnold Klein in 1993. It was served to obtain Michael's medical records during the molestation investigation. Debbie Rowe who worked for Michael's dermatologist, Dr. Arnold Klein, told a deputy she injected Michael frequently. In August 1993, the deputy wrote in an affidavit: "Ms. Rowe observed the back of Jackson's body while she gave him massages to help him sleep. Ms. Rowe also observed Jackson's buttocks on numerous occasions when she gave him injections prior to acne treatments." The type of drug Debbie Rowe administered is not known. Michael had been seeking treatment for his severe acne problem. It was a friend who had called Dr. Klein, a doctor, to help Michael. Dr. Klein saw Michael and noted a butterfly rash on the face and crusting of the scalp. Dr. Klein immediately decided that Michael had Lupus and a biopsy confirmed his suspicions. Dr. Klein told Michael his disease was difficult to treat. He told Michael: "Vitiligo is a side effect of Lupus." He noticed Michael's whole body began to speckle, specifically his hands but also his face. Dr. Klein and Michael decided to use creams to lighten the darker portions, and destroy the remaining pigment cells.

The decision to make Michael lighter was taken because his skin had more white patches than darker ones. If they would have chosen to try to match his original skin, he would have looked even more unreal. "In some cases like with Michael, the skin will try to restore its own pigment. But it just cannot do it at the rate that it's being destroyed," Dr. Klein told Larry King many years later. He said: "White blotches could become freckled with darker patches." When Michael and his doctor had gotten the Vitiligo to a manageable state, the treatment became about maintaining the recurrences of Michael's original pigmentation. After Michael eluded to Oprah that he had a skin disease, he instructed Dr. Arnold Klein, to release an official statement disclosing the King of Pop's Vitiligo. "His face is white because he has had this disease, and instead of having it spotted like a cow or something like that, he just decided to just do the whole thing, because he could afford to do it," Michael's mother Katherine said. "You could not imagine how devastating this disease would be for anyone? People constantly make jokes about Michael and his skin, forgetting that he is a human being. This man has done so much for musical culture in America and the world. He also supports the most charities of any other celebrity. He is controlling his Vitiligo in the best way he can and the best way he feels comfortable with, but he still has patches to this day on his face and body."

    A few months after the allegations became breaking news, Michael had almost stopped eating and lost approximately 10 pounds (4.5kg) in weight. He had canceled the remainder of his *Dangerous World Tour* and began taking painkillers, Valium, Xanax and Ativan to deal with the stress of the allegations made against him. Not much later Michael went into rehabilitation. The singer's spokesperson told the press: "Michael is barely able to function adequately on an intellectual level." Michael booked the whole fourth floor of the clinic and was put on Valium IV.

Singer-songwriter Lisa Marie Presley, the daughter of Elvis Presley, had first met Michael in 1975. During one of Michael's family engagements at the MGM Grand they had been talking to each other shortly. Through a mutual friend they were reconnected again in early 1993. Lisa Marie explained by the time the child molestation accusations became public: "I believed he didn't do anything wrong and that he was wrongly accused and yes I started falling for him. I wanted to save him. I felt that I could do it." Lisa Marie called Michael as much as she could, almost every day. Although she described him after a phone conversation as high, incoherent and delusional, she tried to persuade Michael to settle the allegations out of court. She was one of the loving persons to tell Michael he should go into rehabilitation to recover.

Also in 1993, Michael Jackson pens *Nourish This Child*, an introduction to a family cookbook called *Pigtails and Frog's Legs* from Neiman Marcus. Chuck Jones illustrated the book with delightful culinary sketches and did a caricature of Michael which appeared in the book. Michael: "To a child, food is something special. It isn't just a delicious taste or the vitamins that build a healthy body. Food is love and caring, security and hope - all the things that a food family can provide. Remember when you were little and your mother made a pie for you? When she cut a slice and put it on your plate, she was giving you a bit of herself, in the form of her love. She made you feel safe and wanted. She made your hunger go away, and when you were full and satisfied, everything seemed all right. Because that satisfied feeling was in the pie, you were nourished from a deep level. Food is something we all need physically, but so is the love, the deeper nourishment, that turns us into who we are." Although Michael's legal situation wasn't stable at that time, Neiman Marcus spokeswoman Liz Barrett told the press: "Sales of the book were unaffected by Michael's situation."

Michael visited a hospital in Santiago on October 22, 1993, and made it possible for 5000 underprivileged children to visit the Reino Aventura Park, where the whale Keiko ('Free Willy') was living. On October 28, 1993, he was guest at a children's party at the Hard Rock Cafe in Mexico City.

Michael's sister La Toya announced, while being in Africa, on November 15, 1993, that her brother was under a lot of stress. Wearing a huge wig and big sunglasses, she told the press sadly: "He is very unhappy." She said she didn't want to comment for her brother, and declined to answer further questions about him.

On November 17, 1993, Michael rejected the *Scopus Award*. He was nominated for this award, which was planned to be given him on January 29th, 1994.

The November release of *Michael's Greatest Hits* was postponed and the album was now scheduled for release in mid 1994. On November 23, a huge collection of videos was released from the *Dangerous* album. The video cassette was originally scheduled for release in the beginning of 1993 but Michael had not find any time to finish the product. Included was the original and complete version of Michael's *Black and White*. The new version included racial slurs and Michael is being seen smashing out windows. On the tape is also a sneak peak at the making of the video *Black and White*. We can see Michael having fun on the set with stink bombs and wipped cream. There is behind the scenes footage of *Jam*, *In the Closet*, *Remember the Time*, and videos from *Will*

You Be There, *Who Is It* (never been seen by his fans from the United States), *Heal The World* (two versions), *Gone Too Soon* (his tribute to his dear friend Ryan White) and Michael's performance at the 1993 Super Bowl.

Michael sold for $20 million (£12.2 million) the broadcast rights to his *Dangerous World Tour*, to HBO. This record-breaking deal still stands. The video *Dangerous: The Short Films* sold strongly and outlets couldn't keep enough video cassettes on the shelves. The cassette debuted on Billboard's Top Music Video chart at number 4 and stayed for weeks in the top five. Michael's video *Will You Be There* was included at the beginning of the movie *Free Willy*, that was just released on home video. The film spent a few months in the top five of Billboard's Top Video Sales chart. The movie was peaking at number 2, where it spend nine weeks. On November 24, Michael announced he had just closed the biggest music publishing deal in history.

Not much later Michael received a court document that raised allegations that he was involved in inappropriate behavior with a young boy, named Jordan Chandler. The December 1993 declaration was sworn by the then 13-year-old California boy who sued Michael for sexual battery, willful misconduct, emotional distress and some other things. The declaration included a graphic account of alleged sexual encounters with Michael at Neverland and various hotels.

Michael had vanished after canceling his *Dangerous World Tour* and said he was addicted to pain-killing drugs and was reported to be in hiding at a French ski resort. His lawyer said it would take 6 to 8 weeks to treat Michael's addiction to the painkillers. The Heal The World Foundation United Kingdom supported on December 16, 1993, Operation Christmas Child, delivering toys, sweets, gifts and food to children in former Yugoslavia.

A long awaited statement about his allegations was made by Michael on December 22, 1993, which was carried live by CNN, MTV and E!. Michael said: "Good afternoon. To all my friends and fans, I wish to convey my deepest gratitude for your love and support. I am doing well and I am strong. As you may already know, after my tour ended, I remained out of the country undergoing treatment for a dependency on pain medication. This medication was initially prescribed to soothe the excruciating pain that I was suffering after recent reconstructive surgery on my scalp. There have been many disgusting statements made recently concerning allegations of improper conduct on my part. These statements about me are totally false. As I have maintained from the very beginning, I am hoping for a speedy end to this horrifying experience to which I have been subjected. I shall not in this statement respond to all the false allegations being made against me, since my lawyers have advised me that this is not the proper forum in which to do that. I will say I am particularly upset by the handling of this mass matter by the incredible, terrible mass media. At every opportunity, the media has dissected and manipulated these allegations to reach their own conclusions. I ask all of you to wait to hear the truth before you label or condemn me. Don't treat me like a criminal, because I am innocent."

He then said: "I have been forced to submit to a dehumanizing and humiliating examination by the Santa Barbara County Sheriff's Department and the Los Angeles Police Department earlier this week. They served a warrant on me which allowed them to view and photograph my body, including my penis, my buttocks, my lower torso, thighs, and any other areas that they wanted. They were supposedly looking for any discoloration, spotting, blotches or other evidence of a skin color disorder called Vitiligo which I have previously spoken about. The warrant also directed me to cooperate in any examination of my body by their physician to determine the condition of my skin, including whether I have Vitiligo or any other skin disorder. The warrant further stated that I had no right to refuse the examination or photographs and if I failed to cooperate with them they would introduce that refusal at any trial as an indication of my guilt. It was the most humiliating ordeal of my life - one that no person should ever have to suffer. And even after experiencing the indignity of this search, the parties involved were still not satisfied and wanted to take even more pictures. It was a nightmare, a horrifying nightmare. But if this is what I have to endure to prove my innocence, my complete innocence, so be it. Throughout my life, I have only tried to help thousands upon thousands of children to live happy lives. It brings tears to my eyes when I see any child who suffers. If I am guilty of anything, it is of believing what God said about children, *Suffer little children to come unto me and forbid them not, for such is the kingdom."*

Michael's sister La Toya said 5 days after Michael's attempt to explain his situation: "I can't remain silent." La Toya had charged that brother Michael has molested young boys over the years at the family's home and that her mother Katherine knew about it. She made her shocking statements first at a news conference in Tel Aviv, Israel. Ironically she defended her brother earlier on national television. She said: "I will not be a silent collaborator in his crimes against small, innocent children." She told the press that she was a victim of child abuse herself and knew how the alleged victims would be scarred for life. Katherine had shown her checks that her brother Michael had made out to the families of some boys. "I don't know if these children were apparently bought from the parents by Michael or not," she announced. But her father and mother denied those allegations. Katherine Jackson said: "She is doing it for money, she and her so-called husband, Jack Gordon. That's how they make their money."

Katherine described Jack as a "money-hungry mongrel." Her father Joe said at a news conference at their home that La Toya's charges are "ridiculous. It's a lie!" Katherine added: "I wouldn't let anything like that go on in my home and she knows it. They're (La Toya and her husband) just jumping on the bandwagon."

Jermaine said the family still loved La Toya. He asked her to come back because at a time of crisis, "there is a need for families to stick together." He said also at the news conference: "La Toya is our sister and she knows people will listen to her." La Toya who was aware of that, appeared on the Today show and told host Katie Couric: "I do know he'd have boys over all the time and they'd stay in his room for days. Then they would come out and then there'd be another boy and he'd bring someone else but never two at a time. My mother is very much aware of all the children, all the boys who've stayed there. She's the one who'd always call him *faggot*. She said 'I can't stand it. He's nothing but a, *faggot*.' Now, she's denying it. And that's what hurts." La Toya, who knows brother Michael better than the other siblings said Katherine is denying all of it because Michael financially supports most members of the family. "If she were to tell the truth, Michael would drop everything and she would probably be out on the street," La Toya said. Because Michael and La Toya remained at the family home while most of the others married early and moved out, La Toya was always close to Michael. She told reporters: "When my brothers would come over to the house, Michael would say, 'have them make an appointment.' I'd have to make excuses saying, 'he's busy.' He didn't want to be bothered." La Toya said about the large sums of money, "The amounts were *substantial*," but La Toya could not say with any degree of certainty what it was for.

An affidavit from former Santa Barbara Sheriff's Department deputy Deborah Linden had been filed to secure court permission to photograph Jackson's private parts. Jordan Chandler had told police that Michael frequently masturbated him. According to this affidavit, Jordan told officers that Michael justified the illicit acts. He told them: "Michael said it was 'okay and natural because other friends had done this' with him." Michael allegedly told Jordan that, "masturbation is a wonderful thing." He also told Jordan that if he ever spoke about the incidents, he would be "placed in Juvenile Hall". According to Jordan's statement they both would get in trouble.

A document also described a confrontation between Jordan's father Evan and Michael. The father suspected that the singer may had been assaulting his son during sleepovers. He tracked Michael down to his "hideaway apartment" in Los Angeles and asked him: "Are you fucking my kid?" Michael of course became very upset and told father Evan that he had never used that word. The documents revealed that Santa Barbara Sheriff's Department deputy Deborah Linden noted that Michael did not answer the question or deny the allegation. The boy further stated he could provide a detailed description of Michael's penis as a way of proving the pair had been intimate. Jordan said that Michael's body included distinctive "splotches" on his buttocks and one on his penis, "which is a light color similar to the color of his face." Jordan's information was precise, pinpointing where the splotch fell while Michael's penis was erect, the length of Michael's pubic hair, and that Michael was circumcised.

Elizabeth Taylor said this about Michael's drug abuse: "I have suffered and dealt with the same kind of medical problem now affecting my friend Michael Jackson. Because of that, because of our friendship, when Michael started to call to ask if I could help, I was glad to intervene. I traveled to Mexico City where I saw for myself that Michael was in desperate need of specialized medical attention. Because of my own experience with addicting to prescription medicines, I was able to make a number of calls in search of the best and most appropriate treatment for Michael, and he is now undergoing such treatment in Europe. Out of respect for his privacy, which I know to be extremely important at this time, I have not spoken in public about our movements or about Michael's exact location. And because of my regard for him, and my concern for his health, I will continue to be silence. I will only repeat that I am only a friend of Michael Jackson, and I love him like a son, and I support him with all my heart."

Personalities of the press came forward and said anything that purported to support charges that Michael sexually molested a 13-year-old boy as alleged in a lawsuit filed by the boy's father. Michael's father was furious. The father of the King of Rock, Pop and Soul told in a long distance conference call to JET: "There are people trying to destroy our son... We love him and we support him. We're out here fighting them!" Katherine told about her son and the recent angry accusations by her daughter La Toya, whose career as a recording artist was launched by her father and her first album, *La Toya* produced by Michael: "I'm going to tell you something which was never brought out and all these people know it, especially these White People. That's not La Toya talking. That is

Jack Gordon (La Toya's husband). I think he has brainwashed her and when La Toya gets up there, she is like a crazy person. She is not the same girl." Her father agreed: "He's manipulating her and he's doing everything he possibly can to get into her family and keep the family all messed up. All these accusations she's making never happened. None of this. That's why we didn't understand it. It's like a different La Toya." Katherine Jackson asserted: "What that I think is this. He has brainwashed La Toya because I know what she is saying is not true. Other people out there don't know this, but I know. It's just hard to take when you got a daughter out there saying these things. People will say, 'Well, she is part of the family and she's not going to lie on the family.' But my daughter is out there lying. I think that she thinks she is telling the truth because she has been so manipulated and brainwashed."

Years after Michael's case with Jordan in 1993, The Smoking Gun published official documents about the molesting case on the internet. Michael issued a statement noting that he "has respected the obligation of confidentiality imposed on all the parties to the prior proceedings, yet someone has chosen to violate that confidentiality" and use the boy's statements to "further sully" the star's character. Michael added that, "it should be remembered that at the time, the confidentiality obligation was a mutual one, designed as much to protect" the boy as Michael himself. Michael concluded, "Whoever is now leaking this material is showing as much disregard for [the boy] as they are determination to attack Michael."

Jordan declared in the documents he met Michael when he was 5 years old at a restaurant. He declared that he met Michael again in 1992 at his stepfather's car rental business, Rent-a-Wreck.

His stepfather had called Jordan and told him Michael Jackson was at Rent-a-Wreck and that he should come down and see him. Later, Jordan learned from his stepfather that Michael's car had been broken down and that he was at Rent-a-Wreck to get another car while his was being repaired. Jordan stated that Michael began calling him on the telephone. From about May of 1992 until about February 1993 Jordan received a lot of telephone calls from Michael. He stated: "For at least part of this time Michael was on tour and he would be calling me from various places throughout the world. On occasion these telephone conversations lasted as long as three hours." He said they talked about video games, the Neverland Ranch, water fights, and famous people that he knew.

Jordan: "In about February 1993, my mother, Lily (my half sister), and I went to Neverland at the invitation by Michael Jackson. The three of us stayed together in the guest area. I did not spend the night with Michael Jackson. This was a weekend trip. I spend the entire weekend with Michael Jackson. We went on jet skis in a small lake he had, saw the animals that he kept at Neverland, played video games and went on golf cart rides. One evening he took Lily and me to Toys 'R Us and we were allowed to get anything we wanted. Although the store was closed, it was opened just for our visit. In late March 1993, my mother, Lily and I went to Las Vegas as a guest of Michael Jackson. We flew on a private airplane. We stayed at a large suite at The Mirage Hotel. My mother and Lily shared a bedroom. We stayed at The Mirage Hotel about a week. One night Michael Jackson and I watched The Exorcist in Michael Jackson's bedroom. When the movie was over, I was scared. Michael Jackson suggested that I spend the night with him, which I did. Although we slept in the same bed there was no physical contact. From that time, whenever Michael Jackson and I were together we slept in the same bed. We spend two or three additional nights in the same bed at Las Vegas. Again there was no physical contact. After I returned from the Las Vegas trip, my friendship with Michael Jackson became much closer. My mother, Lily and I started making frequent trips to Neverland. At Neverland I would always sleep in bed with Michael Jackson. I also slept in bed with Michael Jackson at my house and at hotels in New York, Florida and Europe. We were together until our relationship ended in July 1993."

He continued: "During our relationship, Michael Jackson had sexual contact with me on many occasions. Physical contact between Michael Jackson and myself increased gradually. The first step was simply Michael Jackson hugging me. The next step was for him to give me a brief kiss on the cheek. He then started kissing me on the lips, first briefly and then for a longer period of time. He would kiss me while we were in bed together. The next step was when Michael Jackson put his tongue in my mouth. I told him I don't like that. Michael Jackson started crying. He said there was nothing wrong with it. He said that just because most people believe something is wrong, doesn't make it so. Michael Jackson told me that another of his young friends would kiss him with an open mouth and would let Michael Jackson put his tongue in his mouth. Michael Jackson said that I did not love him as much as the other friend. The next step was when Michael Jackson rubbed up against me in bed."

He also stated: "The next step was when we would lie on top of each other with erections. During May of 1993, my mother, Lily and I went with Michael Jackson to Monaco in Europe.

Michael Jackson and I both had colds so we stayed in the room all day while my Mother and Lily were out. That's when the whole thing really got out of hand. We took a bath together. This was the first time that we had seen each other naked. Michael Jackson named certain of his children friends that masturbated in front of him. Michael Jackson would then masturbated in front of me. He told me that when I was ready, he would do it for me. While we were in bed, Michael Jackson put his hand underneath my underpants. He then masturbated me to a climax. After that Michael Jackson masturbated me many times both with his hand and with his mouth."

According to Jordan, who received $20 million (£12.2 million) from Michael for this statement, Michael was into nipples. Jordan stated: "Michael had me suck one nipple and twist the other nipple while Michael Jackson masturbated. On one occasion when Michael Jackson and I were in bed together Michael Jackson grabbed my buttock and kissed me while he put his tongue in my ear. I told him I didn't like that. Michael Jackson started to cry. Michael Jackson told me that I should not tell anyone what had happened. He said this was a secret. My relationship with Michael Jackson ended when my father obtained custody of me in July 1993 and I started living permanently at my father's house. I declare under penalty of perjury that the foregoing is true and correct." Executed on December 28, 1993, at Sante Monica, California. Signed: J. Chandler.

Mainly because of the revealing 'penis pictures', lawyers advised Michael to pay the boy a certain amount of money instead of fighting in court. The two sides announced four months after the Los Angeles Superior Court lawsuit was filed, that the matter had been settled. No criminal charges were ever filed in connection with the teenager's charges. Michael admitted no wrongdoing. He noted that the cash was to settle claims for "damages for alleged personal injuries arising out of claims of negligence" and not for "claims of intentional or wrongful acts of sexual molestation." The agreement stated that Michael finally elected to settle "in view of the impact the action has had and could have in the future on his earnings and potential income." A civil case was settled out of court in early 1994 when Michael paid Jordan Chandler a reported $20 million (£12.2 million).

Three years later Jordan Chandler's stories of the relationship were described in detail in a book written by journalist, Victor M Gutierrez. The book was said to be based on a diary Jordan had kept at the time and included details of alleged sexual encounters between Michael and Jordan. Jordan Chandler's father started in 1996 a claim for around $60 million (£36.6 million), claiming Michael Jackson had breached an agreement never to discuss the case. A court ruled Michael Jackson's favor in 1999 and threw out the lawsuit.

On the weekend of Martin Luther King Jr.'s birthday, Michael gave a party for more than 100 underprivileged children at his Neverland Ranch. 'The Jackson Family Honors' was televised on February 22, 1994. The earnings of the show were given to their own newly formed charity, Family Caring for Families.

In May 1994, Michael married with Lisa Marie Presley (born February 1, 1968). Lisa Marie, also known as the Princess of Rock 'n' Roll was the only child of musician Elvis Presley and Priscilla Presley. Previously, Lisa Marie married her musician boyfriend Danny Keough on October 3, 1988. They had two children together, Riley Danielle (born May 29, 1989), and Benjamin Storm (born October 21, 1992). In April 1994, Presley announced that she and her husband Keough were separating. Only 20 days after her divorce from Keough, she married Michael on May 26, 1994, in the Dominican Republic. Lisa Marie filed for divorce in January 1996, but the couple remained friendly. In 2003 she said she was "not proud" of her brief marriage to pop superstar Michael Jackson in the mid-1990s. She told Rolling Stone Magazine: "I can't say what his intentions were, but I can tell you mine was that I absolutely fell in love with him and fell into this whole thing which I'm not proud of now." She wasn't happy that Michael left her for weeks alone and had told reporters that her father Elvis Presley had cosmetic surgery on his nose. When she finally demanded a divorce, Michael refused to speak to her. She told Rolling Stone: "It just got really ugly at the end. I'm not into Michael-bashing at all. I know people want to know what that was about, and I'm trying to say it without making him a bad guy. It's hard to do, because it was such a bad situation." Lisa Marie's experiences with Michael sent her into a breakdown, mentally and physically, which she took to writing songs to overcome.

In April 12, 1994, on occasion of the 2nd *Children's Choice Award* ceremony at Cit Center (Center for Information Technology) in New York, Michael was presented with the *Caring For Kids* award. This award is to honor celebrities, who take time for young people. 100,000 children and young people from 8 to 18 years old gave Michael their vote of confidence. The *Children's Choice Awards* are sponsored by Body Sculpt, a charity organization, that offers drug-prevention programs for young people. On August 6, 1994, Michael and his wife Lisa Marie were visiting two children's hospitals in Budapest. They distributed toys to the ill children.

In September 1994, Michael went into the studio to record his new album *HIStory* which was originally to be called *Decade*. The first recording started in September 1994 and would carry through March of the following year. The album would include several previous Jackson hit songs and several new recordings from songs he had been written later in his career. Michael wrote most of the songs attacking the press for "scandalizing" him. Songs that attacked the tabloids included *Scream*, a duet between Michael and his sister Janet, *Tabloid Junkie* and *This Time Around*. He asked fans to not "feed into the tabloids".

The Rolling Stone wrote in a biography about Michael: "With the passage of time, however, and especially since 1993, it is Jackson's personality that has dominated headlines formerly dedicated to his prodigious artistic accomplishments and humanitarian efforts. His charity work was enormous and focused always on his highly publicized identification with children. Infatuated with E.T. and Peter Pan, Jackson seemed a kind of childlike extraterrestrial: benign (if in an eerie way), either sexless or sexually ambiguous, neither black nor white. Secluded by his celebrity, he appeared to touch down to earth only on stage or on videotape; fanatically private, he generated endless gossip. In 1993, and a decade later in 2004, with Jackson facing allegations of child molestation, his career was rocked with scandal as gargantuan as his fame."

Chapter 3

The Fame

Michael merged in 1995 his ATV Music catalog with Sony's publishing division, creating Sony/ATV Music Publishing, but he retained half-ownership of the company. Michael earned $95 million (£58 million) upfront as well as the rights to even more songs. He almost immediately released his first double album *HIStory: Past, Present and Future, Book I*, on June 20. The first disc is a singles collection and the second disc is a studio album. The album is still the world's best-selling multiple-disc album of all-time, with 20 million copies (40 million in terms of units) sold worldwide. *HIStory* received a *Grammy* nomination for best album and won one *Grammy* for *Best Music Video — Short Form* for *Scream*. Disc 1, *HIStory Begins* is a greatest hits album containing 15 tracks. It was in 2001 reissued as *Greatest Hits – HIStory Vol. I*. The second disc, *HIStory Continues*, contained 15 brand new songs. Michael's *HIStory* has been certified for more then seven million shipments in the United States alone. The album debuted at number 1 on the charts.

Michael received additional help from many producers. Dallas Austin worked on *This Time Around*, R. Kelly on *You Are Not Alone*, and Jimmy Jam and Terry Lewis worked on different songs for the album. As always, Michael wanted to feature guest stars. Other than his sister, he asked rapper

The Notorious B.I.G. to put down a rap verse in *This Time Around*. Soul group Boyz II Men sung background vocals on *HIStory* and Shaquille O'Neal, the famous basketball star put down a verse on *2 Bad*. Michael himself wrote *They Don't Care About Us*, *Earth Song*, *Stranger in Moscow*, *D.S.*, *Money* and *Little Susie*. The first single released from the album *HIStory* was the double A-side *Scream/Childhood*. *Scream* was a duet, performed with Michael's own sister Janet. *Scream* was the first of several more tunes Michael produced with Jimmy Jam and Terry Lewis. They worked on *2 Bad*, *HIStory* and *Tabloid Junkie*. Janet who agreed to do a duet with Michael after she felt that she "had also made it to the top" was outraged by its success. *Scream* was the highest debut on the Billboard Hot 100 at number 5, and the single received a *Grammy* nomination for *Best Pop Collaboration with Vocals*. The second single was released in August 1995 and was a ballad. *You Are Not Alone* was written by Rob Kelly. The recording was not only seen as a major artistic and commercial success, but it also received an *American Music Award* nomination and a *Grammy* nomination both for *Best Pop Vocal Performance*. Commercially, the song was a significant success. It holds the *Guinness World Record* for the first song ever to debut at number 1 on the Billboard Hot 100 chart. And it was certified platinum by the RIAA.

The music video for *You Are Not Alone* was controversial with an almost nude Michael Jackson and his then-wife Lisa Marie Presley. Rob wrote the song in response to difficult times in his own personal life after the loss of close people in his life. For Rob working with his idol Michael Jackson was like a dream come true. He said: "I was psyched... I feel I could have done his whole album. Not being selfish. I was just that geeked about it. It was an experience out of this world... It's amazing to know that five years ago I was writing songs in a basement in the ghetto and now I'm writing for Michael Jackson." At first Michael contacted Rob Kelly to see if he had any material available. Rob decided to forward a bare demo tape to Michael, who liked the song. Michael decided to co-produce it with Kelly and told Rob he was interested in the song because it also linked to recent events in 'his' personal life. In one scene, Michael originally appeared in complete nudity. Just before the video was aired a decision was made to use special effects to remove or cover these aspects. It's the first high profile video where Michael's wig is cut relatively short. Some people said the video was bizarre and that Michael's nudity made no sense.

In the extended version that appeared on *HIStory on Film, Volume II* we notice Michael looking as a guardian angel over his wife and some special effects were used to give Michael white feathery wings. Lisa expressed herself regretting about doing the video, saying she was "sucked up in the moment. It was kind of cool being in a Michael Jackson video. Come on!" The brothers Eddy and Danny Van Passel from Belgium claimed a few years ago that they had written the melody of *You Are Not Alone* in 1993. A Belgium court ruled in 2007 that mister R. Kelly had plagiarized the 1993 song *If We Can Start All Over* when composing *You Are Not Alone*. The court transferred rights of Michael's hit to the brothers. Airplay of the hit has been banned in Belgium and the judgment is only recognized in Belgium. Michael's third single released from *HIStory* was *Earth Song*. It topped the United Kingdom singles chart for six weeks over Christmas 1995. The single sold a million copies and made it Michael's most successful single in the United Kingdom.

In August 17, 1995, Michael was chatting with fans on the internet. It was one of the few times Michael appeared in a chat box. Michael answered questions from different fans from all around the globe. About things that bothered him from all the bad press Michael wrote: "Despite of what the press says about celebrities and myself in general, I move ahead. I don't pay attention to that tabloid junk - it's garbage. I have my dreams. I am a visionary and I am very resilient. I feel as if I have a suit of armor around me, like a rhinoceros skin. I am here to do what I am supposed to do." Someone asked: "What is the one thing you missed the most in your youth?" Michael answered: "Probably the simple little things that kids do like having a friend over or going to the park or even trick-or-treat, or Christmas, or birthday, and when we were little we didn't have any of those things. We had to hear about them. Some of the kids who take them for granted. I haven't celebrated my birthday yet. Maybe someday I will." VanishR29 asked: "How do you feel about technology like the internet and it's effect on society?" Michael Jackson reacted: "I think it is wonderful. It is a wonderful way to correspond, it's growing and this is the tip of the iceberg. In the next year we will see some amazing growths in technology and I hope that I'm around to see it. I pray that we continue to serve the world in a positive way, not a negative way and not hurt anyone because it is wonderful." Even Beevu: "Do you come up with the ideas for all of your videos?" Michael Jackson: "A lot of them I do come up with. A lot of the concepts do originate with me. After singing *Thriller* I knew that I wanted to do a short film. A simple guy goes out on a date and confesses to her that he's different. I wanted to transform into different things. It was fun. I had so much fun making that. *Beat It* is another concept that I came up with.

Confrontation, two gangs, West Side Story. I wanted real gang members. I wanted to see real truisms in the walk, in the character, in the clothes. And I think it came across." Pelon: "What has been your proudest musical achievement?" Michael Jackson wrote: "One of them? It is really a difficult question to answer because I am not a women, but writing a song is like conceiving a child. I love all the songs. *We are the World* is one of the most favorite things that I've done. I am proud of that... it has reached a lot of people, it has touched a lot of people. My secretary called when I was in the car and said: 'Pull over'. And it was like a prayer when all of the radio stations played it. I had tears." Brian: "Is your new album doing as well as expected? Go MJ!!" Michael Jackson answered: "Yes, I am overly excited about how well the album is doing. It is the fastest selling album in my career. Despite what the press is saying. Unprecedented 7 million worldwide sold in the first week!" Darkan: "Are you ever going to tour America?" Michael Jackson: "I'm not exactly sure, we kind of play it by ear, kind of spontaneous. It would be nice, but I'm not sure." Spin Cycle asked: "Michael, thanks for coming. What is your favorite song on your newest CD?" Michael Jackson admitted: "Probably *Earth Song*, *Stranger in Moscow*, *Little Susie*, I love songs with heart." Bruce Ross: "How has your marriage to Lisa Marie changed your life?" Michael Jackson: "I think I find it more fun to appreciate what family really means. The fact that even though there were 10 of us Jacksons and we were always doing things at different times and I am really learning the real meaning of love. Giving 100% of yourself all the time. Putting up with one another. So far it has been pretty joyous." Ally W: "Hi Michael. You have an amazing voice. Whose music has helped influence your music most?" Michael Jackson surprised: "Thank you for the compliment. That is very nice. To be honest, my first love and appreciation for music was classical, in kindergarten. I used to listen to Tchaikovsky every day. The great writing of Richard Rodgers and Oscar Hammerstein, and many others. I love the show tunes."

On November 2, 1995, Michael received the award *Diamond of Africa*. At the end of 1995, Michael collapsed during rehearsals for a televised performance and was rushed to a hospital. Sources revealed the incident was caused by a stress related panic attack. On March, 30, 1996, The Ark Trust-Foundation, who wants to draw the attention of the public eye on animal's problems, presented the *10th Genesis Award*. Michael was presented with the *1995 Doris Day Award* and received the award for the *Earth Song* video which draws attention to the plight of the animals. Michael wanted to free dolphins who had been locked up for years. He believed there should be legal guidelines about the way dolphins have to live in zoos and parks. Little Bela Farkas received a new liver in March of 1995. Michael and Lisa Marie met this 4-year-old boy during their trip to Hungary in 1994. Michael did everything to help Bela whose only chance to live was getting a new liver. The Heal The World Foundation covered the surgery and the cost for caring. On June 21, 1996, Michael donated a four-times platinum disc of *HIStory* in aid of the Dunblane appeal at the Royal Oak Hotel, Sevenoaks in England. On July 18, 1996, in Soweto, South Africa, Michael laid down a wreath of flowers for youngsters who had been killed during the fights involving Apartheid. In September 1996, the first Sports Festival 'Hope' was held for orphans and disadvantaged children. 3000 children and 600 volunteers took part in the Sports Festival and Michael Jackson was a special guest. On September 6, 1996, Michael visited the children's unit of a hospital in Prague. On October 1996, Michael visited a hospital for mentally challenged children in Kaoshiung, Taiwan, and offered 2,000 free tickets to the sold out performance in Kaoshiung. Michael donated the proceeds of his Tunisia concert to The National Solidarity Fund, a charity dedicated to fighting poverty on October 1, 1996. On October 3, 1996, Michael visited a children's hospital and brought small gifts for the patients during a *HIStory* tour visit in Amsterdam. A room in the hospital (for parents who want to be with their children) was named after Michael. On November 1, 1996, Michael donated most of the earnings from a *HIStory* concert in Bombay, India, to the poor people of the country. On November 7, 1996, before his first concert in Auckland, New Zealand, Michael fulfilled the wish of little Emely Smith, who was suffering from cancer. She just wanted to see him. On November 25, 1996, Michael visited the Royal Children's Hospital in Melbourne, delivering toys, signing autographs and visiting with children. On December 9, 1996, during a *HIStory* tour visit in Manila, Michael visited a children's hospital. He announced that a part of his concert earnings would be donated to the renovation of the hospital. On January 25, 1997, Michael waved his personal fee for his Bombay appearance and donated $1.1 million (£1.7 million) to a local charity helping to educate children living in slums. On April 4, 1997, British magazine OK! published exclusive photos of Michael's son Prince. The magazine paid about 1 million pounds for the photos. Michael donated the money to charity. On June 18, 1997, Michael signed the Children in Need book auctioned by the charity UNESCO.

  Ghosts which premiered at the 1996 Cannes Film Festival and released in 1997, was a short film written by Michael Jackson and Stephen King. The video for *Ghosts* which was directed by Stan Winston, is over 38 minutes long and holds the *Guinness World Record* as the world's longest music video. It was released theatrically in the United States in October 1996, as for the United Kingdom, it debuted at the Odeon Leicester Square in May 1997. The film had 'the look and feel' of *Thriller*. It featured many special effects and dance moves choreographed to original music, which Michael all authored.

On September 7, 1996, Michael started his *HIStory World Tour* and finished it on October 15, 1997, more then 1 year later. The huge show was performed to over 4.5 million fans in 35 countries. Michael and his band performed 82 concerts in 58 cities. It became Michael's most successful tour in terms of audience figures. Michael positioned throughout Europe identical statues, to promote *HIStory*. The statue illustrated Michael's newest clothing style, influenced by military imagery.

Blood on the Dance Floor: HIStory in the Mix was a 1997 remix album by Michael Jackson. The successful album was made up of eight remixes from Michael's previous studio album *HIStory*. It included five new songs. Michael's new material dealt with themes such as drug addiction, women and paranoia. Michael and Teddy Riley created the track *Blood on the Dance Floor* in time for the 1991 release of the album *Dangerous*. However, it did not appear on that record and was minimally altered before commercial release in 1997. Even though the album received minimal promotion, particularly in the United States, worldwide sales stand at six million copies as of 2007, making it the best selling remix album ever released.

Michael said the following of his work and future influence: "Music has been my outlet, my gift to all of the lovers in this world. Through it, my music, I know I will live forever." The album contains eight remixes from *HIStory*; *Scream Louder, Money, 2 Bad, Stranger in Moscow, This Time Around, Earth Song, You Are Not Alone* and *HIStory*, and five new songs, all related to drugs and paranoia, *Blood on the Dance Floor, Morphine, Superfly Sister, Ghosts* and *Is It Scary*. *Morphine* contained an audio clip from *The Elephant Man*, courtesy of Paramount Pictures. On *Morphine*, Michael was the sole arranger, including the classical, vocal and orchestral arrangement. Michael also played solo percussion and drums and joint guitar credit alongside long time collaborator Slash. Andrae Crouch's choir also collaborated on *Morphine*. The song's central theme is Michael's drug usage. Michael had an ongoing drug addiction. He saw his health deteriorate significantly. Some lyrics of the track show clearly a message that Michael wanted to share:

>Trust in me
>Just in me
>Put all your trust in me
>You're doin' morphine...
>Go on babe
>Relax
>This won't hurt you
>Before I put it in
>Close your eyes and count to ten
>Don't cry
>I won't convert you
>There's no need to dismay
>Close your eyes and drift away

(© Lyrics by Michael Jackson *Morphine* (1997), excerpt provided as citation.)

The New York Times acknowledged that promotion was stronger internationally, where Michael had more commercial force and popularity. Michael effectively no longer needed the United States market to have a hit record. By June 1997, only ten percent of sales from Michael's prior studio album came from within the United States. Stephen Thomas Erlewine, of Allmusic, had a negative reaction to the record. Stephen said that all five new tracks were, "embarrassingly weak, sounding tired, predictable and, well, bloodless." He described *Blood on the Dance Floor* as a "bleak reworking of *Jam* and *Scream*." The Cincinnati Post described in a review the lead single as a "lackluster first release, dated, played-out dance track." The review described *Ghosts* and *Is this Scary* as "classic Jackson paranoia," and in *Superfly Sister*, Michael took inspiration from Prince. *Blood on the Dance Floor* was the only track from the remix album performed on the *HIStory World Tour*. Throughout the music video that came with *Blood on the Dance Floor*, Michael shows a sexual attraction towards the dancing woman, played by Sybil Azur. Michael strokes her ankle, calf, knee and thigh, and at one stage looks up her dress. The woman is then seen opening a flick knife as the pair engage in a final courtship dance. The music video won the Brazilian TVZ Video Award: *Best International Music Video of the Year*.

Rolling Stone was of the opinion that at the age of 43, Michael performed "exquisitely voiced rhythm tracks and vibrating vocal harmonies." Nelson George stated: "The grace, the aggression, the growling, the natural boyishness, the falsetto, the smoothness, that combination of elements mark him as a major vocalist." Vincent Paterson, who collaborated with the singer on several music videos said that, "Jackson conceptualized many of the darker, bleak themes in his filmography."

Deborah Jeanne Rowe met Michael when he was diagnosed with Vitiligo in the mid-1980s, acting as his dermatologist's assistant. 'Debbie' currently lives in Palmdale, California. It was announced that Debbie was pregnant from Michael in 1996. The two were married on November 14, 1996, in Sydney, Australia. Both had been married before. Debbie divorced Richard Edelman in 1988, while Michael divorced Lisa Marie Presley in 1996. Only three months after the -secret- marriage, Debbie gave birth to son Prince Michael Joseph Jackson (born February 13, 1997) and the following year to daughter Paris-Michael Katherine Jackson (born April 3, 1998). Michael and Debbie divorced on October 8, 1999, with Debbie giving full custody rights of the children to Michael. It was Michael who wanted to have children *badly*. Debbie, as reported, received an $8-million (£ 4.9 million) settlement, and a house in Beverly Hills, California. According to court documents, Debbie had signed a prenuptial agreement and therefore could not obtain an equal division of community property under California law. Debbie went in 2001 to a private judge to have her parental rights for the two children terminated. After Michael was charged -again- with multiple counts of child abuse, she went to court another time to have the decision reversed. Michael wanted to have more children but Debbie said: "I had so many problems when I was pregnant with Paris. After that I couldn't have any more children."

After his first son was born, Michael talked to Barbara Walters on ABC News, in 1997. He expressed clearly that he couldn't handle the people of the paparazzi. Barbara said: "Up until last week the most photographed people in the world were Princess Diana and Michael Jackson.

Now only one remains to talk about what it means to live under that kind of scrutiny. Since the allegations of child abuse made against Michael Jackson four years ago, he has been, if possible, even more pursued. By the way, we checked with the district attorney's office in Los Angeles and Santa Barbara and learned that there is no active case against Mr. Jackson today." She sat down with Michael in Paris. Michael showed openly his grief about Diana's death and talked about paparazzi and other stuff.

"Michael Jackson himself is notoriously shy about giving interviews, but on my way home from covering Princess Diana's funeral, I met with him in Paris to discuss the paparazzi and his personal recollections of the Princess. When it comes to the paparazzi, Michael Jackson says he feels a bond with Princess Diana. The paparazzi have been a part of his life since he was a small child, the youngest of the Jackson 5. He has been a superstar for 3 decades. At 39, he continues to sing and dance all over the world and the paparazzi follow him all over the world. He has been on a European Tour for the last five months playing for over 2 million people. The night Princess Diana died, Michael Jackson canceled his concert, but his last two concerts were dedicated to her. He does not pretend that she was a close friend. She was a fan," said Barbara on the show.

Michael told Barbara how he and Lady Diana met in London. "I met her first at a concert, in London. She was very kind, very loving, very sweet," Michael said. Barbara asked what they talked about. Michael: "I wrote a song called *Dirty Diana*. It was not about Lady Diana. It was about a certain kind of girls that hang around concerts or clubs, you know, they call them groupies." Barbara said: "Groupies." Michael: "I've lived with that all my life. These girls, they do everything with the band, you know, everything you could imagine. So I wrote a song called *Dirty Diana*. But I took it out of the show in honor of her royal highness. She took me away and she said, 'Are you going to do *Dirty Diana*?' So, I said, 'No I took it out of the show because of you.' She said, 'No! I want you to do it... do it... do the song.'" Barbara said surprised: "So she had a sense of humor with you?" Michael: "Yeah, of course. And she told me it was an honor to meet me. And I said, 'It's an honor to meet you.'" Barbara asked Michael how he first heard of her death? Michael said: "I woke up and my doctor gave me the news. And I fell back down in grief and I started to cry. The pain, I felt inner pain, in my stomach, and in my chest. So, I said, 'I can't handle this, it's too much.' Just the message and the fact that I knew her personally. Then on top of that one I said, 'There's another one, real soon. I feel it coming, there's another one. It's another one coming and I pray it's not me. Please don't let it be me.' And then Mother Theresa came..." Barbara asked if Michael was psychic? Michael: "I don't want to say that, but I've done it before." Barbara asked him: "And you thought it might be you?" Michael said: "Yes. I've been living that kind of life all my life. The tabloid press, that kind of press, not the press, the tabloids, the paparazzi, that type. I've been running for my life like that, hiding, getting away. You can't go that way 'cause they're over there, well lets go this way and pretend we're going that way, and we'll go that way. Someone should say, 'Hold on! Stop! This person deserves their privacy. You're not allowed to go in there!' I go around the world dealing with running and hiding. You can't. I can't take a walk in the park. I can't go in the store. You can't. I have to hide in the room. You feel like you're in prison."

Barbara asked what have been Michael's most intrusive thing and what was the worst? Michael: "They have always been... they go as far as to hide things in places. They'll slide a machine up under the toilet." Michael made the sound of a camera. "Tch, tch, tch, tch... and you go, 'Oh my God!' They've done that," he said. Barbara said: "When you came into this hotel you had to come in, or you felt you had to come in, through the kitchen." Michael: "I've been doing it for years. In many lobbies, I've never seen the front door. Never." Barbara asked: "Did you ever try to outrace the paparazzi?" Michael asked her: "To outrace them?" Barbara admitting: "Yes." Michael told Barbara that they followed him. He said: "They chase us on their scooters." He made the sound of scooters. Barbara: "Cutting in front of you?" Michael said: "Yes. And I have to say to the driver, I say, 'Slow down.' I jump in and I say, 'You're going to kill us.' I say, 'Slow down.' I've done that many times, 'You're gonna kill us.' So he jumps out of the car and yells at these people."

Barbara told Michael: "You know, there is an argument that you rely on publicity to sell your albums, for your concerts, that you want it." Michael: "When I approve of something, yes." Barbara said: "But you can't always control the press. You can't approve everything. You can't invite them in again and again, and then at a certain point, close them out." Michael said he could. Barbara asked him: "Well how do you do that? What's that line?" Michael said: "By doing that. This is their time for this... and this you should not do. You should not say, 'He's an animal, he's a...' You should not say, 'He's Jacko'. I'm not a 'Jacko'. I'm Jackson." Barbara asked him how he felt about that people called him Jacko. Michael: "Yeah, 'Wacko Jacko', where did that come from? Some English tabloid. I have a heart and I have feelings. I feel that when you do that to me. It's not nice. Don't do it. I'm not a 'Wacko'." Barbara: "There are those that would say that you add to the attention." Michael: "No, I don't." Barbara: "Well, the masks, the mysterious behavior." Michael didn't think so. He said: "There's, no, there's no mysterious behavior. There's a time, when I give a concert. I like to have as many people who would like to come can come and enjoy the show. And there's a time, when you like to be in private, when you put on your pajamas and go to sleep, cut the light and you lay down, that's your private space. You go to the park. I can't go in the park, so I create my own park, you know, at Neverland, my own water space, my movie theatres, my theme park, that's all for me to enjoy."

    Barbara said: "I don't want this to sound insulting. I'm just gonna be straight with you. But you are somewhat eccentric to say the least. The way you dress, the way you look, it invites attention. The whole appearance as you grew up was, larger than life, more extreme. Don't you think that draws the paparazzi to you?" Michael was shaking his head: "No. No, maybe I like to live that way, maybe I like to dress that way. I don't want the paparazzi, really. But if they do come, be kind and write the right, kind of thing to write." Barbara: "Michael, is it the journalist's role, or the role of the press to be kind?" Michael is looking disturbed and surprised. He asked: "To be kind??" Barbara explained: "Because the press also has to look into things, be tough. It can't always be kind." Michael said seriously: "What you saw, what happened to Lady Diana, you tell me. There should be some boundaries, some kind of way. The *star* needs some space. Some time to relax. He has a heart, he's human."

Barbara wanted to know why Michael canceled the concert he was about to do when you heard of Diana's death. Michael said sadly: "Yes." Barbara asked: "And when you finally did a concert, you dedicated it to her. What did you say?" Michael: "In my heart I was saying, 'I love you Diana. Shine. And shine on forever, because you are the true Princess of the people.' And in words I did not say it, but I said it for three minutes in showing a big picture on the JumboTron screens, Sony, big huge screens, and her picture was there shining, and the crowd went bananas. And I played the song *Smile* and *Gone Too Soon*." Barbara asked kindly if Michael could show us some of the lyrics. Michael said: "Shiny and sparkly, and splendidly bright, here one day, gone one night, Gone too soon."

Barbara said: "You have said, 'I grew up in a fishbowl. I will not allow that to happen to my son.' Yet, when your son was born, you sold pictures to the National Enquirer and to other European papers, tabloids. Why did you do that?" Michael asked surprised: "Why??" Barbara repeated Michael saying: "Why?" Michael: "Because there was a race. There were some illegal pictures out. Illegally, somebody had taken pictures of a baby, millions of dollars. It said, 'Here's Michael's son'." Barbara agreed and asked: "And it wasn't, as I recall." Michael shaking his head: "And it wasn't. So, I took pictures of the baby. I said, 'They're forcing me to get his pictures.' There were helicopters flying above us, flying over my house, flying over the hospital, and, machines and satellites all over. Even the hospital said, 'Michael, we've had every kind of celebrity here, but we've never had it like this. This is unbelievable.' And so I said, 'Here, take it.' And I gave the money to charity." Barbara asked: "So, rather than, what you're saying is, what you did was to get them off your back." Michael: "Yeah, and now they want to do it again, and I don't want, maybe I don't want to show him to the world like that. I want him to have some space, where he can go to school. I don't want him to be called 'Wacko Jacko', that's not nice. They call the father that. That isn't nice, right?" Barbara asked Michael how he was you going to prevent that people would say, 'That is Wacko's son.' Michael said: "That's the thing." He waited and said: "That's the idea. Maybe you should come up with a plan to help me." Barbara: "You're his daddy." Michael: "There you go. They created that. Did they ever think I would have a child one day, that I have a heart? It's hurting my heart. Why pass it on to him?"

Barbara asked Michael if he liked being a father. Michael said: "I love it!!" Barbara asked if Michael was very involved with him. Michael answered: "Yes!" Barbara: "Do you want more children?" Michael laughed and said: "Yes." Barbara told Michael: "You have been in the spotlight since you were a baby yourself." Michael: "Yes." Barbara asked: "If your son shows any talent, by the way, does he show any talent at nine months?" Michael answered: "Well, I'll tell you this much, when he's crying, to keep him from crying, I have to do one thing." Barbara asked: "What?" Michael: "I have to stand in front of him... and dance." Barbara surprised: "Really?" Michael admitting: "Yes. And he stops crying. His tears turn to laughter, and he's happy. He smiles." Barbara started to laugh and asked: "And do you do your moonwalk with him?" Michael: "Yeah. I do all kind of movements." He dances while staying seated and laughs. Barbara wondered and said: "And then he stops crying?" Michael: "And then he stops crying!" Barbara told Michael he must do a lot of dancing. Michael laughed and said: "I do a lot of dancing, yes." Barbara had a serious question and asked Michael: "Michael, if this little boy says, 'Daddy, I want to go on stage'..." Michael started laughing and slapped his legs. Barbara asked: "After what you've been through?" Michael: "I'd say, 'Hold on, now. Hold on. If you do go that way, expect this... expect this... expect that.'" He counts on his fingers. Barbara: "You'd lay it all out?" Michael agreed: "I'd lay it all out. I'd say, 'See you're gonna get all this.'" He looked to the cameras and other equipment. "And all this and all this," he continued pointing to lights. "You are ready to do that?"... "Yeah, I can't wait."... "Then I would say, 'Go... and do it better than I did.'" Barbara said: "But know what you're in for..." Michael agreed: "Know what you're in for." Barbara said after Michael left the building: "Our interview was over. We had told no one it was happening, nor had the Paris hotel. But when Jackson tried to sneak out through a back door, there was a huge crowd... already waiting."

Heal the World, the charity set up by superstar Michael Jackson, was under scrutiny in Augustus of 1997 after the Charity Commission found a "significant" amount of its United Kingdom income went on administration. The organization Heal the World was set up in 1992 with the aim of raising 60 million pounds in a year. In June 1997, Channel 5's, What's The Story program revealed that the charity had not made a single charitable donation since 1994. President of Heal the World International, Richard Fowler, said that the United Kingdom charity had been made semi-dormant to cut costs, but would soon be revived. A Charity Commission spokeswoman confirmed that the accounts of the organization had been studied and that contact would be made with Heal the World. She said: "Some charities do have high start-up costs through the nature of what they do and obviously we have to make sure we have to make sure that money is being spent on the purpose that the charity was set up for."

Michael received recognition in the 2000 edition of the Guinness Book Of World Records for breaking the world record for the *Most Charities Supported By a Pop Star*, being a global humanitarian, lending his support to 39 charity organizations either with monetary donations through project sponsorships. Michael Jackson: "I've been in the entertainment industry since I was six-years-old... As Charles Dickens says, 'It's been the best of times, the worst of times. But I would not change my career...' While some have made deliberate attempts to hurt me, I take it in stride because I have a loving family, a strong faith and wonderful friends and fans who have, and continue, to support me."

One such friend was Brett Ratner who met Michael in 1998 when he was finishing his first *Rush Hour* picture. Chris Tucker was doing a scene and tried to do a Michael Jackson-style dance. When Brett had test screenings of the film, the scene of Chris got one of the biggest laughs in the picture. Brett knew this scene was going to make him and Michael look great. He said: "I loved it, it was really funny." Brett also knew he had to clear the thing with Michael before he could put the sequence in the movie. Brett however couldn't get in touch with Michael and even tried to call him at Neverland but never got anywhere. Brett told a friend from Miami: "My editor was talking to the projectionist who ran the final screening and it turned out that he was Michael's personal projectionist. So I gave him the print and asked him to play the beginning of the second reel for Michael, which had Chris' dance in it." Two days later Michael called Brett. Brett heard the voice of Michael Jackson for the first time on his phone and was thrilled. Michael told Brett he'd watched the whole movie and loved it, especially the scene Chris did with his dance. Michael then told Brett: "You have my permission to use whatever you want." Michael invited Brett to his ranch and so Brett had walked in. Brett said about his first time on Neverland: "All his giraffes and other animals. They were all out there to greet me." Brett stayed at the ranch and became close friends to Michael. Brett: "We both had this almost childlike fascination with movies, music and all kinds of entertainment." Long time friend Chris Tucker, who would sometimes come along, would play Michael's old records and dance along to them, with Chris and Michael together. Brett said he and Michael spend days and nights together, having dance-offs in the game room at Michael's house, watching movies together, sitting around in their pajamas, eating ice creams and drinking soft drinks. Brett documented the sittings and asked Michael about what kind of music he loved as a kid. Michael would ask Brett how he started in the business and Brett would ask Michael the same question. "When you were with him, you really felt like God was within him. He was an amazing, superhuman kind of person, but he always treated you as an equal. He would be your friend and he never asked for anything in return," Brett said.

On September 1998, Michael visited 5 year old Aza Woods, who suffered from cancer, at the Hilton Hotel in Las Vegas. Michael introduced Aza to the attraction Star Trek: The Experience and spent the rest of the afternoon with the little boy. Finally Michael invited Aza to spent some time with him at his Neverland Ranch. On November 16, 1998, Michael arrived in Harare, Zimbabwe. He was a member of the American Delegation invited by the Minister of Defense. The delegation praised the government of Zimbabwe for helping to keep the peace in this area. On May 1, 1999,

Michael was presented with an award for his humanitarian activities at the Bollywood awards in New York. The award was signed: "Though he comes from the young American tradition, Michael is the embodiment of an old indian soul. His actions are an expression of the philosophy of Weda, which asked to work for the people - not for one's own interests." On September 4, 1999, Michael presented Nelson Mandela with a check for 1,000,000 South African rand for the Nelson Mandela Children's Fund. On January 22, 2000, during Christmas 1999, a violent storm ravaged the park of the Chateau de Versailles and destroyed 10,000 trees in the park. The estimated cost for rebuilding the park was around $20 million (£12.2 million). Some celebrities were supporting the restoration of the park. French officials were reporting that Michael Jackson was one of them. He was one of the first people to donate money to this cause. On October 28, 2000, Michael painted a plate to be auctioned for the Carousel of Hope Ball benefiting childhood diabetes research. On March 6, 2001, Michael donated a black hat, a birthday phone-call and a jacket worn at the Monaco Music Awards in 2000 to the Movie Action for Children auction, an event being given by UNICEF with all proceeds going to UNICEF's efforts to prevent mother-to-child HIV transmission in Africa. On March 26, 2001, Michael handed out books to young people at a Newark, NJ theater. The event, which helped to launch the Michael Jackson International Book Club, part of his new Heal the Kids charity, aimed to promote childhood reading and encourage parents to return to reading bedtime stories.

In 2001, Uri Geller who has written 15 books, including three novels, and is often seen with famous pop stars and other world leaders asked Michael a favor. He asked him to be best man when he renewed his wedding vows in 2001. Michael liked the idea of traveling to the United Kingdom and told Uri, 62, he was coming. Daily Mail wrote about it: "Eccentric pop superstar Michael Jackson finally made it to spoon-bender Uri Geller's wedding yesterday - two hours late. The best man held up the Jewish ceremony in which his paranormal friend was renewing his marriage vows to his wife, Hanna, 50." More then 100 guests sipped champagne while they waited on the beloved music legend. Among the people waiting were former F1 racing car world champion Nigel Mansell, singer Patti Boulaye, broadcaster Sir David Frost and Dave Stewart from the Eurythmics. According to Daily Mail, Michael finally swept into Uri's $9 million (£5.5 million) Thames-side mansion in Sonning, Berkshire at 3 p.m., arriving in convoy in a Chrysler people carrier with blacked out windows. Uri Geller, probably the world's most famous paranormalist, said Michael did not mingle with guests, but was seated with him and Rabbi Boteach. The day before Michael turned up three hours late for an engagement at the Oxford Union and missed a specially arranged dinner with six Dons. Edwin Cline, the Mayor of Liverpool told reporters that Michael was late because his entourage did not get back to his London hotel until 5 a.m.. This was after his address to the Oxford Union. "It was all Michael's fault," Mr Cline said and added, "We had the reception before the wedding - that made it a bit unusual. I didn't get to talk to him. You couldn't get anywhere near him because of his bodyguards. But his body language was very good to everybody that was there. He waved to people and clapped back when they clapped him. It was a bit unreal but nice."

The article in Daily Mail further read: "The guests were treated to a lavish, kosher banquet in a marquee in Geller's garden, according to caterer Carole Sobell. The centerpiece was a cascade of fruit with two enormous melons, inscribed with 'Uri' and 'Hanna' at its heart. Diners sampled dishes including sushi, smoked salmon and falafel to the gentle strains of an eastern European instrumental group." Uri Geller, who claimed Michael Jackson was keen to be knighted after seeing his friend Steven Spielberg awarded with the honor in 2001, said he and his friend Matt Diddes were extremely concerned about Michael's drug abuse at that time. "Michael had told him he was still suffering from jet lag but Uri knew better. Matt explained years later that Uri confiscated injection equipment from his room and whisked it away. He also remembers Michael was desperate to clone himself. Michael became "obsessed" with the idea of creating a "mini-version of himself" after attending a conference on human cloning with Uri in Las Vegas in 2002. Some people say Michael lost his "sense of reality" at that time.

Michael's chauffeur Al Bowman, who drove both Michael and Uri to the event in 2002, told reporters: "Jackson was very excited. He bounced out of that conference like a small child. He was smiling and on a high. I heard him and Uri talking in the back of the limo. He was talking about the prospect of being cloned. He grabbed Uri by both arms and told him, 'I really want to do it Uri and I don't care how much it costs.'" The conference was held by Clonaid, the scientific arm of the Raelian movement, a bizarre sect that believes cloning is the key to eternal life. The spoon bending psychic himself admits the bending of cutlery has long been in the repertoire of many magicians. However, Uri asserts that he "really" bends using psychic powers, whereas others use tricks. He once said: "Sure, there are magicians who can duplicate it through trickery. But the real ones... there's no explanation for it." Uri, who told to Timesonline.co.uk that for the past 35 years or so he never carried a wallet because money does not mix with his philosophy, ideology or spirituality, "so I decided I wouldn't touch it ever again." Uri also talked Michael into flying to the moon to do his moonwalk there.

Michael was so excited and called up Uri one night to say: "Uri Geller, it's Michael calling. When you get this message, please know that I pray we do the moon trip. I want to be the first one to do it in the pop world. Now I hear that 'N Sync and all these people are trying to go. I want to be first... please. And let's do hands across England and let's think of some other wonderful things(?), I love you." Uri released the voice mail message revealing Michael's excitement at being told his dream of rocket travel was absolutely possible. Michael was already in advanced talks with a space scientist in a desperate bid to do the moonwalk on the moon. Michael became obsessed with beating his pop star rivals into space. He wanted to top them by actually making it to the moon to do his famous dance move - in a ten-year $2 billion (£1.2 billion) project. The whole plan was thwarted after Michael was arrested and charged with child molestation in 2003 after Uri invited Martin Bashir over in Michael's house.

Usher, a young new star who performed with Michael Jackson for the *Michael Jackson: 30th Anniversary Special* concert video in 2001 told Time Magazine later in his career: "The first time I got a chance to meet Michael was on stage at Madison Square Garden. There were tons of people on the stage and I just remember losing my mind. Like, Oh my God, that's Michael Jackson right there. I was just over his right shoulder. And then when I finally got a chance to get on the stage with him, I was just shut down. He had the type of magic that you just bowed to." Usher told him: "I love you... and I know you've heard it a million and one times from fans all over the world, but you've meant so much to me as an entertainer, and I love you, and I've admired you all these years." Michael said, "Thank you", in a very calm, meek voice. Usher said: "He was like: 'Thank you so much, Usher. What you do is great; you're great. What you do is not easy, the singing and dancing is not easy. Most performers can't do that, and you've been able to do it, and I'm very impressed by you.'"

In the days after the September 11 terrorist attacks, Michael planned a fundraising single that would be sold through McDonald's Corp. He had made long-time friend F. Marc Schaffel executive producer. The special project which some of the country's top performers had committed to would raise money to help the grieving families. However, Marc had never produced a musical recording before and had no experience in the record business. He was devoted to the project and started to invest money in the project. He was assembling a choir of superstars to sing with Michael on the single *What More Can I Give*. The single would feature artists from Ricky Martin to Reba McEntire to Mariah Carey. But the FBI was investigating Marc's background. Sources said that a FBI probe was launched in the autumn of 2001 after the agency received a complaint from a person who provided a copy of a videotape that allegedly included footage of boys performing sex acts. The footage was filmed by Marc Schaffel in Budapest. Los Angeles Police Department detectives were given a copy of the tape. Michael's representatives received a copy as well. What Michael's handlers discovered triggered a major damage-control effort and brought a halt to the project. Marc said: "I have produced and directed dozens of gay pornography videos. It's no secret that my background is in the adult film business." He added: "I don't keep anything in my life hidden. I'm Michael's friend." Michael's representatives said that when they found out about Schaffel's background, they immediately broke ties with him. Marc's lawyer, Tom Byrne, denied in 2003 that his client had done anything wrong. He said: "Mr. Schaffel has nothing to do with child porn."

The song was recorded in September 2001 and featured more than 35 other artists. Its goal was to raise $50 million (£30.5 million) for numerous charities in response to the September 11, 2001 attacks. Hollywood.com's Erika Gimenes wrote on September 21: "With plans to record a fund raising song titled *What More Can I Give?* Michael Jackson has lined up support from today's hottest acts to aid survivors and families of victims of the recent terrorist attacks the United States suffered earlier this month. The question is: Could Jackson recreate the success of his 1985 tribute tune *We Are the World*? Our answer: Definitely."

Michael said on a press release: "I believe in my heart that the music community will come together as one and rally to the aid of thousands of innocent victims. There is a tremendous need for relief dollars right now and through this effort, each one of us can play an immediate role in helping comfort so many people." Hollywood.com wrote: "While some may think that Jackson's effort to record a new song is only intended to increase interest in his comeback efforts, the King of Pop has always been involved in charitable organizations. In October 1998, tenor Luciano Pavarotti and Jackson's close friend Elizabeth Taylor joined the superstar in a series of concerts Jackson organized and headlined to benefit the World Peace Foundation for Children (WPFC), in hopes of providing aid to needy children and families around the world. Other musicians were doing their part to pay tribute to the victims by donating to different relief funds." Michael told ABCNews.com: "Music is capable of touching people's souls, and it's time we use that power to help us begin the process of healing immediately." Michael was inspired to write the song after meeting with former South African president Nelson Mandela in 1999.

Michael said the song was intended to "find solace in the wake of the attack on America and to create a sense of global unity in the face of mindless violence and mass murder." The recording included performances by Michael and other stars like 3LW, Aaron Carter, Anastacia, Beyoncé, Billy Gilman, Brian McKnight, Bryton, Carlos Santana, Celine Dion, Cristian Castro, Gloria Estefan, Hanson, Jon Secada, Luther Vandross, Mariah Carey, Michael McCary from Boyz II Men, Mýa, 'N Sync, Nick Carter from Backstreet Boys, Reba McEntire, Ricky Martin, Shakira, Shawn Stockman from Boyz II Men, Thalía, Usher, Tom Petty, Ziggy Marley and Jesse McCartney. The Spanish version included stars such as Alejandro Sanz, Cristian Castro, Joy Enriquez, Juan Gabriel, Julio Iglesias, Laura Pausini, Luis Miguel, Olga Tañón and Rubén Blades. The charity single was finally abandoned by Michael's advisors. Interviews and internal records indicate that it was Michael's manager or attorney who quietly asked Sony to bury the charity project after discovering that Michael had signed over the rights to the single to Marc Schaffel. McDonald's Corp. backed out of the multimillion-dollar agreement to sell the single in its restaurants, and so the release of the single was pulled. The fast-food chain feared fallout from customers also because of Michael's involvement in a 1993 child molestation case. On October 21, 2001, the song was performed at a 9/11 benefit concert called *United We Stand: What More Can I Give?* It was Michael's last brand new song performed. The making of the song was shown at the 2003 *Radio City Music Awards*, where Michael was presented with a humanitarian award.

Michael's representatives announced that Michael Jackson's first studio album in six years, *Invincible* was due to hit stores on October 30. One representative said: "Fans can get a feel for Michael Jackson's new sound when the short film *You Rock My World*, starring Marlon Brando, Chris Tucker, Michael Madsen and Michael Jackson, premieres on music cable channels." MTV, VH1, MuchMusicUSA and Black Entertainment Television (BET) played the long versions and added it to regular rotation. *Invincible* (number 1), was featuring the singles *Butterflies* (number 14, 2001), *You Rock My World* (number 10, 2001), and *Cry*. The album sold almost 8 million copies worldwide, but Michael once again found himself embroiled in controversy when he decided not to renew his contract with Sony.

Marc Schaffel, the executive producer of Michael's aborted *What More Can I Give* fund-raising single sold the rights to the project for $1 million (£610,000) to a Japanese company. He kept half of it for himself. In February 2002, just three months after Michael's advisors fired Marc Schaffel, a bizarre transaction was negotiated quietly between Tokyo-based Music Fighters Corp. and F. Marc Schaffel. Representatives for Michael, Marc Schaffel and Music Fighters confirmed the sale. The deal included a provision under which Marc Schaffel was paid a $500,000 (£305,000) fee. As reported, Michael's representatives lobbied Sony Music to refuse permission for its stars to appear on the single. But Marc then cut a $1 million (£610,000) deal. The company Music Fighters Corp. agreed to pay more than $400,000

(£244,000) in bills to vendors associated with the project. Bizarre is that Michael had not only blamed Sony Music and its chairman, Thomas D. Mottola of being a racist and for the poor showing of his *Invincible* album, but he also accused Sony of blocking the release of the charity single, *What More Can I Give*. Michael said that Sony Music failed to adequately promote his latest recording. He had accused Sony and other record companies of conspiring to cheat particularly black artists out of royalty payments.

April 25, 2002, Michael Jackson performed at a fundraiser for the Democratic National Committee at the Apollo Theater in Harlem, helping to raise nearly $3 million (£1.8 million) towards voter registration. On September 15, 2002, Michael donated 16 exclusively autographed items consisting of CD's, videos and 2 cotton napkins to aid in the support of the victims of a severe flood in Germany. These items were auctioned off for charity and managed to raise €3.935 ($ 3,814). On October 12, 2002, Michael Jackson invited more than 200 Team Vandenberg members, who recently returned from overseas deployments, and their families to his Neverland Ranch. This was to show his appreciation for the sacrifices the military in his community make. In November , 2002, Michael donated an autographed teddy bear dressed in his likeness to Siegfried & Roy's celebrity teddy bear auction. This auction helped Opportunity Village which is a non-profit organization based in Las Vegas (USA) that enhances the lives of individuals with intellectual disabilities and their families. Michael's autographed teddy bear raised $5,000 (£3,000) for the charity. On November 21, 2002, Michael donated a jacket to the The Bambi Charity Event in Berlin which raised $16,000 (£9,800).

Chapter 4
Kids & Allegations

In many ways Michael felt the Martin Bashir interview damaged him deeply. Michael was initially persuaded by his friend Uri Geller, to let Martin become part of his entourage for eight months. Uri Geller said: "Michael liked Martin and he was happy to have him around. I said to him, 'Michael, maybe it's time to open up to the world,' and so he did." Martin Bashir had scored a momentous public relations coup with Diana's Panorama interview in 1995. And Michael liked *The Princess of Wales*. Michael believed unprecedented access to his personal life would help him win public sympathy. Michael hoped he could repair a reputation that had become heavily tarnished. But Michael showed a big error of judgment on his part. The unflattering television documentary by British journalist Martin Bashir caused an uproar when Michael admitted he shared his bed with young cancer victim Gavin Arvizo. Michael told the audience he wanted to help Gavin Arvizo, then 12. He admitted sleeping with more children at his Neverland Ranch in California. No any singer ever made such a confession before.

In the film, *Living With Michael Jackson*, Michael talked openly about sleeping with boys, including the *Home Alone* star Macaulay Culkin and his brother Kieran when they were 12 and 10.

Michael said: "I slept in a bed with many children." He told the reporter: "It's not sexual, we're going to sleep. I tuck them in, it's very charming, it's very sweet." The footage of him holding hands and cuddling Gavin seemed odd through the cameras of Martin Bashir. Michael's many donations were not shown and no charity organizations were mentioned. "We should have send a kid to do the interview, that would have been more revealing," someone said close to Michael. We heard Michael saying: "Peter Pan represents something very special in my heart. He represents youth, childhood, never growing up, magic. To me, I just have never grown out of loving that or thinking that is very special. I am Peter Pan in my heart." Michael told Martin more or less the same things he told Oprah years ago. Michael told Martin he feared his father Joe Jackson because he used to watch him and his siblings rehearse their dance steps with a belt in his hand. He told Martin he had no surgery on his face or changed his appearance on purpose, claiming that the media was ignorant about what they didn't understand.

In the documentary Martin didn't show he really understood Michael wanted to help a patient that was suffering. Martin asked Michael: "When you are talking about children, we met Gavin - and it was a great privilege to meet Gavin because he's had a lot of suffering in his life - when Gavin was there he talked about the fact that he shares your bedroom?" Michael responded: "Yes." Martin asked: "Can you understand why people would worry about that?" Michael: "Because they are ignorant." Martin: "But is it really appropriate for a 44-year-old man to share a bedroom with a child that is not related to him at all?" Michael: "That's a beautiful thing." Martin: "That's not a worrying thing?" Michael: "Why should that be worrying, what's the criminal, who's Jack the Ripper in the room? There's some guy trying to heal a healing child. I'm in a sleeping bag on the floor. I gave him the bed because he has a brother named Star, so him and Star took the bed and I went along on the sleeping bag?" Instead of understanding what Michael was trying to say, Martin wanted to get all the details about other sleep-overs. He asked Michael: "Did you ever sleep in the bed with them?" Michael: "No. But I have slept in a bed with many children. I slept in a bed with all of them, when Macaulay Culkin was little: Kieran Culkin would sleep on this side, Macaulay Culkin was on this side, his sisters in there. We all would just jam in the bed, you know. We would wake up like dawn and go in the hot air balloon, you know, we had the footage. I have all that footage." Martin was surprised: "But is that right Michael?" Michael: "It's very right. It's very loving, that's what the world needs now, more love more heart!" Martin: "The world needs a man who's 44 who's sleeping in a bed with children?" Michael: "No, you're making it - no, no you're making it all wrong." Martin: "Well, tell me, help me." Michael: "Because what's wrong with sharing a love? You don't sleep with your kids? Or some other kid who needs love who didn't have a good childhood?" Martin: "No, no I don't. I would never dream." Michael: "That's because you've never been where I've been mentally."

A little later in the documentary we hear Martin speaking to Gavin. Martin: "What is it, Gavin, about Michael that makes him connect so well with children? What is it?" Gavin: "Because he's really a child at heart. He acts just like a child, he knows how a child is, he knows what a child thinks. See, because I think that you don't necessarily have to be a child just because society says that 18 and up you have to be an adult. Doesn't really matter. You're an adult when you want to be one." After Gavin's sister talked about her brother, Martin asked Gavin: "When you stay here, do you stay in the house? Does Michael let you enjoy the whole premises?" Gavin: "There was one night, I asked him if I could stay in his bedroom. He let me stay in the bedroom. And I was like, 'Michael you can sleep in the bed', and he was like 'No, no, you sleep on the bed', and I was like 'No, no, no, you sleep on the bed', and then he said 'Look, if you love me, you'll sleep in the bed'. I was like 'Oh mannnn?' so I finally slept on the bed. But it was fun that night." Michael: "I slept on the floor. Was it a sleeping bag?" Gavin: "You packed the whole mess of blankets on the floor." Martin: "But Michael, you're a 44-year-old man now, what do you get out of this?" Gavin: "He ain't 44, he's 4!" Michael: "Yeah, I'm 4. I love, I feel, I think what they get from me, I get from them. I've said it many times, my greatest inspiration comes from kids. Every song I write, every dance I do, all the poetry I write, is all inspired from the level of innocence. That consciousness of purity. And children have that. I see God in the face of children. And man, I just love being around that all the time."

Michael told Martin Bashir in 2003 about his oldest son: "Like he said, he didn't have a mother." Martin asked Michael: "Do you not think, though, that your children would benefit from contact with their mother?" Michael: "No, because, because she doesn't? It is private information. She doesn't, she can't handle it!?" Martin: "She can't handle her own children?" Michael: "She'd prefer them to be with me than with her." Martin: "Did you know that she didn't want to have relationships with the children when you married her?" Michael: "Yes, she did it for me. She did it for me." Martin: "So - just so I understand this correctly; she knew that Michael Jackson loves children and she knew that

Michael Jackson wanted children..." Michael: "Yes, that's why. She said you need to be a daddy." Martin: "Right, she said you needed to be a daddy more than she needed to be a mother?" Michael: "Yeah. And she wanted to do that for me as a present." Martin: "As a present, what do you mean?" Michael: "As a gift, I used to walk around holding baby dolls..." Martin: "Really?" Michael: "Yes, because I wanted children so badly." Martin: "What you've just said is that your wife gave you two children as a present because she knew that you wanted to be a father?" Michael: "Yeah. It was a lovely gesture." Martin: "It is an incredible gesture." Michael: "Yes, there are surrogate mothers who do that every day. That happens every day in the world, it is happening right now." Martin: "Is that how Blanket was born?" Michael: "I used a surrogate mother and my own sperm cells. I had my own sperm cells in my other two children. They are all my children but I used a surrogate mother and she doesn't know me, I don't know her. And so he was born." Martin: "How did you select the mother, out of interest?" Michael: "It didn't matter to me as long as she was healthy. I didn't care what race as long as she is healthy, as long as she didn't have eye... and her vision is good, and her intellect, I want to know how intelligent she is." Martin: "Would you have conceived a child with a black woman?" Michael: "Of course." Martin: "But I have seen Blanket and I think it is safe to say that his mother was probably white." Michael: "No, you are wrong." Martin: "I am wrong?" Michael: "You are wrong." Martin: "So Blanket's mother is black. But blanket is so light?" Michael: "Black people were called colored people because we come in all colors from very white, as white as my hand, to very dark, as dark as your shirt. My father has blue eyes. And when they see Paris, they always say Debbie but that could be my father's genes, you know." Martin: "Really?" Michael: "Of course." Martin: "So when do you think you are going to have your next child?" Michael: "I wish I could have it today." Martin: "Really?" Michael: "I am thinking about adopting two kids from each continent around the world." Martin: "A boy and a girl from every continent?" Michael: "From every continent. That is my dream."

The conversations of Michael led a few months later to an investigation by the Californian authorities and his prosecution on 10 separate charges, including four of molesting a minor. The film was first screened in February 2003, in the Netherlands and it was a broadcasting sensation. I remember waking up and seeing pictures on the front of all the newspapers. Michael's story made again headlines all over the world. The film was first watched by more then 1 million viewers in the Netherlands and a few days later it was watched by 15 million ITV1 viewers in the United Kingdom. Another 38 million viewers watched it in the United States, when it was screened by the network ABC, who bought it for 3.5 million pounds. Michael was furious and made a formal complaint to television -watchdogs-. Michael accused Martin Bashir of 'utterly betraying' him and his friendship with Uri Geller was over. Michael told in a videotaped statement: "Martin Bashir persuaded me to trust him that this would be a honest and fair portrayal of my life and told me he was the man that turned Diana's life around."

Uri told me on the telephone that Michael didn't want to see the footage before it was broadcast. He told me Michael believed him and he trusted Martin 100%. Michael issued a statement through a London press relations company. The statement said: "Michael is devastated and feels utterly betrayed by the

British television program, *Living With Michael Jackson*, presented by Martin Bashir and broadcast in the United Kingdom on Monday, February 3, 2003, which he regards as a gross distortion of the truth and a tawdry attempt to misrepresent his life and his abilities as a father." Michael was concerned that Martin Bashir and Granada Television had broken the trust he placed in them. "In particular, he felt he had obtained their assurance that his children would not be featured in any way in the broadcast program. Michael repeatedly asked Bashir to stop filming his children, and was promised by him that the footage of his children would be taken out in the final edit but, Bashir said, shooting should not be stopped because "it would break the continuity of filming". Michael is deeply upset that the program sensationally sets out to use two or three pieces of footage giving a wholly distorted picture of his behavior and conduct as a father. Michael feels particularly devastated that he has been treated so badly by Martin Bashir, whom he let into the Jackson family home on a number of occasions over eight months, in the belief that Bashir wished to make a genuine documentary of his life. Michael believes that what was eventually broadcast was a salacious ratings chaser, designed to celebrate Martin Bashir, and which was indifferent to the effect on Michael personally, his family and his close friends. Michael originally consented to grant Bashir extended access to the Neverland Valley Ranch, his family and Michael himself, because he wanted to give the world a faithful representation of the truth about his life. Michael believed that the program Bashir has produced is a travesty of the truth. Michael would never have consented to participating in this film if he had been aware of how Bashir was going to falsely portray him. Michael believes that this program was intentionally produced and edited with a view to broadcasting sensationalized innuendo. Michael feels deeply angry that the program could have led viewers to conclude that he abuses children in any way. Michael Jackson has never, and would never, treat a child inappropriately or expose them to any harm and totally refutes any suggestions to the contrary. Michael would never betray the trust that a child, or their parents, might place in him."

Michael was moved to make the following personal statement: "I trusted Martin Bashir to come into my life and that of my family because I wanted the truth to be told: 'Martin Bashir persuaded me to trust him that his would be an honest and fair portrayal of my life and told me that he was 'the man that turned Diana's life around'. I am surprised that a professional journalist would compromise his integrity by deceiving me in this way. Today I feel more betrayed than perhaps ever before; that someone, who had got to know my children, my staff and me, whom I let into my heart and told the truth, could then sacrifice the trust I placed in him and produce this terrible and unfair program. Everyone who knows me will know the truth which is that my children come first in my life and that I would never harm any child. I also want to thank my fans around the world for the overwhelming number of messages of support that I have received, particularly from Great Britain, where people have e-mailed me and said how appalled they were by the Bashir film. Their love and support has touched me greatly.'" These comments were excerpts from a videotaped statement from Michael Jackson. The statement was released after the airing of the Bashir television special in the United States. "It breaks my heart that anyone could truly believe that Michael would do anything to harm or endanger our children: they are the most important thing in his life," Debbie Rowe, Michael's ex-wife and the mother of two of his children said. Michael got his revenge later when footage was aired on American television of Martin. But maybe it was too late, though. Martin said, "that Neverland was a 'dangerous place' for children." Martin was also heard to tell Michael: "Your relationship with your children is spectacular. It almost makes me weep when I see you with them because your interaction with them is so natural, so loving, so caring."

The investigation into Michael's private life was again under way. Bashir's career was booming as a result of his coup. Within months after the making of the film, Martin Bashir took up a deal with ABC, said to have been worth $1 million. He became an anchor on 20/20, the American equivalent of Newsnight. Later, Bashir told people that the star had not idea what he was getting himself into. "As far as Michael Jackson's concerned, he signed three contracts," Martin said. "He knew exactly what was happening and the film didn't emerge in the way that he'd hoped."

While audiences and critics around the world were concentrated on the extraordinary portrayal of Michael's home life, people in the United States were questioning the ethics used by Martin Bashir to win Michael's trust. USA Today described Bashir's interviewing style as 'unduly intrusive' and The New York Times wrote about his 'callous self-interest masked as sympathy.'

Prosecutors alleged that following the broadcast of the Bashir documentary, Michael and five associates plotted to control and intimidate the Gavin's family to get them to go along with damage-control efforts, including holding them against their will at Michael's ranch. The molestation charges related to alleged incidents between Michael, Gavin and his brother after the

Bashir documentary aired. Michael denied the sexual abuse allegations. He said that the sleepovers were in no way sexual in nature. Michael's friend Elizabeth Taylor defended him on Larry King Live. She told Larry: "We were in the bed, watching television. There was nothing abnormal about it. There was no touchy-feely going on. We laughed like children and we watched a lot of Walt Disney. There was nothing odd about it."

Something odd about Michael, according to Reuters, was this story: "Report: Jackson put 'curse' on Spielberg. Voodoo rituals, prosthetics and bleaching," reported that Michael, according to Vanity Fair, wears a prosthetic nose and once paid $150,000 (£ 91,500) for a 'voodoo curse' to kill director Steven Spielberg despite being deep in debt. Vanity Fair reported that in 2000 Jackson attended a voodoo ritual in Switzerland where a witch doctor promised that Spielberg, music mogul David Geffen and 23 other people on the entertainer's list of enemies would die. The article stated that Michael underwent a 'blood bath' as part of the ritual, then ordered his former business adviser Myung-Ho Lee to wire $150,000 (£91,500) to a bank in Mali for a voodoo chief named Baba, who sacrificed 42 cows for the ceremony. Vanity Fair reported that Jackson 'wears a page-boy wig and a prosthesis' that served as the tip of his nose. The magazine interviewed a source close to Jackson who said that without the device, Jackson resembles a mummy with two nostril holes. The magazine also revealed Michael's extravagant lifestyle and 'declining record sales have left him $240 million in debt'. The article relied in part on court filings in a $12 million (£7.3 million) lawsuit against Michael by his former business adviser Myung-Ho Lee. Since the mid-1990s Michael had relied on a series of multimillion-dollar loans to cover his expenses. In addition to the lawsuit by his former business adviser, Michael was also enmeshed in a $21 million (£ 12.8 million) court battle with German concert promoter Marcel Avram over canceled *Millennium* concerts. He also has been sued by Sotheby's auction house for $1.6 million (£976,000). Vanity Fair reported that Michael must pay off the principal on a $200 million (£122 million) loan within a few years. According to the article this will be nearly impossible unless Michael would sell his most valuable asset, the Beatles song catalogue. Vanity Fair calculated Michael would run up nearly $4 million (£2.4 million) per year in expenses from his Neverland Valley Ranch.

Martin Bashir, who was with Michael on shopping trips, agreed Michael could spent too much. He told The (London) Sunday Times newspaper, "Michael spent $6 million (£3.6 million) in Las Vegas on 'everything from 10-foot-tall glass urns to oversized marble chess sets'. He's already got three of these." Martin observed Michael's expenditure is tacky and extravagant. About the Berlin incident, which received worldwide condemnation and for which Michael later deeply apologized, Martin said: "Not one of his entourage was prepared to tell him it was ludicrous and dangerous." Martin said in the program about Michael: "In many ways he is charming. In others he is a disturbing individual whose financial power enables him to do what he wants, when he wants."

November 20, 2003, Michael was arrested and charged with child abuse and released on $3 million (£1.8 million) bail. District Attorney Thomas Sneddon said he expected to file "felony child molestation charges against Michael" within a week. The child abuse investigation was immediately placed with the Sensitive Case Unit.

The reason for this is that the department guidelines dictate that if "one of the clients in the referral is a public figure" or if the case's allegations "would be certain to generate media interest if they became known outside of DCFS," the matter requires utmost secrecy. Formal charges against Michael were filed in December 2003.

Michael smiled and waved to fans flashing a V-sign as he left the Santa Barbara County Jail in a black Suburban, escorted by three sheriff's motorcycle officers. Mark Geragos, Michael's Defense Attorney said: "He's come back specifically to confront these charges head-on. He is greatly outraged by the bringing of these charges. He considers this to be a big lie." Santa Barbara County Sheriff's deputies who raided Michael's Neverland Ranch found powerful narcotics, vials and IV bags containing what could be anesthesia. Among the items they collected were, A vial of Versed (a powerful sedative), several IV bags containing 'a milky white fluid, located in a small cardboard box on top of the bathtub', a vial of Promethazine (an antihistamine with strong sedative effects), a bottle of Alprazolam (generic for Xanax, a powerful anti-anxiety drug), a bottle of Percocet (a painkiller), a vial with Demerol in it, a bottle of Prednisone (a steroid), Ery-tab (an antibiotic), IV stands, Oxygen tanks, a prescription for Alprazolam, prescriptions for Xanax that had been filled, a syringe and numerous loose pills outside bottles. Fans were showing their support for Michael after the entertainer was accused of child molestation.

CNN anchor Kyra Philips talked in CNN's Breaking News to Jermaine Jackson after Michael was arrested. The interview aired November 20, 2003. Kyra asked if Jermaine was all right and said: "And I understand that you are coming to us from Las Vegas. I am assuming that you were with your brother as he was shooting this music video. I guess, first of all, I want to ask you how are you feeling right now? I know you have been a big supporter of your brother. You have always come out publicly and supported him. What's going through your mind right now?" Jermaine who supported Michael throughout his career said: "Well, first of all, I'd like to say the whole family supports Michael 100 percent, 1,000 percent. Michael is innocent. And just to let you know how I feel, I'm very disappointed in the system in which things were done. At the same time, Michael is in very strong spirits because he is innocent." Kyra worried, "What has he told you?" Jermaine: "We're tired of people... I'm sick and tired of people speaking on my brother's behalf and my family's behalf who do not know us. So you put these people on national TV, on international TV, and they say these things, and the public is saying, oh, wow, is he really like this?" Jermaine was angry and started a great speech to support his brother. "My brother is not eccentric," Jermaine said with tears in his eyes. "We had an incredible, wonderful childhood. And what they're doing is bringing him down with the very thing that he loved, his children and family. My brother is about peace. They don't know us. But this will reveal itself. But I'm sick and tired about everybody saying these things about my family." Jermaine was ready to stand up for his brother. He said: "We will fight, and we will stand up. And everybody that knows this family around the world will support us. Because, at the end of the day, this is nothing but a modern day lynching. This is what they want to see, him in handcuffs. You got it. But it won't be for long, I promise you."

Kyra tried to calm down Jermaine and said: "Jermaine..." Jermaine said: "I'm sick and tired."

Kyra: "And believe me, I..." Jermaine: "Sick and tired of this." Kyra: "... I have no idea what you are going through. I am definitely not in your shoes." Jermaine: "No, you don't know." Kyra: "No, you're right. You are right." Jermaine: "You don't walk in my shoes or my family's shoes." Kyra agreed and said: "You are absolutely right." Jermaine: "You don't walk in our shoes, but you put these people on national television to say things. They don't know our family." Kyra admitted: "And that's why we have you..." Jermaine: "We are a family and we will continue to be a family. That's my love right there. And we support him 1,000 percent. I have nothing else to say. Goodbye." Kyra: "Jermaine, please stay with me. Jermaine, please stay with me. Jermaine, are you still with me?" But Jermaine hang up. Kyra continued: "OK. Well, as you can understand, wow. A lot going through our minds right now. Jermaine is probably watching right now there in his hotel room in Las Vegas, and we appreciate you coming on the air and talking with us. Obviously, a lot of emotions right now soaring through the minds and the hearts of the Jackson family. A very difficult time for this family. But Jermaine Jackson coming forward, expressing how he is frustrated with how this is being handled. But we do have to lay out the facts right now. And that is, that his brother, Michael Jackson, has surrendered to the police. He is in the custody of Santa Barbara Sheriff's Department right now facing allegations of child molestation. However, for the first time, we heard from a family member, Jermaine Jackson, Michael's brother, sticking by his brother, expressing the love among his family. That they are supporting him, and are they're by his side. And coming forward believing, Jermaine Jackson saying that his brother is innocent."

Ed Bradley was a board member of Jazz at Lincoln Center and was instrumental in helping create the new facility for that genre of music at Lincoln Center. Ed was a principal correspondent for CBS Reports (1978-1981), after serving as CBS News' White House correspondent (1976-1978). Ed Bradley was also anchor of the CBS Sunday Night News (November 1976-May 1981) and of the CBS News magazine Street Stories (January 1992-August 1993). The pioneering black journalist who was a fixture in American living rooms for more than a quarter century on 60 Minutes, died in November 2006 after a battle against complications from chronic Lymphocytic Leukemia. He was an intelligent and friendly gentleman who was also known for his impeccable clothing and style. The well-respected CBS News Correspondent called Michael for an interview after his arrest. Ed sat down with Michael on Christmas Day at a hotel in Los Angeles, one of several cities where Michael had been in seclusion since authorities in Santa Barbara officially charged him with seven counts of sexual molestation and two counts of using an "intoxicating agent", reported to be alcohol, to seduce the alleged victim. Out on bail and awaiting trial, Michael spoke out finally about his arrest, his accuser and the bizarre charges that had made his life a shambles. Ed asked what Michael's response was to the allegations that were brought by the district attorney in Santa Barbara, that he molested this boy? Michael: "Totally false. Before I would hurt a child, I would slit my wrists. I would never hurt a child. It's totally false. I was outraged. I could never do something like that." Ed asked: "This is a kid you knew?" Michael said: "Yes." Ed: "How would you characterize your relationship with this boy?" Michael: "I've helped many, many, many children, thousands of children, cancer kids, leukemia kids. This is one of many." Michael said his accuser he had invited to his Neverland Ranch was among thousands of children he had invited to play in his amusement park, visit his zoo, watch movies, play video games, and feast on their favorite foods.

Ed asked why Michael developed Neverland. Michael said: "Because I wanted to have a place that I could create everything that I never had as a child. So, you see rides. You see animals. There's a movie theater. I was always on tour, traveling. You know? And, I never got a chance to do those things. So, I compensated for the loss by..., I have a good, I mean, I can't go into a park. I can't go to Disneyland as myself. I can't go out and walk down the street. There's crowds, and bumper to bumper cars. And so I create my world behind my gates. Everything that I love is behind those gates. We have elephants, and giraffes, and crocodiles, and every kind of tigers and lions. And..., and we have bus loads of kids, who don't get to see those things. They come up sick children, and enjoy it. They enjoy it in a pure, loving, fun way. It's people with the dirty mind that think like that. I don't think that way. That's not me." Ed asked: "And, do you think people look at you and think that way today?" Michael told Ed that if people have a sick mind, 'yeah'. If people believed the trash they read in newspapers, 'yeah'. He continued: "Just because it's in print doesn't mean it's the gospel. People write negatives things cause they feel that's what sells. Good news to them, doesn't sell." Michael told Ed his relationship with this boy he first met a year ago was positive. Michael said he was determined to help him with his battle against cancer. He added: "When I first saw him, he was total bald—headed, white as snow from the chemotherapy, very bony, looked anorexic, no eyebrows, no eyelashes. And he was so weak, I would have to carry him from the house to the game room, or push him in a wheelchair, to try to give him a childhood, a life. Cause I felt bad. Because I never had that chance, too, as a child. You know? That the— and so, I know what it— it felt like in that way. Not being sick, but not having had a childhood. So, my heart go out to those children I feel their pain." Michael told the reporter he tried to help in the healing process by taking the boy around the grounds of Neverland to Michael's favorite places. Michael said: "He had never really climbed a tree. So, I had this tree that I have at Neverland. I call it, 'My Giving Tree.' Cause I like to write songs up there. I've written many songs up there. So, I said, 'You have to climb a tree. That's part of boyhood. You just gotta do it.' And I helped him up. And once he went up, up the tree, we looked down on the branches. And it was so beautiful. It was magical. And he loved it. To give him a chance to have a life, you know? Because he was told he was going to die. They told him. They told his..., his parents prepare for his funeral, that's how bad it was. And I put him on a program. I've helped many children doing this. I put him on a mental program."

Ed asked some further in the conversation: "What was going through your mind when you're taken into a police station, in handcuffs, to have a mug shot taken, that you know is gonna be shown around the world?" Michael answered: "They did it to try and belittle me, to try and to take away my pride. But I went through the whole system with them. And at the end, I wanted the public to know that I was okay, even though I was hurting." Ed asked Michael: "What happened when they arrested you? What did they do to you?" Michael said: "They were supposed to go in, and just check fingerprints, and do the whole thing that they do when they take somebody in. They manhandled me very roughly. My shoulder is dislocated, literally. It's hurting me very badly. I'm in pain all the time.

This is..., see this arm? This is as far as I can reach it. Same with this side over here." Ed: "Because of what happened at the police station?" Michael: "Yeah. Yeah. At the police station. And what they did to me, if you, if you saw what they did to my arms, it was very bad what they did. It's very swollen. I don't wanna say. You'll see. You'll see."

Michael explained that police put the handcuffs at a certain position, knowing that it was going to hurt, and affect his back. He told Ed: "I can't move. I — I — it keeps me from sleeping at night. I can't sleep at night." Michael who only wanted to help a victim of cancer ended up being handcuffed and was locked up in a toilet. Michael: "Then one time, I asked to use the restroom. And they said, 'Sure, it's right around the corner there.' Once I went in the restroom, they locked me in there for like 45 minutes. There was doo doo, feces thrown all over the walls, the floor, the ceiling. And it stunk so bad. Then one of the policemen came by the window. And he made a sarcastic remark. He said, 'Smell, does it smell good enough for you in there? How do you like the smell? Is it good?' And I just simply said, 'It's alright. It's okay.' So, I just sat there, and waited."

Ed couldn't believe the story: "For 45 minutes?" Michael: "Yeah, for 45 minutes. About 45 minutes. And then, then one cop would come by and say, 'Oh, you'll be out in a second. You'll be out in a second.' Then there would be another ten minutes added on, then another 15 minutes added on. They did this on purpose." Ed asked Michael: "How did you feel when they went into Neverland, I mean, with a search warrant? I mean, what were they looking for? What did they take?" Michael told him: "My room is a complete wreck. My workers told me. They said, 'Michael, don't go in your room.' They were crying on the phone, my employees. They said, 'If you saw your room, you would cry.' I have stairs that go up to my bed. And they said, 'You can't even get up the stairs. The room is totally trashed.' And they had 80 policemen in this room, 80 policemen in one bedroom. That's really overdoing it. They took knives, and cut open my mattresses with knives. They just cut everything open."

Ed wanted to know from Michael if they took anything from Neverland? Michael: "I'm not sure what they took. They never gave me a list." Ed: "But you're saying that they destroyed your property?" Michael told him they locked everybody out of the house. He said: "They had the whole house to themselves to do whatever they wanted. And they totally took advantage. They went into areas they weren't supposed to go into, like my office. They didn't have search warrants for those places. And they totally took advantage. And the room is a total, total wreck, they told me. I don't think I wanna see it. I'm not ready to see it yet." I've been back there. But not in my bedroom. I won't live there ever again. I'll visit Neverland. It's a house now. It's not a home anymore. I'll only visit there. What time is it? Cause I'm hurting. You know what? I'm — I'm hurting. I have to go pretty soon anyway. Yeah. Okay. I don't feel good."

After Michael had to defend himself again against accusations of child molestation in the interview with 60 MINUTES host Ed Bradley, a doctor found Michael unconscious after being secretly summoned to his rented Beverly Hills home in the middle of the night. Hours earlier, more than 27 million viewers in the US had watched the interview. It is been said Michael collapsed from a morphine overdose after working himself into a frenzy of anxiety over the TV interview. The doctor recalled in an interview with The Mail on Sunday, the events of the early hours of December 29, 2003. He warned Michael's family that Michael should seek help for his obvious addiction. The doctor, who asked not to be named, told The Mail on Sunday: "I'd been treating Michael's brother Randy for several months when I was awakened by a phone call from him at 1.51 a.m. I was told someone wasn't well and that they couldn't call 911 [the US emergency services number] for security reasons." The doctor continued: "Randy sent a car to pick up the doctor, who lived nearby. When I got in it, I asked the driver who was sick and he said, 'Michael'. Once at the house, the doctor led to a first-floor bedroom where he found the singer, wearing pajama bottoms, propped up in bed, but unconscious. Michael did not respond to his name but his heartbeat was regular." Randy asked the doctor if he was going to make it. The doctor checked Michael's breathing and blood pressure, and finally Michael seemed to murmur something. The doctor couldn't understand what Michael was saying but Randy heard Michael saying 'he needed to use the bathroom'. Randy and the doctor each took an arm to get him to the bathroom. The doctor: "We then helped him back to bed. His frame was light but not severely malnourished. He probably weighed about 11 stone."

Randy said Michael had been under severe stress because of the television program which had aired that night. Randy told the doctor that an earlier TV documentary had caused all manner of problems. According to The Mail on Sunday, the doctor remained in the house until nearly 4 a.m., regularly checking on his famous patient. Randy told the doctor he couldn't call anyone but his own doctor when Michael collapsed because he was terrified of the publicity. The doctor told: "It was all cloak-and dagger-stuff and once people in the house realized Michael was going to be all right there was a palpable sense of relief. But I was deeply disturbed by the event. I told Randy that his brother should voluntarily go to a rehabilitation center to deal with his obvious addiction problem. I advised that Michael must be kept upright that night in case he vomited and inhaled the material, which could possibly cause his death. I told them that his body would break down the narcotics and that he would be fine in several hours."

The doctor left strict instructions that he or the emergency services should be called if the singer showed further signs of distress. He told The Mail on Sunday he also asked that Jackson be brought to his surgery later that day for an evaluation. He said: "I wanted to discuss with Michael directly the damage he was doing to his health and the very real concerns I had for his well-being. I never heard from any of them again."

Santa Barbara District Attorney Thomas W. Sneddon Jr., who led the investigation into allegations that Michael molested boy in 1993, said to be more eager than ever to "get" Michael. Fans of Michael have known that D.S., a track on *HIStory*, was a pointed reference to Santa Barbara District Attorney Thomas W. Sneddon Jr. Michael actually appears to call out the name *Tom Sneddon*, in the song, even though the lyric sheet says the name is *Dom Sheldon*. On the *HIStory* album, these are the lyrics that appear:

> "DOM SHELDON"
> They wanna get my a**
> Dead or alive
> You know he really tried to take me
> Down by surprise
> I bet he missioned with the CIA
> He don't do half what he say
> Dom Sheldon is a cold man
> Dom Sheldon is a cold man
> Dom Sheldon is a cold man

Dom Sheldon is a cold man
He out shock in every single way
He'll stop at nothing just
to get his political say
He think he bad cause he's BSTA
I bet he never had a social life anyway
You think he brother with the KKK?
I know his mother never taught
him right anyway
He want your vote just to remain DA.
He don't do half what he say

(© Lyrics by Michael Jackson *D.S* (1994), excerpt provided as citation.)

During a January 19, 2004 interview with Santa Barbara Sheriff's Department officials, a detective asked the boy about conversations he had with Jackson about girls and any related guidance offered by the performer. The boy, 13, replied that Jackson would "always, like, try to give me advice about the birds and the bees." However, the boy told investigators Michael didn't know much. He said: "I knew more than he did." District Attorney Thomas W. Sneddon asked if the boy had ceased drinking alcohol after leaving Neverland Ranch for the last time. The accuser stated: "That period of my life, I went to AA. That period of my life is over." To "make sure the record is clear." Attorney Sneddon asked if the boy was joking about attending Alcoholics Anonymous. "I'm just joking," replied the accuser.

Law enforcement sources told in February 2004: "In connection with the pop star's arrest on multiple counts of child molestation, Santa Barbara authorities have raided the home of a gay pornography producer Marc Schaffel." Police sources said F. Marc Schaffel, Michael's advisor who produced and sold footage of Michael holding hands with a boy at his Neverland Ranch to Fox TV in February 2003, was tracked by Santa Barbara detectives since November 2003, when they received a phone call from the FBI in Los Angeles informing them that F. Marc Schaffel was under investigation for alleged involvement in child pornography in Budapest. Sources said the latest charges against Michael renewed the agency's interest in Marc's activities. Law enforcement sources said the FBI investigated last year a videotape, filmed and produced by Marc Schaffel that involved alleged child pornography. Marc came in the spotlight when The Times reported that Marc had produced Michael's charity single, *What More Can I Give*. Santa Barbara detectives did not receive a copy of Marc's sexy video until December 2003, after Gavin Arvizo featured in the Fox TV footage of Martin Bashir's documentary alleged to police that Michael had molested him. A grand jury indicted Michael, 46-year-old, in April 2004 on charges of molesting the boy, giving him alcohol and conspiring to hold him and his family captive in 2003. Michael did not testify during the trial and pleaded not guilty to the charges. Michael's profile was examined by mental health professional Dr. Stan Katz during the investigation. Dr. Katz spent also several hours with the accuser. The assessment made by Dr. Katz was that Michael had become a regressed 10-year-old and did not fit the profile of a pedophile.

Roger Friedman of FoxNews.com reported in April 2004 new details on the case, including word that Santa Barbara District Attorney Tom Sneddon changed the dates of the alleged acts from occurring between February 7th and March 10th, 2003, to now February 20th and March 12th, 2003. He also reported that the accuser's mother arrived and remained in a wheelchair during the grand jury proceedings even though a source said,

"There was nothing wrong with her." Roger Friedman also reported that the appearance of Michael 's accuser before a grand jury did not go well for the prosecution. 10 years ago, Santa Barbara District Attorney Tom Sneddon's case against Michael depended on the grand jury believing the veracity of a young boy. Two grand juries in 1994 did not conclude that Michael had molested anyone. The boy who testified recently, also did not make a good witness. His own lawyer cut off the questioning when he saw things were getting rough. And a source said his mother was back in a mental hospital.

The *Trial of the Century* began in Santa Maria, California, two years after Michael was originally charged. During the trial the singer became dependent on morphine and Demerol, a dependency which he subsequently overcame. Michael suffered strongly from stress-related illnesses and severe weight loss. The Sun wrote that Michael needed money and had mortgaged his own songs to raise $50 million (£30 million). He borrowed the cash using the rights to hits like *Thriller* and *Billie Jean* as security, the magazine reported. The news came after prosecutors at his sex-abuse trial claimed Michael was crippled by $270 million (£164.8 million) of debts. Michael took out the $50 million (£30.5 million) loan two years ago, according to a biography of Paul Russell, who is Michael's pal. According to Sun, Michael borrowed $110 million (£67.million) from banks in 1999 against his $500 million (£305 million) back catalog of Beatles songs he owns. The damage to Michael's career was incalculable. Even though the trial was a bargain, costing a little more than $30 million (£18.3 million) in legal bills, Michael was left with no money. There was no money to make restart his career. The joint venture with record company Sony kept him from bankruptcy. Sources said Sony had been paying Michael's bills for the last years. Michael was in hock to Sony for hundreds of millions and no bank would give him any money.

The trial lasted nearly five months, until the end of May 2005. Michael was acquitted on all counts. Michael's former lawyer Tony Capozzola claimed after the trail in Britain's Daily Mirror: "Michael Jackson was petrified he might be sent to jail during his 2005 trail for child molestation." He said: "I was worried he would do something stupid." Tony Capozzola oversaw Michael's defense during the 2005 case and even hinted he would rather kill himself than be imprisoned. "He would constantly say, 'Tony, do you think I'm going to jail? I need you to be honest with me.' He would break down, his voice would tremble and he'd be sobbing. He never said, 'I'm going to kill myself,' but Michael said, 'I can't go to jail, I just can't.' He implied that he would have to find another way out," he said. Tony tried to help Michael and said: "I tried everything to keep his mind away from that, but I was worried. In court, Michael was completely quiet, the perfect defendant. He wasn't arrogant, he didn't say a word. He just sat there frightened."

Michael denied all charges, and was eventually acquitted of all counts, but Tony claims the stress of the case affected the singing legend's mental health. He told Daily Mirror years after the trial: "Michael was terrified that he might be convicted and go to jail, that was his worst fear. He called me many, many times after court, he called me late at night. He was very emotional and crying in a lot of the calls, it was a really tough time for him, he was unstable. Michael was frightened to be in custody, he knew that if he went to prison as a child molester, terrible things would have happened to him. He was scared he would be attacked and even molested by other prisoners. Physically he was very frail and very frightened about that." The lawyer also said: "He could not understand society's evil thoughts about him because of his mental set, he was Peter Pan. He would ask, why people think he is evil. He could not believe why people thought he was guilty." Tony further said: "I had to be very blunt with him." He told him: "Because you're a 48-year-old man and you got interviewed by Martin Bashir and told him you sleep with children. That doesn't go on in America or in most civilized countries, a man does not sleep with children." Michael then said: "That's society's problem and not mine." And Tony said: "In other words they are the dirty old men."

Friend Uri Geller said he had burst into tears when he heard the news and was "overjoyed" at the result. Uri: "I am just so emotional. I am just so pleased. In an indirect way I started all this, introducing Martin Bashir to Michael Jackson and now all I can say is 'Thank God'. I'm just so relieved and so happy for Michael Jackson. The nightmare is over. This ordeal that he went through all these months is finished, it's behind him. Thank God he survived this." Uri felt partly responsible for the 16-week trial and everything that happened to him and Michael: "In a way, yes. We both felt betrayed."

Prosecutors had charged Michael with four counts of lewd conduct with a child younger than 14; one count of attempted lewd conduct; four counts of administering alcohol to facilitate child molestation; and one count of conspiracy to commit child abduction, false imprisonment or extortion. Michael's prosecution rested on accounts provided to investigators by the teenage boy, his younger brother, older sister, and the children's mother. According to The Smoking Gun:

"If the harrowing and deeply disturbing allegations in these documents are true, Jackson is a textbook pedophile, a 46-year-old predator who plied children with wine, vodka, tequila, Jim Beam whiskey, and Bacardi rum. A man who gave boys nicknames like Doo Doo Head and Blowhole and then quizzed them about whether they masturbated and if "white stuff" came out. A man who conducted drinking games with minors and surfed porn with them on a laptop in his Neverland Ranch bedroom, noting that if anyone asked what they were looking at, the kids should just say they were watching "The Simpsons." A man who frequently talked sex with his little companions and explained that "boys have to masturbate or they go crazy." A man who told one pajama-clad boy that he wanted to show him how to "jack off". When the tipsy child declined the demonstration, Jackson announced, "I'll do it for you," and buried his hand in the boy's Hanes briefs, size small. And a man who emphasized to his little friends that these activities were "their little secret" and should not be disclosed to anyone, even if a gun was at their head."

The Smoking Gun had compiled an authoritative, behind-the-scenes account of the prosecution's case against Michael. Documents showed how the children received alcohol from Michael: "While their sister did not witness any sexual abuse, nor was she ever invited to stay in Jackson's bedroom, she told investigators that the entertainer provided her and her brothers with wine at Neverland and also said that her siblings each confided in her about Jackson's explicit sex talk. The older boy, she said, told her that Jackson gave them tequila and Skyy vodka and asked her not to tell their parents about his drinking."

Michael's defense team said the mother was a scheming grifter who had fabricated the abuse accounts and programmed these tawdry tales of masturbation and soiled underwear into her children. The boys ultimately reported that Michael often concealed the pair's wine, which Michael called Jesus Juice, in cans of Diet Coke and Sprite. In addition, the sister of the boys told detectives that the older boy said Michael would touch his behind outside his clothes, something that made her brother feel uncomfortable. The family's story changed shortly after the mother hired legal counsel in mid-2003. Before that, the family denied any improprieties by Michael in interviews with Los Angeles child welfare officials and Santa Barbara Sheriff's deputies.

According to an internal government memo, child welfare officials and confidential investigation by Los Angeles police concluded that allegations Michael Jackson sexually abused a cancer-stricken boy were "unfounded." According to the memo, the child was questioned in February by a social worker assigned to the Sensitive Case Unit of L.A.'s Department of Children & Family Services (DCFS). The boy "denied any form of sexual abuse." He said that he never "slept in the same bed as the entertainer." The boy, and his 12-year-old brother, who also denied sexual abuse, expressed "a fondness for the entertainer and stated they enjoyed visiting his home, where they would often ride in the park, play video games, and watch movies."

In an official memorandum from Jennifer Hottenroth, Asistant Regional Administrator for the Department of Children & Family Services, on November 26, 2003, we read that the mother of the boy stated (in February 2003) that she believed the media had taken everything out of context. The children's mother said that one of her boys was in stage 4 cancer and had received a year of chemotherapy in addition to having his spleen and one kidney removed. Mother stated that *the entertainer* was like a father to the children and a part of her family. The family first came in contact with 'the entertainer' through a performer at The Laugh Factory who learned that her son had wanted to meet *the entertainer* who then initially met him in the hospital. As per the sexual abuse allegations, the mother stated that her children were never left alone with the entertainer. She further stated that her son has slept in the same room as the entertainer but they did not share a bed. The entertainer would sleep on the floor. Their sister told a social worker that she accompanied the boys on "sleepovers at the entertainers home," but had "never seen anything sexually inappropriate between her brothers and the entertainer."

This family had one prior child abuse referral investigated by Department of Children & Family Services in October 2001 as a result of allegations of domestic violence between mother and father. These allegations proved to be substantiated. The children and the mother admitted to physical perpetrated by the father. At the time of the referral, the father had been arrested and the mother had a restraining order against him. This referral was subsequently closed in November 2001. As with many DCFS investigations, the abuse case involving Michael began with a call to the agency's child abuse hot line. According to the memo, a Child Abuse Referral was phoned in on February 14, 2003, by a school official from the Los Angeles Unified School District. The school official lodged allegations of "general neglect by mother and sexual abuse by an entertainer." The school official identified both the cancer patient, then 13, and his younger brother as the "referred children." Published reports have indicated that the older boy was taunted by classmates after the documentary of *Living with Michael Jackson* aired on ABC. During the February 6 program, the boy was seen resting his head against the singer's shoulder.

    Michael's lawyers consistently portrayed Michael as a naive victim of the accuser's family. They said the family were grifters with a habit of wheedling money out of the rich and famous. On March 10, the first day Michael's accuser took the stand, Michael arrived late for court as the judge threatened to revoke the singer's $3 million (£1.8 million) bail. He finally came to court in pajamas and slippers. His father and a bodyguard supported him claiming he had a back injury severe enough to require a short hospital visit. The boy testified in graphic detail about what he claims were molestations by Michael on two separate occasions in the first months of 2003. Gavin admitted however during cross-examination, he told an administrator at his school that nothing happened between him and Michael. Michael's trial was full of salacious testimony and dramatic moments. More than 130 people testified. Prosecution witnesses included Gavin's mother. She was on the stand for three days. Also included was a former security guard who testified that he saw Michael engaged in oral sex with another teenage boy. At the end of the trial, prosecutors showed a police videotape in which the accuser told detectives Michael gave him wine and masturbated him as many as five times. It took nearly 14 weeks before the jury, eight women and four men ranging in age from 20 to 79, got the case. Throughout the course of seven days, the jury deliberated about 32 hours before finally reaching its decision. Michael told about his trial on child molestation claims: "It is the hardest thing I've ever done in my life." Michael declared he was "completely innocent." He said his trial on child molestation charges has brought him to the lowest emotional point of his life, and he asked his fans around the world to pray for him.

During an interview with the Rev. Jesse Jackson, Michael said he believed to be the victim of a conspiracy. He declined to elaborate, citing the court-imposed gag order that prevents him from discussing his trial in detail. But Michael added, that he believed he was the latest of several "black luminaries" to be unjustly accused, citing former South African President Nelson Mandela and some former heavyweight boxing champions. Jesse Jackson met with bankers on Michael's behalf and told him to reduce spending. He also suggested charging for admission to Neverland Ranch. Jesse Jackson told the Chicago Tribune: "There were all these decisions that he had to make. I was simply one voice that had some access to him. I do not credit myself with having the determining voice."

Adrian McManus, who used to work at Neverland Ranch as a housekeeper claimed Michael used to lock boys in his bedroom for days, plying them with booze before sexually abusing them. He told the News of The World: "Every night I went home feeling sick to my stomach. He was a lonely, deranged, sick human tragedy. And he wasn't playing at being a boy again, this man was molesting boys. He was at his happiest when he had little boys with him. He would lock himself in his bedroom for days at a time with them. He acted inappropriately with at least ten boys. He would buy dozens of these baby bottles for the older kids. It was obvious he was drinking and slipping wine into their drinks. Michael filmed the boys with cameras and videos, and packed photo boards with their naked bodies. I saw Michael kiss and touch Jordan Chandler. They both bounded into the bedroom, soaking wet, after playing under the waterfall at the side of the house. Then Michael just lent forward slowly and kissed Jordan on the lips. Michael then moved his hand down. I froze and realized that my boss was a pedophile. On one of my first days Michael said very calmly, 'You know Adrian if you do or say something I don't like, I will have someone take care of you, but it wouldn't come from me.' I took that as a death threat."

Refuting prior testimony from two former Neverland Ranch employees, actor Macaulay Culkin told jurors that Michael never touched him inappropriately during stays at Michael's estate. Macaulay, wearing a black suit, took the stand early in the morning. Defense Attorney Thomas Mesereau, an American trial attorney and former amateur boxer, asked about allegations that Jackson fondled him. The actor said these were false. During direct testimony, the *Home Alone* star testified that he could not believe trial witnesses had made the abuse allegations. He also added that prosecutors have never contacted him to ask about the truth of these claims.

Macaulay said of Michael, "I've never seen him do anything improper." Prosecutor Ronald Zonen asked the actor about a trip he once took to Bermuda with Jackson and other friends. Macaulay confirmed that Michael gave him an expensive Rolex watch, but discounted the gift's significance: "It wasn't anything all that crazy to me. I was not a person without means, so it wasn't anything that was all that awe-inspiring." Prosecutors have alleged that as part of a pedophilic "grooming" process, Michael gave expensive gifts to his underage male targets, as well as their family members. Alleged abuse victims Wade Robson and Brett Barnes told jurors that Jackson never molested them. When Macaulay was asked whether Michael could have fondled him while he was sleeping, he said: "As far as I know, he's never molested me." Zonen asked asked Macaulay how many times he bunked with the King of Pop and if Macaulay slept with more 35-year-old men. Macaulay said: "Not that I remember," but I wasn't really friends with a lot of 35-year-olds who actually understood me." During his 16 minutes on the stand he testified that Michael could relate with the actor's worldwide fame and the fact that some people sought to personally profit from their association with him. "He gets it," Macaulay said.

The star was invited to counter testimony from former Neverland employees Adrian McManus and Phillip Lemarque. Maid McManus told jurors that she saw Michael once kiss Culkin on the cheek while, "he had his hand kind of by his leg, kind of on his rear end." Lemarque claimed that he saw Michael fondle Culkin while the pair played a video game in Neverland's arcade sometime in 1991. In his April 8 testimony he also said that he saw Jackson's left hand inside Culkin's pants.

The New York Daily News reported Macaulay Culkin's father, Kit, accompanied Macaulay and his other children during their Neverland visits. Kit had written his innermost thoughts about the time his family spent with Michael. "My kids never slept with Michael," Kit Culkin writes. "Whenever at Neverland, they always had their own quarters. Michael's bedroom was almost always an open place to hang out in, as was most all of the rest of the house." Kit explained his children would sit on the bed as would he, to play cards or checkers. He writes: "But then we would do so most everywhere else also. They might of occasion fall asleep there, just as they might of occasion fall asleep most anywhere else. None of my children, either by word or action or sense of feeling, ever reported or otherwise conveyed to me that pedophilia was a part of the menu at Neverland, or anywhere else that they might happen to be with Michael."

Publicist Max Clifford said: "I'm not surprised at the verdict. Obviously Michael Jackson fans must be delighted and he must be hugely relieved. But I think there are a lot of things that came out in the trial which have left a bad taste in the mouth of the general public. I don't think it is a foregone conclusion that Michael Jackson is, if you like, back on top. Certainly some of the stuff that emerged has really left a big question mark with a lot of people. Although he has been found innocent of all charges, I think that the verdict is still slightly mixed for the world's public."

Upon hearing the findings, Michael's family members reached out to touch one another and to support Katherine Jackson. She sobbed at hearing the first "not guilty." Michael stared at jurors with no visible signs of emotion at the reading of the verdicts. The judge read a statement from the jury after the verdicts. It stated: "We the jury feel the weight of the world's eyes upon us." The jurors asked to return to their "private lives as anonymously as we came." Michael dabbed both his eyes with a tissue after he heard the good news, while fans cheered, wept and hugged outside the courtroom. Michael was followed by attorney Thomas Mesereau leaving court after his acquittal. The California jury had exonerated Michael of the child molestation, conspiracy and alcohol charges that could have sent him to prison for nearly 20 years. Thomas Mesereau Jr. told reporters on his way out of the courthouse: "Justice was done. The man's innocent. He always was." Thomas Mesereau Jr. defended Michael by attacking the motivations of his accusers. He told jurors there was a lack of direct evidence.

"It's important that allegations of abuse are fully tested in courts. However, it's equally important that this doesn't deter people from raising their concerns about child abuse. It's vital that everybody is vigilant about inappropriate behavior towards children. Children need to understand that behavior that makes them feel uncomfortable isn't acceptable and that talking to someone they trust could help stop any abuse they suffer," said Mary Marsh, director of the NSPCC. Santa Barbara County District Attorney Thomas Sneddon said after the reading of the verdict he would accept the decision. "In 37 years [as a prosecutor], I've never quibbled with a jury's verdict, and I'm not going to start today," Thomas Sneddon said. Debbie Rowe's attorney released a statement from her. It read: "Debbie is overjoyed that the justice system really works, regardless of which side called her to testify at the trial." The trial was a losing battle for Michael. Some late night comedians derided him as a pedophile, and prosecutors who lost the case against him never accepted the jury verdict. Michael had no money left, felt driven to give up his Neverland Ranch and left the country.

According to the Jewish Telegraphic Agency Debbie Row, mother of Michael's children, who is Jewish, feared that Michael's nanny and some of Michael's siblings were exposing the children to teachings of the Nation of Islam. In 2005, court documents noted that "Because she is Jewish, Deborah feared the children might be mistreated if Michael continued the association." On the stand of a case, which was called People v. Jackson case, she explained that she had been allowed limited visits to her own children for only eight hours every 45 days. She sold her Beverly Hills house for $1.3 million (£800,000), and bought a ranch in Palmdale, California. In 2006, Debbie sued her ex-husband for one immediate payment of $195,000 (£119,000) and one payment of $50,000 (£30,500) to pursue a child custody case. Michael was also ordered to pay her $60,000 (£36,600) in legal fees. During the trial Jermaine, Michael's brother, connected Michael to Sheikh Abdullah. Jermaine said: "I was happy because he was so down. He was scared. Nobody else called. So Michael was spending hours on the phone with Abdullah. He was the one who was sending the money for the lawyers." The Bahraini sheikh allowed Michael and his family to stay in his palace. Only last year Abdullah sued Jackson in the London High Court for $7.8 million (£4.7 million) for reneging on a music contract that would have paid back this and other loans. Grace Rwaramba (Grece Rwaramba), Michael's nanny and a big fan of Michael since the 80s, told Britain's Times Online that Michael was ignoring the case. Grace would later recall: "When Sheikh Abdullah sued Michael in 2008, Michael said in the beginning, 'Oh, I never got money from him.' He tried to frame me that I took the money." Sheikh Abdullah called Grace one day and asked for her bank account. Grace asked why he needed her bank account, "I said why?" Sheikh Abdullah said he was sending money to Michael through her account. He sent $1 million. Then another $35,000."

In October, Michael's attorney Thomas Mesereau Jr. told the press: "The pop singer has made the Middle Eastern nation of Bahrain, not Neverland Ranch, his permanent home." He declined to comment on speculation that Michael planned to sell his ranch. He further stated: "The singer is very happy in his new home. He's looking much better. He's with his children and he's moving on in life. He's living permanently in Bahrain. He has friends there who have been very loyal and helpful to him in a difficult period of his life. Michael's attorney said he saw Michael a few weeks ago in London, where the singer is reportedly working on a charity single to benefit the victims of Hurricane Katrina. He said of the singer: "He looks really well."

Grace who took care of Michael and his children in Bahrain left all her Michael Jackson pictures, postcards, records, t-shirts and glove to Sister Patrick (her dorm mother) and to Toni Barboza (her little sister), hoping that they would learn to love him too, when she left her hometown years ago. She was determined to marry Michael when she would grow up. She wanted to have her own Jackson 5 generation with Michael. But Michael tried to blame his nanny for his overspending. In 2005, Katherine, the mother of Michael needed cash too. According to Times Online Michael told Grace to give his mom her ATM card. So Katherine was cashing out of the machine every day. Grace: "I checked it." So Grace told Katherine that the Internal Revenue Service (IRS) might find out, and said she wasn't happy with the situation. Grace who wrote in 1985 she likes Michael Jackson, her family, day dreaming and traveling, told journalist Daphne Barak a few years later in London: "I said, You, Michael and I, we will all go to jail! You know that we didn't report to the IRS about that gift. I told her I had all the documents." Katherine immediately called Michael. From that moment Michael stopped denying he knew about the money. Grace who spoke 4 years later in London about her time in Bahrain said: "When we lived in Bahrain, we had no money at all. Everything was paid by Abdullah, and Michael owed so much money to people." TV journalist Roger Friedman said: "For one year, the prince underwrote Jackson's life in Bahrain, everything including accommodation, guests, security and transportation. And what did Jackson do? He left for Japan and then Ireland. He took the money and moonwalked right out the door. This is the real Michael Jackson. He has never returned a phone call from the prince since he left Bahrain."

In 2006 Sony BMG released *Visionary: The Video Singles* to the European market; a series of 20 of his biggest hit singles of the 1980s and 1990s. Each single was issued weekly over a five-month period in DualDisc format (DVD video on one side, CD audio on the other). The whole group of discs was made available as a boxed set afterwards. The box set was released in the United States on November 14, 2006.

Rumors of financial problems for Michael became frequent after the closure of the main house on the Neverland Ranch as a cost-cutting measure. A prominent financial issue concerned a $270 million (£164.7 million) loan secured against his music publishing holdings. After Michael constantly delayed repayments on the loan, a refinancing package was shifted the loans from Bank of America to debt specialists Fortress Investments. Sony proposed Michael a new deal. Michael could borrow from Sony an additional $300 million (£183 million) and reduce the interest rate payable on the loan. It was giving Sony the future option to buy half of Michael's stake in their jointly owned publishing company (leaving Jackson with a 25% stake). Michael agreed to a Sony-backed refinancing deal, but details about any deal were never made public. Despite these loans and according to Forbes, Michael was still making as much as $75 million (£45.7 million) a year from his publishing partnership with Sony alone. In May 2006, the State of California closed Michael's Neverland Ranch and fined him $69,000 (£42,000) for not offering his employees insurance.

One of Michael's first documented public appearances since his trial was in November 2006, when he visited the London office of the Guinness World Records. Michael was awarded the *Diamond Award* on November 15, 2006, for selling over 100 million albums at the *World Music Awards*. Michael was scheduled to perform *We Are the World* but only managed a few lines before he left the stage. Michael Jackson earlier took a break from rehearsals for the *World Music Awards* to drop into the office of Guinness World Records. He asked to visit the building in north west London to receive his collection of World Record certificates. Michael was presented with certificates for eight accolades, including the most recent for the *Most Successful Entertainer of All Time*, *Youngest Vocalist to Top the US Singles Chart* and *First Vocalist to Enter the US Single Chart at Number One* for *You Are Not Alone*. He also holds the record as the *First Entertainer to Earn More Than 100 million Dollars in a Year*, *Highest Paid Entertainer of all Time* ($125 million-£76.2 million in the 1989 Forbes list), *First Entertainer to Sell More Than 100 Million Albums outside the US*, *Most Weeks at the Top of the US Album Charts* (non-soundtrack for *Thriller*) and *Most Successful Music Video* (*Thriller*).

Michael who was fan of Guinness World Records since childhood arrived at the office wearing his signature black shades, trousers with yellow piping and three quarter length dinner jacket. Michael was, like always, followed by an army of screaming fans from his hotel. He received not only his record certificates but also a copy of the latest edition of the *Guinness Book of World Records* and a special edition from the year he was born. Michael enjoyed with his children a midnight shopping trip to Top Shop while staying in London. His last live performance in Britain was at the 2006 World Music Awards. Following the death of James Brown, Michael returned to the United

States to pay his respects. Michael, along with more than 8,000 people, paid tribute during Brown's public funeral on December 30, 2006. Michael nearly stole the show when he made a surprise appearance at the last stop on James's so-called Farewell Tour. Rev. Al Sharpton delivered a eulogy and Michael bent down to kiss James' forehead and proclaimed him "my greatest inspiration."

In February of 2007, rumors were spreading that Michael sneaked into Prince's show, following the NBA All-Star Game in Las Vegas. Michael was interested in Prince's run of shows at the Rio Nightclub. Michael's partner at the party was actor and comedian Chris Tucker. It was Chris who helped Michael get involved with the Arvizo family in 2001. It leaded to Michael's eventual involvement with the family and more badly to his trial for child molestation and conspiracy. It took in fact concrete testimony from Chris and his ex-girlfriend to exonerate Michael.

Michael also had rekindled a friendship with Carol Lamere. She was the woman who introduced him to the Arvizos. Carol became the girlfriend of the father of Michael's accuser, David Arvizo. She also became a host to Arvizo's daughter, who lived with Carol for long stretches. The girl, then 16, didn't want stay with her mother, the now-infamous Janet Jackson. She even had replaced good old friend of Michael, Karen Faye, his long time makeup artist. In November 2004, Carol Lamere was interviewed by Defense Investigator Scott Ross about Michael. She told the investigator that she warned Michael about the Arvizo family but his secretary, Evvy Tavasci, didn't pass along the message. She also told him that Janet Arvizo was quite skilled at manipulating her kids. She was gifted at playing poor to get money out of strangers and she could get her children to say anything she wanted. The report stated: "Carol's opinion of Janet is that she should be in a mental institution."

Others were worried that Michael was somewhere lost. -Reconnect MJ- published a forum (reconnectmj.wordpress.com/my-mission/) saying: "My Mission. No, I'm not bored! I don't have too much time at hand, I don't need attention. I don't want to bad-mouth anybody or gossip! I'm not a fanatic and I'm not a know-it-all. And especially: no, I'm not a hater (BIG "no" there). Now that we've cleared up what I'm not, let's see what I am! I am concerned! I'm concerned about Michael, his life, his wellbeing, his career. Concerned about his associates, concerned when I see his actions (or non-actions). Concerned when I think about his future, his legend, his artistry. Concerned to see more and more friends and fans leaving. And especially concerned when I compare the Michael Jackson he was a few years ago to the Michael Jackson I see now! I want to help a friend and don't just sit here and watch how he alienates himself from... well, basically himself! Lets put it this way: If a good friend or a family member has been though a hard time – harder than anybody could probably ever imagine – this person will react in his own very special way. If he goes into isolation and doesn't find back to himself or even puts himself into a position of dependence and external control, then it's time to act! This is the moment when friends need to help! So if my friend changes, isolates himself, if he sits in his room and the outside world becomes strange and incalculable, I will not watch and accept when he says *Leave me alone*! Michael remained true to himself for 48 years! He did it his way and we all always admired him for his courage and power to do whatever he believed in, no matter how hard it was! He reinvented himself without losing his basic characteristics. His way to move, to stage-manage, to express himself, to communicate and interact, to stand up for and pass on his believes to thousands of people has always been unique and fascinating. But all of that seems to be under a big dust now. I don't care about a new album, I don't care about sold-out concert tours. I accept changes, I accept mistakes! I don't demand the character "King of Pop", but I don't accept the loss of Michael Jackson! Whoever thinks we will not lose the Michael we all know and love and that all will be fine as soon as a new album is out, didn't understand a very important thing: my mission is the human being, not the artist production! Therefore I don't want to just sit back and wait for a wonder from Mr. Incredible, actually I don't see Mr. Incredible at all, I see someone who's alone with a broken heart! And I want to take as many people as possible with me on my mission, because it should be OUR mission!"

For Akon, there's one star brighter than the rest and that is Michael Jackson. Akon and Michael spent time in a Las Vegas studio writing and recording songs for Michael's comeback album. Only two of the songs they recorded have surfaced: a remix of Michael's *Wanna Be Startin' Somethin'* that appeared on the 25th anniversary edition of Michael's *Thriller* album and *Hold My Hand*, a track featuring both Akon and Michael but written by Claude Kelly. Michael and Akon recorded 'days' of materials. Akon said in 2009, in MTV's *Michael Jackson's Human Nature* special: "My favorite moment was the day we actually met, because I didn't expect him to be that cool. I expected him to be this diva, just hard to deal with, rarely speaks, got to send his message through someone else, you know? Because these are the stories you hear." Akon was highly surprised: "So I'm going upstairs [to meet him], I knock on the door, his bodyguard opens and says, 'OK, he's waiting to meet you.' I walk in and Michael is in this spinning chair, but it's facing backwards, so I walk in the room, but his back is turned, and the guard says, 'Hey, Mike, Akon's here.' So he spins around, like it was choreographed, so right away I was like, 'Oh boy.' But as soon as he turns around, gets up, 'Yo, what up, man?!' and I was like, 'What up, Mike?' and he gave me a pound, we hugged each other. He's like, 'Yo, I've been waiting to meet you for so long, this is a great honor, thanks for showing up, thanks for making the time.' And in my mind I'm like, 'You know, I should be thanking you for making the time.' Akon had a great, incredible time that day: "It was the craziest thing, because we sat down, we talked about Africa, we talked about my foundation [Konfidence], we talked about the music, we talked about girls. He was extremely funny, he told jokes, and he liked to have fun." Akon couldn't stop about his meeting with Michael. About Michael he said: "He's incredible. He's a genius. Just to be in the same room [with him], I felt everything I wanted to accomplish in life has been achieved. That aura... that's how incredible that aura is... The way he thinks. Some artists think regional, some think national, I was thinking international. He thinks planets! It's on another level!"

In September Michael, who was rumored to be in New York to shoot a cover spread for Italian Vogue, sat for three hours in a chair until a stylist perfected his coif. The Insider said Michael had been "holed up in a fancy Midtown hotel since Thursday afternoon 'with an enormous entourage' and left only once, at 5 a.m., to take part in the 10-hour shoot for the fashion."

In February 2008, *Thriller* was reissued again as *Thriller 25*, an expanded version of the best-selling album, including five remixes featuring contemporary artists, Akon, Fergie, Will.I.Am and Kanye West, a previously unreleased song, a DVD and other bonus material. *Thriller* ranked on Rolling Stone magazine's *500 Greatest Albums of All Time* list in 2003, number 20. *Thriller* was listed by the National Association of Recording Merchandisers at number 3 in its *Definitive 200 Albums of All Time*.

      Stuart Backerman, a publicist who stopped working for Michael after Michael was arrested in 2003 was so worried about Michael's addiction to painkillers that he published his emotions on a website. Stuart stated: "Thank you, Mr. Backerman. An Open Letter To Michael From Stuart Backerman. It read: "I was your official spokesman and worked for you for almost two years, doing the best job I could, believing that you had a gift to share with the world. When I resigned, I stated that I loved both you and your fans, who have over the years exhibited a truly amazing display of loyalty and devotion to you, both as a person and to the values that they believe you exemplify. Though that declaration might have seemed excessive at the time, it was uttered from the heart, since I believe we are all perfect in the eye's of our Creator, an expression of that divine force that animates all life in the Universe. Michael, artists like yourself have a special gift to express that energy, which you have done so well in your remarkable life and career. But that said, it doesn't matter how many millions of records you have sold, how many TV specials you make, how much homage you receive, what really matters is the pact you have made with yourself, the inner self, not the celebrity who the world knows as Michael Jackson... I'm worried about you Michael, and wish that as a result of these difficult few years you could experience in your personal life that state of grace where there is no difference between the singer and the song. Michael, I don't want to set myself above you, like so many people are inclined to do. I don't want to preach to you, since I know your life hasn't been easy and that you've sacrificed greatly for the success you've achieved, creating a musical and charitable legacy like few other artists. But it is written, 'For what shall it profit a man, if he shall gain the whole world, and lose his own soul?' Michael, You have given much to the world, and have much still to give. I believe it is time to make a new beginning. I believe that if you sincerely do so, the whole world will accept and respect the new energized and contented Michael Joseph Jackson."

On Augustus 29, 2008, ABC News' reporter Chris Connelly asked Michael over the phone how he was going to celebrate his 50th birthday. Michael said: "Oh, I'll have a little cake with my children and we'll probably watch some cartoons." ABC said that 'Michael is still the biggest star in the world, and one of the most private.' Chris asked: "As you look back on your career Michael, what would you have done differently?" Michael: "I am still looking forward to doing a lot of great things, so that's hard, I think the best is yet to come in my true humble opinion." He told Chris he was watching a James Brown show, "I am just watching a little James Brown show right now." Chris: "Is that right?" Michael: "I love James Brown, yes." Chris Connelly asked Michael also questions about how he looked back at his career: "As you look back on 50 years in your career, at what point in your career do you think, you were the happiest." Michael answered: "The happiest...? The recording of *Thriller* and the *Off the Wall* albums, that meant very much to me and seemed to be received so beautifully by the public and the world, I enjoyed it very much." Decades later it is fair to ask Michael if he can still dance like he did before. Michael told ABC News: "Yes!! Because I am expanding a lot of the avenues, people see some of the things I do and say why don't you show this to the world, people don't know you do these things. Well maybe I will."

Michael told Chris he admired other artists to like Chris Brown and Justin Timberlake. "I really admire what they are doing," Michael said. Chris: "Is there anything you sacrificed by having this amazing career, 40 years and counting?" Michael explained: "A lot of hard work sacrificing your time and your schedule and your childhood, you know, giving up your life for the medium." Chris: "Would you like them to have the same kind of upbringing you did in terms of getting into show business at an early age? Or do you want to say whoa, take a moment, enjoy your childhood?" Michael: "I am letting them enjoy their childhood as much as possible. I really do, I let them go to the arcade and go to the movies and do things. I think that comes naturally. You know I want them to get to do things I didn't get to do." Chris: "It must mean a lot for your kids to be able to do the things you weren't able to do, huh?" Michael: "Yes, I get pretty emotional when I see them having a wonderful time, when they scream and they are happy and they are running. It makes me emotional." Chris asked: "You know, when most people turn 50, the AARP finds them and sends them a AARP card - Have you gotten an AARP card in the mail?" Michael started laughing and said: "Not that I know of...(laughing)."

In late 2008, a shadowy figure emerged as Michael's 'official spokesman'. He said he was Dr. Tohme Tohme. Dr. Tohme Tohme has been described as a Saudi Arabian billionaire and an orthopaedic surgeon. In fact he is a Lebanese businessman who doesn't have a medical licence.

At one point, Dr. Tohme claimed he was an ambassador at large for Senegal. However the Senegalese embassy said: "We have never heard of him." Also it is to believed Dr. Tohme is connected to Nation of Islam. The mysterious financier, who helped save Neverland from foreclosure and who served as Michael's adviser and confidant in the final years of his life told The Associated Press in 2009 how and when he entered Michael's orbit.

"For the last year and a half, I was the closest person to Michael Jackson," he told the news service. Dr. Tohme was inspired to help Michael because he saw that he was a "wonderful human being" and a "fine father to his three children." He told The Associated Press: "I'm a private man. A lot of people like the media and I don't. I respect the privacy of other people but lately nobody respects mine." Though Dr. Tohme apparently uses the title 'Dr.' and has a medical degree, there is no record of Dr. Tohme practicing medicine in the United States. Dr. Tohme said that one of the first things he did when he took over Michael's business was to fire many members of Michael's staff, including security guards. Dr. Tohme wanted to build a fence around Michael and protected him from others who wanted to control Michael's finances. Dr. Tohme also said he fired nanny Grace Rwaramba twice, on Michael's orders. According to his financial adviser Michael didn't use drugs and kept himself on a strict, healthy diet that included no red meat or alcohol.

Dr. Tohme said he was contacted in 2008 by Michael's brother Jermaine to help rescue Neverland from falling into foreclosure. The pair traveled to Las Vegas and met Michael there. Dr. Tohme liked Michael immediately. Dr. Tohme said he helped negotiate a deal with his close friend, the chairman of Colony Capital. Colony Capital agreed to buy the mortgage on the home and kept it out of foreclosure. Michael and Dr. Tohme had great plans for the future. Among the deals he said Michael and he negotiated about were deals for a *Thriller* Broadway show, the subject of a lawsuit from the director John Landis, and deals for an animated series based on *Thriller*. He said a clothing line was going to be produced including "moonwalk shoes", and Dr. Tohme said he was working to renegotiate the terms of some of Michael's main assets, Michael's share of the very lucrative Sony-ATV Music Publishing Catalog. Some people believe Dr. Tohme and Michael met already years ago after Michael left the country in 2005.

According to Julien's Auctions: "An array of treasures from Michael Jackson's Neverland Ranch ranging from Michael Jackson's iconic white-jeweled glove to the grandiose entry gates to Neverland Ranch are being presented in a tour de force public exhibition boasting 1390 Lots conducted by Julien's Auctions." The idea was to start with a highlights tour to major cities worldwide. An article on the website of Julien's Auctions tells us: "This monumental four-day public exhibition to be conducted by Julien's Auctions April 14th–25th, 2009 at 9900 Wilshire Boulevard adjacent to the legendary Beverly Hilton Hotel, offers an astounding array of Fine & Decorative Art items, paintings and life size bronze and marble sculptures to Memorabilia from the Life & Career of Michael Jackson. The exhibition also includes Amusements, Arcade Games & Disneyana, Entertainment Memorabilia and Garden Statuary and Furniture from the life and career of the King of Pop Michael Jackson and his Neverland Ranch." It further read: "King of Pop: A Once in a Lifetime Public Exhibition Featuring Property From the Life and Career of Michael Jackson and Neverland Ranch, April 14th – 25th,

2009." Michael was furious and immediately wanted to stop the auction. He called up Dr. Tohme and asked him for help.

New York auctioneer Darren Julien filed in March 2009, an affidavit in Los Angeles Superior Court. Darren described a meeting he had with Dr. Tohme's business partner, James R. Weller. James told Darren: "If you refuse to postpone [the auction], you would be in danger from 'Farrakhan and the Nation of Islam; those people are very protective of Michael.'" He also told that Michael and Dr. Tohme wanted to give the message that 'your lives are at stake and there will be bloodshed'. Weeks later Dr. Tohme accompanied Michael to a meeting at a Las Vegas hotel with chief executive of the AEG Group, Randy Phillips.

The article on Julien's Auctions' website also said: "Michael Jackson began his assent to the zenith of international pop culture in the 1970's as the stand-out member of the Jackson 5. His aspirations for success as a solo artist would be realized beyond anyone's wildest imagination in the following decade with the release of his albums *Off The Wall*, *Thriller*, and *Bad*. His altruistic personality and undeniable musical talent proved him capable of reinventing everything from music industry conventions to age-old racial barriers, becoming the first black entertainer to be embraced by the new crossover audience of the MTV generation. "The King of Pop" became one of the defining aspects of 1980's popular culture. His highly acclaimed, extravagant worldwide tours propelled him into the international spotlight, earning him recognition and respect from millions of fans around the world. Michael Jackson's innovations reach far beyond his groundbreaking musical aesthetic extending from short film to high fashion and influencing countless generations to come." It said about Neverland: "Neverland Ranch is named after Peter Pan's magical island whose youthful inhabitants never grow up and was created in 1988 when Michael Jackson purchased the 2,700-acre property in central California's wine country. Neverland became an awe-inspiring wonderland containing larger-than-life superheroes, a custom made horse-drawn carriage and antique automobile replicas, top-tier 19th century paintings and sculpture, exquisite furniture and fine art, renowned international awards and Michael Jackson's iconic concert costumes. Michael Jackson was an enthusiastic and avid collector of everything from exquisite antiques to prized entertainment and popular culture memorabilia. Julien's Auctions is proud to present all these items and much more for sale to the public in this once-in-a-lifetime auction of the property of Michael Jackson and the contents of his Neverland Ranch." The King of Pop's possessions, that would have been on display were organized by the self-styled King of Pop.

Dr. Tohme believed that the best thing Michael could do to make money, was to restart his career with a new *Michael Jackson World Tour*. Michael refused at first but Dr. Tohme told him he could make so much money, that he would never have to tour again. Michael refused again and said he could only do a few concerts. Dr. Thome told him he was thinking of making a movie from the concerts and told Michael eventually a new album could be recorded. Michael didn't believe in touring in the United States. He said, that if he wanted to do a concert, he wanted to perform in London. He said, he wanted to think about it. "Do that," Dr Tohme told him. Michael had some money left from his trip to Bahrain and wanted to start paying back his debts. Ultimately, Michael agreed to the tour but decided to do only ten concerts in London. He passed a rigorous 4½-hour medical before signing the deal in March, according to promoters of the shows at the O2, in Greenwich, South-East London. The O2 Arena, which can hold up to 20,000 people had become a venue of choice for big-name acts and comeback performers. Britney Spears was due to play there for eight nights in June, Prince did a 21-day series of shows at the arena in 2007. Led Zeppelin played a one-off reunion gig there the same year.

Michael announced plans for a series of live concerts in London this summer, in what would be his last press conference at O2 Arena in London on March 5, 2009. Michael finally returned to the stage after eight years. Tickets were expected to sell quickly for all the shows, despite concerns Michael may not be up for a return to the spotlight. He told a crowd of screaming fans that he would play a series of concerts before retiring from public performance. He said, as the fans screamed: "This is it. This is it. These will be my final shows, performances, in London. This is it. And when I say this is it, I mean this is it. This is really it. This is the final curtain call, OK? See you in July." He was wearing his trademark sunglasses and a silver-embroidered black military-style jacket. The 10-concert stand would begin July 8, 2009. British music writer and broadcaster John Aizlewood said about his return to the stage: "These concerts are a huge opportunity for rehabilitation. Because of what's happened to him and how he's lived his life over the last 20 years, he's made it very difficult for people to out themselves as Michael Jackson fans. This is Michael Jackson playing his greatest hits, some of the greatest hits in the history of music, live. It is a great event. I think even Michael Jackson won't blow it." Bookmakers, like William Hill already took bets on whether Michael would show up for his first gig. It was offering 5/1 odds that Michael would not, and spokesman Graham Sharpe anticipated brisk business. He said: "Once people start buying tickets they may well want to have a bet that he won't show up as a form of insurance."

"Michael Jackson is taking drastic steps to improve his looks, he's reportedly had hair transplants," Showbizspy.com stated. "The *Thriller* singer, 50, is said to be petrified of being back in the public eye," the article said. Michael opted for the treatment in a bid to make him feel better about himself and boost his confidence. "Ever since Michael announced his comeback there has been a lot of speculation on whether it will be a flop," a source told newspaper The People. As Michael is set to play 50 gigs at London's huge O2 Arena later this year, "he needs all the confidence he can get." The source added: "Everyone just hopes he doesn't take the surgery any further." Michael's health was rumored to be as precarious as his 'troubled' finances. Michael had struggled to pay his debts after his financial empire crumbled rapidly following his arrest in 2003. People believed he had lung disease or an infection acquired during nose surgery.

On May 20, AEG announced that the first London shows had been delayed for five days while the remainder had been pushed back until March 2010. AEG denied that the postponements were health-related. The crew needed more time to mount the technically complex production. But Michael wasn't eating much and had problems sleeping. Michael told staff members he had nightmares and was worried of being murdered. He was worried of disappointing his fans and in fact he was terrified to return to the stage. There were many reasons to worry. Michael's drug habits had significantly intensified in his final months. Rumors emerged that Michael was sick, this time with skin cancer. Concert promoter AEG Live repeatedly declared in the press that the change in schedule had "absolutely nothing to do with Jackson's health." Michael's erratic behavior have often overshadowed his music. His last major tour was the *HIStory World Tour* in 1996-1997. Michael had not played a full concert since 2001.

The Sun reported, according to Ian Halperin who falsely stated that Michael had long problems, that Michael Jackson was -indeed- homosexual and even had -numerous- -flings- with a string of male lovers, using some rather bizarre tactics to keep his secret safe. The new book released in the wake of Michael's death, is insisting that 'virtually everybody' around Michael knew he was gay. The book, *Unmasked: The Final Years of Michael Jackson*, says that Michael would sneak out of his home very late at night dressed as a woman to go hook up with various male lovers. Biographer Ian Halperin even claims to have tracked down two of those alleged male lovers. One lover, Ian Halperin claimed, who Jacko was 'madly in love' with met the singer for liaisons at a grungy motel. He wrote that the hotel was "all the debt-ridden star could afford." A 'secret' lover even would have told the biographer: "The very first time he had sex with me he said, 'The King of Pop's going to lick your lollipop'. I still laugh thinking about that." The other Michael lover the writer tracked down was a Hollywood waiter/aspiring actor known only as 'Lawrence'. He told Michael and him met almost every night for three weeks at his Hollywood Hills home in a short but passionate affair. He added: "He was very shy. But when he started to have sex, he was insatiable." Ian claims to have interviewed many acquaintances and supporters who told him Michael was absolutely gay. He stated: "Virtually everybody has told me. Even those who are his most ardent defenders, people who maintain he is innocent of the molestation charges, insist that he is homosexually inclined." The book doesn't give any detailed information. Sources in the book have no names or are called by the first name. Most of the stories seems to be fabricated and make Michael and his life looking even more odd. Ian stated that at first he didn't believe Michael was not guilty. He is one of those reporters that most probably believed what other reporters had written about Michael. Michael hated *those type* of reporters. As reported, Michael never left his house for decades, without security around. He was too afraid to hit the streets by himself, neither has he invited people over. And above all, he didn't call himself The King of Pop, Jacko or something else. He liked candy but didn't like lollipops.

An AEG promoter told reporters: "In June, Michael Jackson approved a line of official merchandise for you, his fans... A variety of official merchandise commemorates this incredible talent and preserves the legacy that is Michael Jackson." The line which includes interesting accessories like a wine glass, sleep masks, handbags, belt buckles, and tea sets is said to be launched soon and will be available at places like JC Penney and Target. "It's going to be a 300-piece collection of clothing and accessories," the promoter said.

Michael told fans he is fuming with his concert promoters for booking 50 shows instead of 10. The star told some fans outside his dance studio in Los Angeles, he wanted to take his live extravaganza across the globe - and only perform a few gigs at the O2 in London. A deal was struck for Michael's monster 50-date residency. Michael claimed he only learned of the extra 40 bookings when he awoke to the news one morning. Michael said: "Thank you for your love and support, I want you guys to know I love you very much. I don't know how I'm going to do 50 shows. I'm not a big eater - I need to put some weight on. I'm really angry with them booking me up to do 50 shows. I only wanted to do 10, and take the tour around the world to other cities, not 50 in one place. I went to bed knowing I sold 10 dates, and woke up to the news I was booked to do 50." He is panicking he's not physically strong enough to cope with the grueling schedule. The concerts were due to kick off on July 8. The opening night has already been pushed back five days.

Some people knew it was a disaster waiting to happen. Nobody predicted the rehearsals could actually kill him but nobody believed Michael would end up performing. Everybody in the room was in shock when Michael collapsed during only his second rehearsal. Michael needed medical attention and couldn't go on. And nobody knew what caused it. Michael wrapped up work on an elaborate production called: *Dome Project*. Michael wanted to dazzle his concert audiences with a high-tech show. It could be the final finished video piece overseen by Michael. 3D images, inspired by *Thriller* would flash behind him on stage. They filmed at Culver Studios, which was the set for the classic film *Gone With the Wind*, 70 years ago. Including in the four sets was a cemetery recalling the *Thriller* video. Michael was most days on the set. Vince Pace, whose company provided cameras for the shootings said: "It was a groundbreaking effort. To think that Michael's gone now, that's probably the last documented footage of him to be shot in that manner." The company Stimulated was hired to produce screen content for Michael's comeback concerts in London. At the time of Michael's death, the project was in post-production and would have been expected to be completed in July. The shooting took place from June 1, till June 9, and the sets were exclusively constructed for Michael's production. One set was designed to simulate a lush jungle. Another set was draped in black with an over sized portrait of Michael in his *Thriller* werewolf costume. The last set was built to replicate a construction site with a screen in the back to allow projection. One scene included scantily clad male dancers wearing carpenter's belts. A person close to the project told Michael at one point needed assistance as he descended steps off a stage. Arriving in a caravan of SUVs with security guards in tow, he made quite an impression. The whole team worked extremely hard and the marathon sessions during the five-week project were ending early in the morning. Spokesman for Michael, Michael Roth, who works for Los Angeles-based promoter AEG Live, said he had not heard about the production. "It could be part of the company's contract with Michael," he said.

During the last months of his life, Michael made desperate attempts to prepare for the concert series. According to many people Michael wasn't able to perform 50 shows, mentally and physically. Many felt that the whole London tour was madness. Michael fell victim to something he had experienced since his last trial, stage fright. His mental health crumbled since he knew he was going to perform again. Of course he liked the idea of making money but when he signed for the O2 shows, he wasn't really up to it physically and mentally. Michael was afraid of being murdered or being killed by a gun, while on stage. Michael would sometimes be excited, and full of energy for his shows, but on other occasions he would refuse to respond to anyone around him. In the evenings he didn't like to have his children around anymore and refused to eat and drink. Friend of Michael and former producer Tarak Ben Ammar claimed the hypochondriac pop star had been a victim of "charlatan doctors." He told others about his concerns: "Michael was a hypochondriac and one never really knew if he was sick because he had become surrounded by charlatans who were billing him thousands of dollars' worth of drugs, vitamins. It's clear to me the criminals in this affair are the doctors who treated him throughout his career, who destroyed his face and gave him medicine to ease his pain."

Michael's brothers and sisters were so concerned about his addiction to powerful painkillers they considered forcibly admitting him to a rehabilitation clinic. The plan was abandoned because Michael did not want to get any help from other people, and because of the overwhelming pressure to fulfill his concert commitments in London. Michael agreed to consult a controversial therapist known as *Doc Hollywood*. The family had consulted Californian drugs expert Dr. Howard Samuels, to try to "save Michael from himself", because they knew he would refuse to go into rehab. The family discussed all options with Dr. Samuels. They agreed that Michael would detox at his Hollywood home under medical supervision and then be provided another doctor, who would remain with him for the duration of his upcoming tour until March. Michael himself hired a Texan cardiologist, a *sober coach* to accompany him to Britain to stay with him constantly. This doctor tried to wean Michael off drugs. Michael wanted the doctor to be living in his house as soon as possible. Dr. Murray started to live at Michael's home after quitting his medical practice. A source told Daily Mail: "Michael was adamant he did not have a drug problem and was not going to rehab. But in the end he relented to his family's wishes and agreed to having a sober companion." A *sober coach* is a trained professional who accompanies a patient full-time to ensure they stay off drugs.

Randy Phillips, of AEG Live said: "Michael told me personally that he trusted this man."

Doc Hollywood, Dr Samuels is, according to many celebrities their favorite, because of his unconventional treatment methods. The Wonderland Centre, which cost $58,000 (£35,000) to rent for a month, a private drugs and alcohol rehab facility based in the Hollywood Hills that previously treated stars as Mike Tyson and Lindsay Lohan could have been a great solution for Michael's problems. "No one in the family had realized how serious Michael's problems were until Randy, his youngest brother started staying over at Michael's house. Randy said the family needed to save Michael from himself. Michael's drug use was so severe, yet Michael was in total denial about how bad it was. Randy quickly realized that the situation was grave and that Michael needed urgent medical help or he might die," a source said. The Daily Mail quoted a source saying: "The Jackson family were recommended to call Wonderland as Dr. Samuels is very experienced at dealing with high-profile celebrities. Many celebrities do not want to go into a conventional treatment center because it takes them away from their professional commitments, causes negative Press and means they have to mix with ordinary junkies and of course, they don't like to think of themselves in that way. Initially the family were so worried, they wanted to get a psychiatrist to go to Michael's house to perform a psychiatric evaluation to force him to go to rehab. It is an extremely difficult and lengthy process. When this was explained to the family, it was clearly not an option for Michael. He was having injections of the painkiller Demerol first thing in the morning and last thing at night, along with a host of other powerful drugs. He was refusing to eat and was popping pills constantly." A person can be forcibly admitted to a drug detox facility under California law, if two independent psychiatrists evaluate him and convince a judge that he is a danger to himself or others.

His backing dancers held a private party for Michael. One said Michael was dancing so well, "But he was thin, so very thin. He danced all week but you never saw him eat a thing." Michael had problems with eating, but his big problem was falling asleep. Michael couldn't sleep because of his addiction to a lot of painkillers and other unknown prescription medication. For many years, he was addicted to Demerol and knew of its danger. He wrote a song titled *Morphine* in 1997, with lyrics such as "Demerol. Demerol. Oh God, he's taking Demerol." He knew country singer Tammy Wynette died at 55 of a heart attack after years of Demerol addiction. She once said: "I've depended on Demerol, plus a lot of medications to get me through an awful lot of shows and a lot of pain. I've had physicians tell me many times that I was dependent on pain killers. They would turn around the next week and do surgery and use Demerol." She said she needed the medications to get through her 26 major surgeries and her grueling concert scheduled. Also David Kennedy, the fourth child of Sen. Robert F. Kennedy, died in a Florida hotel suite of an overdose of Demerol, cocaine and the anti-psychotic drug Mellaril in 1984. He was 28 when he died.

Tammy Wynette's Demerol addiction crept up slowly on Wynette. Like Michael, she was treated for her painkiller habit at the Betty Ford Center. The drug is fast acting and comes in the form of a pill, syrup or intravenous injection. It was many years ago regarded as safer and less addicting than morphine. Demerol was even regarded as the magic bullet of painkillers. Side effects can include slow and shallow breathing, a weak heart beat and seizure. Demerol has been used by doctors for patients suffering acute pain. The drug, also known as Pethidine and more than a dozen other names, has a dark and dangerous side. Demerol produces a quick rush leading to euphoria and many users quickly become addicted. It has since largely fallen out of favor and doctors have turned to other drugs.

British journalist and author Ian Halperin, told In Touch magazine that Michael needed a lung transplant and was bleeding in the intestines. He 'revealed' that the pop star was suffering from Alpha-1 Antitrypsin deficiency, a genetic condition that affects the lungs and liver. He further claimed that Michael couldn't see out of his left eye and was so winded that he could barely speak most of the time. All these claims ended up being false. Michael's spokesman, Dr. Tohme Tohme who said he never knew of Michael's drugs problems denied also the health problems, saying that the rumors were a "total fabrication" and that Michael was "in fine health."

Deepak Chopra, Michael's friend wrote in an article that Michael had called him in an upbeat, excited mood. Deepak wrote: "The voice message said, 'I've got some really good news to share with you.' He was writing a song about the environment and he wanted me to help informally with the lyrics, as we had done several times before. When I tried to return his call, however, the number was disconnected. (Terminally spooked by his treatment in the press, he changed his phone number often.) So I never got to talk to him, and the music demo he sent me lies on my bedside table as a poignant symbol of an unfinished life." What was about to happen was yet unknown.

Even though Michael had been plagued by crippling back and leg pain, he had by all accounts a 'emotional and moving' day. Michael had failed to appear at many of the scheduled rehearsals in Los Angeles over the past two months. But he did show up at a full rehearsal at the Staples Center of his scheduled July 13 London concert on the evening before his death. The show was planned as a spectacular performance with Michael suspended on a crane and another great performance was a 3D view of a *Thriller* decor, requiring the audience to put on special glasses.

Michael turned up for five of the last six sessions. Some crew members were worried that the singer was not strong enough to withstand a rigorous performance schedule but others said that the entertainer seemed more joyous and in his element then ever. But Michael told his doctors that he had a lot of pain, and that he knew he was taking too many pills. "I cannot function without them anymore," he told his doctor. "I am in constant pain. I need my medications to be able to perform." Kenny Ortega, the show's choreographer, told the Los Angeles Times: "He was dancing, training, working every day with our choreographer Travis [Payne]. Michael has always been slight. That was his fighting weight. He was getting rest time, coming in and working with the band, guiding the singers, working on orchestrations. He was enthusiastically involved in every creative aspect of this production." AEG's Phillips told Bloomberg News, "I take great solace in the pride and confidence he exhibited in the rehearsals on Wednesday night. This is the memory I will cherish for the rest of my life."

Patrick Woodroffe, lighting designer, watched the final rehearsal and told the BBC4 that the singer seemed frail. He said: "We had rehearsed for the last couple weeks. We put together a complicated show, quite a spectacular show. Of course a huge part of it was him, and I would say for the last week he hadn't really been with us. He would appear, and he would rehearse sometimes, and he would not rehearse." Patrick also said: "I guess that we were nervous whether we would be able to carry off this show at the 02. It was quite an emotional moment when we realized that, well, he had it. And of course we all had a view as to whether he would be able to survive these 50 shows." London was to be just the start of a multi-city world tour.

Before Dr. Murray closed his office to work for the famous popsinger he released a statement for his clients and fans. The statement was send from his office Global Cardiovascular Associates, Inc. on June 15, 2009. It said: "Dear patients and friends. Because of a once in a lifetime opportunity, I had to make a most difficult decision to cease practice of medicine indefinitely. Over the years, I have come to know you both as patients and as friends. It has been more then pleasurable providing you with state of the art quality care and having your trust and confidence. Although the road varied from individual to individual, the challenge was undertaken with dept and concern for each of you and for the most part we were successful. Because of my continued concern for your health, my practice (Global Cardiovascular Associates); thereby giving you the opportunity to continue your care with us or elsewhere if you choose. In my absence, I will continue to manage the practice, and be involved as much as possible but it will be from a distance. On behalf of my family and my staff, I would like to state how much they have appreciated you, as I have. Again, I am deeply saddened to leave you at this point, but please know my absence is not permanent. I wish each and every one of you, continued good health, success, properity and peace. Thank you. Sincerely, Conrad Murray, MD."

Chapter 5

This Is It

Thursday 25, June 2009. It was like always a chaotic scene inside the bedroom of Michael. His, and his children clothes strewn around the stifling hot room and handwritten Post-it notes papering the walls. The messages were seen by a police source after Michael's death. One read: "Children are sweet," and another said: "Children are innocent." A strange tattooed mannequin was in the kitchen. Michael began renting the $100,000 (£60,000) -a-month luxury home in December. The house boasts seven bedrooms, 13 bathrooms and 11 fireplaces as well as sprawling grounds, a guest house and a swimming pool. Michael shared the home with his children, aides and bodyguards. Staff members were not allowed upstairs. Doctor Murray moved in recently. He was told by Michael not to interact with the rest of the staff. He only came to administer Michael's meds, but he was not brought into the rest of the house.

That same day police seized bags of drugs and medical equipment from the house. A women's blouse appearing to be stained with blood was hanging in Michael 's wardrobe and was not seized by police after Michael's death. Lawyer Craig Silverman, who is not involved in the case, said: "It's pretty extraordinary that a bloody shirt would not be taken as evidence." Asked why the shirt, with a price of just $3.99, was not taken in by investigators, a spokesman replied: "I don't know why. Our detectives aren't speaking to the media about the investigation so we won't have an answer at the moment. I don't foresee one for some time." The blouse still had a price label attached, indicating it had not been worn. Some people believe it could have been used to mop up blood. Michael shared the home with his children, aides and bodyguards. Prince watched 'in a trance' when he realized his father was lying dead in front of him.

Daily Mail: "The entire drama was witnessed by the singer's 12-year-old eldest child Prince, who thought his father was clowning around before a doctor began pumping his chest to try to start his heart." A source told Britain's News of The World Newspaper: "An air of crisis swept through the house like a whirlwind. It was terrifically sad. The three children had been taken to another room by their nannies, but they thought their dad was just fooling around. He often played dead and would then jump up and surprise them, so they thought he was just having a bit of fun. But when they saw the emergency trucks arrive, that really shook them." When paramedics were running upstairs, the kids were in shock. "The kids were terrified and started crying and howling for their dad," the source added. According to news articles, "Dr. Murray also believed at first Michael was joking around, as he often did to entertain the kids. Tragically, this was real. Dr. Murray called out to staff members to help him. He tried to talk to Michael to rouse him. It suddenly dawned on Dr. Murray he was in serious trouble. Michael was dragged off the bed and he made a few other attempts to resuscitate Michael."

Michael had been given many different kind of drugs in the night to make sure he would fall asleep, and had been pacing around the house frantically. His show rehearsals had ended after midnight. Michael was so exhausted he couldn't sleep. The doctor, "left Michael's side to go to the restroom and relieve himself." Upon his return, Dr. Murray noticed that "Michael was no longer breathing." Michael never regained consciousness. Dr. Conrad Murray who refused to sign the death certificate at the UCLA Medical Center noticed that Michael wasn't breathing at around 11 a.m. He was then on the cell phone for 47 minutes (?) with 3 separate calls, from 11.18 a.m. To 12.05 p.m. After Michael wasn't breathing for more then 1 hour and 5 minutes he began CPR and at some point ran downstairs and asked the chef to send up Prince Jackson, Michael's eldest son. When he arrived, Dr. Murray showed Michael's son what he was doing and continued performing CPR. The 911 call came in at 12.21 p.m., almost 1 ½ hour after Michael stopped breathing. Some people close to Michael were even in denial about his drug use.

The full transcript of the 911 call from Michael Jackson's home had been released by the Los Angeles Fire Department, 2 days after his death. The call was received by the operator. He asked: "What is the nature of your emergency?" The caller said: "Yes sir, I need an ambulance as soon as possible, sir." Operator: "OK sir, what's your address?" Caller: "Los Angeles, California 90077." Operator: "Is it Carolwood?" Caller: "Carolwood Drive, yes." Operator: "OK sir, what's the phone number you're calling from?" Caller: "Sir, we have a gentleman here that needs help and he's not breathing. He's not breathing and we're trying to pump him, but he's not...." Operator: "OK, OK. How old is he?" Caller: "He's 50 years old, sir." Operator: "50? OK. He's unconscious? He's not breathing?" Caller: "Yes he's not breathing sir." Operator: "OK, and he's not conscious either." Caller: "No, he's not conscious sir." Operator: "Alright, is he on the floor, where's he at right now?" Caller: "He's on the bed, sir, he's on the bed." Operator: "OK, let's get him on the floor." Caller: "OK." Operator: "OK, let's get him down to the floor. I'm going to help you with CPR right now. We're on our way there, we're on our way but I'm going to do as much as I can to help you over the phone. We're already on our way. Did anybody see him?" Caller: "Yes we have a personal doctor here with him sir." Operator: "Oh you have a doctor there?" Caller: "Yes but he's not responding to anything. He's not responding to CPR or anything." Operator: "OK, well we're on our way there. If your guy's doing CPR as instructed by a doctor, he has a higher authority than me. Did anybody witness what happened?" Caller: "No, just the doctor, sir, the doctor's been the only one here." Operator: "OK, so the doctor's seen what happened?" Caller: (aside) "Doctor, did you see what happened, sir?" (To operator) "If you can please...." Operator: "We're on our way, I've dispatched these questions on to our paramedics and they're on their way there sir." Caller: "Thank you sir. He's pumping his chest but he's not responding to anything sir, please." Operator: "OK, we're on our way, we're less than a mile away. We'll be there shortly." Caller: "Thank you sir, thank you." Operator: "OK sir, call us back if you need any help." Caller: "Yes sir."

Frank Dileo received a call around 12.25 p.m. saying that Michael wasn't breathing and hadn't been breathing for a while. Frank immediately went up to the house. He arrived when the ambulance left the property with Michael's body. Michael Jackson was found to be not breathing after fire fighters responded to the 911 call. Michael was transferred to UCLA Medical

Center and later pronounced dead due to cardiac arrest. It was Dr. Conrad Murray, Michael's personal physician in the weeks before he died, who was at his bedside trying to revive the pop star before he was taken to a Los Angeles hospital. Paramedics tried to resuscitate the pop singer but were unable to revive him.

Some people were saying his death was a possible suicide, but no official statement had been made to that effect. One nurse told reporters: "It was clear when he came through the door he was dead. And he had been dead for some time. A long time." It became clear Michael suffered a massive heart attack, which most probably led to his death in the afternoon of June 25. Michael's mother was seen at the hospital in tears, distraught over the death of her son who died tragically and unexpectedly.

In the first moments it was only known that Michael was rushed to the UCLA hospital after suffering a major cardiac arrest. Hundreds of fans gathered around UCLA Medical Center, where the 50-year-old King of Pop had been rushed after collapsing at home. Authorities were seeking to clear up the mystery surrounding Michael's death, including whether drugs could have been a factor.

Manager Frank DiLeo signed the paperwork releasing his body to the Coroner's Office at 2.26 p.m.. Frank had to talk to the family: "It was so sad, so, so sad. All I thought about was that I had to tell his kids their daddy was dead. And that's what I had to do. Agony." Many spectators who stormed the Reagan UCLA Medical Center in California crowed the vicinity and thought initially that Michael had been in a coma.

World's most famous pop singer was pronounced dead in the afternoon of June 25, 2009 at UCLA Medical Center in Los Angeles after falling into a deep coma, following a heart attack.

A coroner for the medical facility has confirmed the hit maker died after suffering a cardiac arrest. Around the circus that surrounded Michael there were three little children, sitting in a cold anteroom, waiting for news of their beloved father. When Michael's manager Frank DiLeo was entering the family waiting room at the Ronald Reagan UCLA Medical Center, he knew he had to impart the most devastating news of his life. Frank said: "I'm sorry children, your father has passed away." One day later he added, "The outpouring of emotion is something I shall live with for the rest of my life. It was the single most painful moment of my life. I cannot tell you how difficult it was. Those children just fell to pieces. The emotions poured forth." Prince Michael, 12, Paris, 11, and seven-year-old Prince Michael II were quiet for a few seconds. Then little Paris screamed: "No, no, Daddy. No, no!" Frank said about Michael: "He was like a son to me. We had our fights but we were together at the end. We loved each other."

Manager DiLeo, hired back for the 02 shows, had his own turbulent past with Michael, being in and out of favor. He refuses to acknowledge that the superstar was unprepared for the grueling task of performing so many shows in London. A friend of Frank said: "Frank said Michael was as good as ever. Frank said he was truly happy on Wednesday night. The rehearsals went on late." And Frank added: "Michael hugged me and said, 'This is great, Frank. It's the team back together again. We're gonna take on London, and the world!'" Michael then returned home exhausted shortly after 2 in the night. Dr. Conrad Murray, his personal physician, allegedly gave him a drug to help him sleep.

La Toya explained 3 weeks later to Daily Mail reporter Caroline Graham how she heard about the tragic news: "I was at home when I received the news that Michael had been rushed to the hospital. I live about three minutes away from Michael in Beverly Hills. I was talking to a friend about the fact that Farrah Fawcett had just passed away. Her death came just after Ed McMahon [famous in America as the sidekick of talk-show host Johnny Carson] died. I said, 'There's going to be another one because they always go in threes.' About an hour-and-a-half later, my father called me from Las Vegas and said, 'Get to the hospital right away. Michael's been rushed to hospital.' I jumped into my car and kept calling my mother's assistant saying, 'How is he? How is he?' But he wouldn't tell me. Finally, I heard Mother in the background asking, 'Who is that?' When she learned it was me, she screamed, 'Why don't you just tell her?' and she grabbed the phone and just screamed as loud as she could, 'He's dead!' I nearly crashed my car. My legs went weak. I couldn't press down on the gas pedal. I got to the wrong entrance at the hospital and was begging the security guys to help me and take my car because I was so weak and faint. They took me up to the area where Michael had been taken. Mother was crying and Michael's kids were crying. I screamed, 'Is it true?' and she said, 'Yes, he is gone.' I couldn't stop crying. I'm screaming and the kids are screaming. My mother was sitting there with all three of them on her lap, just crying. Paris demanded to see her father 'one last time'."

According to Daily Mail, a nurse told La Toya it would help the children grasp the reality that their father was dead. La Toya held Paris's hand as all three children, together with Michael's brother Randy, went into the small ante-room off the emergency room where Michael lay, still warm to the touch. La Toya said: "There was a towel over his face and I lifted it and the kids saw him and Paris said, 'Oh Daddy, I love you.' We hugged and kissed him and the children lifted up his hands. He didn't look like he was gone. His eyes were half open and he looked like he was sleeping. He wasn't cold. The kids had been screaming and crying but once they were in that room and saw Michael they stopped and became calm. We said prayers over him. I asked them, 'What do you want to say to Daddy?' and they said private things to him. Paris was holding his hand. We were all sitting around the bed. His chest was very red from the attempts to revive him. I lifted the covers to see his legs. Everything looked fine."

Family pal Brian Oxman blames 'medication abuse' for Michael's death. The longterm family friend has hinted the legendary superstar was killed by an abuse of prescription drugs, likening his death to tragic star Anna Nicole Smith. He told CNN news, "Michael Jackson is my friend and I am just heartbroken. Everyone is rather speechless. The atmosphere is so very sad. I can't tell you what has taken place, but everyone is very stunned. I saw Randy and Jermaine and I hugged them. I cried with them. No one will confirm anything to me. All I can tell you is that the family members are crying. La Toya, Jermaine and Randy are at the hospital. They are in a room by themselves and they are sobbing."

Brian was adamant Michael's death is down to the people who surrounded the star and claimed that the superstar family have been desperately trying to "take care" of their fragile relative. He explained, "Michael was in perfect health until recently. I believe (his manager) Frank DiLeo was with him at the time (of his heart attack), that is what I have been told. This family has been trying for months and months and months to take care of Michael Jackson. The people who have surrounded him have been enabling him. If you think the case of Anna Nicole Smith was an abuse, that is nothing compared to what has taken place in the life of Michael Jackson. I do not know what medications he was taking, but the reports that we have received within the family are that they were extensive. I don't know the cause of all this. But this is something that I feared. This is a case of abuse of medications, unless the cause is something else."

Jesse Jackson said Michael's mother Katherine was inconsolable. He said: "She said to me, 'I have lost my baby Michael. He was a good boy, no matter what they say about him.'" The atmosphere on the ward was one of devastation. Michael's family were too upset to confirm the sad news. Michael's family rushed to his bedside, but they were all too late to say their goodbyes.

The Reverend Sharpton spoke of Michael as the icon. He showed a photo of himself with Michael soon after the announcement. He spoke of James Brown as being an idol of Michael Jackson. Michael had attended the funeral of James Brown with him saying "who took Michael Jackson to see James Brown." Not much later Apollo, the place were Michael started his career was alive with celebrating Michael Jackson's life with crowds of people doing Michael's 'moonwalk' that made him famous worldwide.

CNN reported that Janet Jackson issued a statement of condolence for her brother, Michael Jackson passing, and was on her way from filming a movie, to be with the Jackson family in California.

Time wrote a few hours later that "the superstar behind such hits as *Beat It, Thriller* and *Billie Jean* appeared to invite speculation, appearing in public wearing a surgical mask, as he did a decade ago, or in a wheelchair, which he used on certain occasions last year." According to the magazine: "The singer was always very thin and appeared frail." Time Magazine also stated: "In 1984, the singer was hospitalized after receiving second-degree burns when his hair accidentally caught fire during the filming of a Pepsi commercial. Jackson reportedly used a hyperbaric oxygen chamber while he recovered and allegedly also slept in the chamber in an effort to halt the aging process — photos of him lying in one were leaked in 1986 — a claim he denied."

Celebrities from all over the world have paid their respects to the legend. Celine Dion who said she loved Michael, was one of the first entertainers to give her reaction on Michael's sudden death. She told ET: "I am so devastated by this terrible news. From the beginning of my career, he was my idol in show business. He was a genius and an incredible artist!! I remember when I was growing up and watching him on TV, and all his videos... I had his poster on my wall... he was so amazing... his singing, his writing, his dancing. We had the same record company, and they knew I was a huge fan, so when things started to happen for me, they arranged for us to meet. I was so nervous, and so excited at the same time, and Michael was so nice. He autographed one of his hats for me... I was so thrilled. Years later, he came to see my Las Vegas show and we spent some time together... and we were really looking forward to seeing his show in London. It's unbelievable that he's no longer with us. It still hasn't sunk in. I guess we're just finding out what happened, but all I can say is that he must have been under an enormous amount of pressure... to do the shows, and to keep on top of everything, plus this was going to be his big comeback. This is a lot of pressure and it can be overwhelming for anyone. I'm sure it was just too much to handle. Right now, along millions and millions of others I am so sad... and I just want to send my prayers and love to Michael's family. I can't imagine how difficult this is for them... to lose someone so special. And it's the same for everyone in the world who loses a loved one. It just keeps reminding us of how precious life is, and that we never know when it's our time. God Bless his soul."

Others followed with moving statements. Gordon Brown: "Very sad news for the millions of Michael Jackson fans in Britain and around the world. The Prime Minister's thoughts are with Michael Jackson's family at this time." The broadcaster Paul Gambaccini paid tribute to the "biggest world star since the Beatles" and told BBC: "Michael would be remembered for his solo career rather than the controversies that dogged him. In decades to come people will look back and remember the historic records. The 'freak show' part of Michael's life would fade into the background." Former Beatle Sir Paul McCartney said: "It's so sad and shocking. I feel privileged to have hung out and worked with Michael. He was a massively talented boy man with a gentle soul. His music will be remembered forever and my memories of our time together will be happy ones."

CNN news provided excellent coverage of the Michael Jackson's passing from the first announcement. The cable news station was also covering the helicopter removal of Michael Jackson from the UCLA hospital to the coroner's office. On Larry King Live on CNN, Smokey Robinson and Suzanne Depasse, who was a conduit of Michael's success, spoke condolences to Michael Jackson. Stevie Wonder and Elizabeth Taylor released statements that they were too distraught to make immediate statements about the passing of Michael Jackson to the media. Larry King was interviewing celebrities about Michael Jackson's unexpected passing. Jermaine Jackson spoke with Larry King Live to express his condolences. Beyonce released her statement about the passing of Michael Jackson. Beyonce said that the event was a "tragic loss." Beyonce statement said that there will never be anything like the magic that is Michael Jackson.

Donna Summers expressed her condolences. She said that Michael Jackson's greatness was his drive for perfection and that he was intent to "up the standard." Tory leader David Cameron said sadly: "Despite the controversies, he was a legendary entertainer. Everyone will be thinking of his family, especially his children, at this time." British actor Stephen Fry, a regular user of Twitter wrote: "Goodness. Michael Jackson. Poor old soul. Oh dear." Uri Geller feared it may have been the 'stress' of his friend's planned comeback tour that killed him. "I'm shocked and devastated. I am hoping this is a dream I will wake up from, but it is not. Michael is dead. For him not to be around, that he's gone, is just surreal. It cannot sink into my psyche. He was a genius," he said. Opera singer Katherine Jenkins said: "Such sad news about Michael Jackson - I've always been a big fan and was really looking forward to seeing the show."

Film director Martin Scorsese told MTV.com: "Michael Jackson was extraordinary. When we worked together on *Bad*, I was in awe of his absolute mastery of movement on the one hand, and of the music on the other. Every step he took was absolutely precise and fluid at the same time. It was like watching quicksilver in motion. He was wonderful to work with, an absolute professional at all times, and, it really goes without saying, a true artist. It will be a while before I can get used to the idea that he's no longer with us." Bruce Forsyth said: "Michael was pure genius and his death at such a young age is nothing short of a tragedy." Chris Moyles reacted: "He was to me what I imagine Elvis was to another generation."

Richard Bacon said he felt a shiver down his spine on hearing the news.

The 74-year-old actress Sophia Loren who was a friend of the singer and a neighbor in Los Angeles, told Italy's ANSA news agency: "There will never be another Michael Jackson again, I am devastated. The world has lost an icon, with his songs he gave the world a treasure. I hope he finds the peace he deserves after so much suffering." Singer/producer P. Diddy stated: "He showed me that you can actually see the beat. He made me believe in magic. I will miss him." Pete Waterman: "He was across the planet even in places they hardly have TV. He became part of culture." Amanda Holden said: "Not just a huge talent but a dedicated father and family man."

Mohamed Al Fayed who said, "It's a total shock. He was such a great character, a legend," remembered Michael on his website: "Michael Jackson was a true genius; when he was on stage, everyone watched him. He had a rare gift that inspired people of every race, in every country, right across the world. We got on well; Michael loved to feel young and had a wonderful childlike quality: he was simple, kind and genuine. We all know he had a troubled childhood, but he also had a big heart and tried to help thousands of deprived and ill children. A few years ago, Michael came to Harrods to do some shopping and I asked him if he would like to watch a game of football with me. He accepted and I remember how excited he was, sitting in my box at Fulham watching the game progress. He enjoyed himself, and it showed, but the last time I saw him, he looked different. I told him he looked ill, but he wouldn't listen. I hope that he is now at peace and that he will be remembered as one of the most influential musical legends the world has ever seen."

Brooke Shields, also issued a statement on his passing. "My heart is overcome with sadness for the devastating loss of my true friend Michael. He was an extraordinary friend, artist and contributor to the world. I join his family and his fans in celebrating his incredible life and mourning his untimely passing," Brooke said. Roger Federer expressed himself saying: "I listened to a Jackson concert from outside a stadium when I was very young. It's sad." Jed Hilly, the executive director of the Americana Music Association, told ABC News.com: "For a long time he was unquestionably the most famous person on the planet." Chris Connelly, an ABC News contributor said that the pop star was "determined to convey that he had greater things ahead of him." He said, thinking of his interview with Michael last year: "The word he spoke with the greatest emphasis was the 'More!' that he exclaimed when I asked if he could still do all his famous moves and hit all those notes at the age of 50." Connelly said: "In an all-too-short life that in so many ways was filled with enigmatic emotions, or troubling ones, his laugh sounded fresh, clear and altogether genuine. If only there had been more of those."

Gotham Chopra regularly blogs at intent.com. Gotham Chopra, Co-Founder of Liquid Comics and son of Deepak Chopra wrote the following moving statement about his friend Michael: "When I was in my second year of college living on campus (at Columbia in NYC) with 4 suite mates, every time the phone rang, there was a race to answer it. Everyone wanted to be the guy to hear the 'hello' on the other side just in case it was my friend Michael Jackson calling. Most of those days, Michael was holed up on top of the Four Seasons, roughly 60 blocks away from where I lived on the Upper West Side of Manhattan just near Harlem. I'd happily drift downtown, gain clearance from security downstairs who knew I was allowed free access to Michael's suite, take the elevator all the way up and start ordering room service and watch movies on Mike's tab. Eventually, Michael and I would get down to work. He was working on a new album and asked me to help him write lyrics for songs. It was an informal relationship - I'd wander downtown with a backpack full of dictionaries, and thesauri, and rhyming books. Michael would hum songs and talk about what he wanted to say with the song and we'd try and marry our skillsets and come up with something.

"We came up with great stuff. Michael swore me to secrecy those days. I happily complied. After we were done with those sessions - they'd usually go until about 2 a.m. or so - Michael would wander into the bathroom and come out with a sack he'd pulled out from under the toilet. In it, he kept several thousands of dollars. He'd ask me how much I wanted. I just sort of shrugged and he'd hand me a couple of thousand dollars. Soon, I'd be packing my dictionaries and thesauri and rhyming books in my backpack, calling my friends and telling them to meet me downtown. Within an hour, we'd be at Flashdancers 'making it rain.' Michael was always envious when I told him about my adventures with my friends. More than a few times, he'd get dressed up - dawning some sort of quasi-disguise - preparing to go with me, only to back down at the last minute or be held back by his security who would shake their heads and plainly say no to his misguided ambitions. Instead, he'd pour himself a tall glass of orange juice and settle in for the night to watch an old movie on TV, telling me to spend a few extra bucks for him. I happily complied."

Gotham had a close friendship with the superstar. He wrote: "My friendship with Michael was very special to me, and I like to think it was the same for him. Over the last few years, it always felt awkward to explain the origins of our friendship - that I met him initially when I was fifteen-years-old and that we instantly hit it off." Gotham had spend days at Neverland Ranch. He brought along his sister, cousins, or other friends. Gotham wrote: "Likewise he'd visit our house in Massachusetts (he was very close to my father as well) where he'd sleep in the guest room. My mom got a great kick out of the fact that every morning Michael stayed, he'd try to make the bed (very badly) and offer to cook breakfast (very badly). Then when I was about 17, Michael invited me on the road with him - he was heading out to Europe on the biggest rock concert at the time (Dangerous tour) and wanted company. I begged and pleaded with my parents to let me go and they eventually said yes. Not a bad way to spend your summer vacation between junior and senior year of High School.

"Over the years, as Michael faced his scandals, I often reflected on my own experiences with him as a teenager. People would ask me if I had endured anything strange or awkward with him. I'd answer truthfully that in all of my years with him, in every single moment, Michael was nothing but dignified and appropriate, never once doing anything that would be deemed scandalous with me. It was really that simple. Check that. Back to those college days. One night he did call me in a panic. He had just gotten married to Lisa Marie Presley and needed advice - sex advice. He was incredibly nervous and said that he wanted to make sure that Lisa was impressed with his "moves." He asked me if I had any advice. I answered with one word: "foreplay." "Really?" He answered. "Girls really like that?" Over the last few years, Michael's and my relationship evolved and matured greatly too. We both became fathers and that was the centerpiece of our most recent conversations the last few months. Returning the favor from my days as his 'lyrical advisor,' he's the one who monikered my half-Indian, half-Chinese son 'The Chindian' which little Krishu Chen Xing Hua Chopra will now forever go by. We'd talk about how great it would be for our kids to grow up together, become as good friends as us, and set the world on fire. Michael admired the fact that I was able to find a wife, keep a wife, and gain her trust. I'd joke it was all about the foreplay! When his daughter Paris befell an accident a few years ago, he called my wife Candice (a physician) pleading for us to come to his house to check her out. We did - Paris had fallen from a tree and cut herself deeply beneath the eye. Michael was devastated and confessed to me that he felt like the world's worst father. I calmed him as Candice helped Paris get up from the bed where she lay so we could take her to the Emergency room to get some simple stitches. When I advised Michael of the plan, he pulled me into the bathroom, pulled a sack filled with thousands of dollars from beneath the toilet and asked me how much I needed for the Emergency room. I shook my head: "this one's on me." RIP in peace my friend."

Chris Martin and his Coldplay band-mates said: "MJ was the best of the best. His music and performances made the world a brighter place. His light will shine on forever." Dame Shirley Bassey said: "I have very fond memories of Michael with one dinner in particular where he renamed me Lady Goldfinger. For the rest of the time I knew him that was my name." Max Clifford, who first met Jackson in the 60s, spoke to the singer three weeks before reality star Jade Goody died of cancer after Michael asked to meet her. Max said: "It is a terrible shock, you wonder if the strain of getting fit for this major tour proved too much. In recent pictures he looked anything but healthy. That's the first thought that went through my mind. When he called to speak to Jade he was anxious to visit her, unfortunately she was too ill but they spoke on the phone and his final words to her were that he wanted to see her and wanted her to come to his show. Sadly she is no longer with us and now he is also no longer with us, it is very sad. He was always someone who seemed to find it difficult to cope with fame. He was a great talent. He was already a superstar when he was in his teens but then he was with four others. Then all of a sudden he was on his own and he did seem to find it difficult to cope." Tina Turner added her condolences: "I am shocked and saddened by Michael's passing. I, along with his millions of fans, looked forward to seeing him tour one more time. Now, may he rest in peace."

Michael's nanny Grace, who was introduced to Michael by Deepak, Gotham's father, spoke with journalist Daphne Barak on the night Michael had passed away. "I love my babies. I miss my babies. I used to hug them and laugh with them," she said. She explained there were periods when the singer was virtually penniless adding that Michael's children 'froze' when Michael was around. "Michael didn't like me hugging them," she said. "But they needed love. I was the only mother they knew." In the interview Grace described one occasion when Blanket performed a concert of Michael's songs for her. Michael heard Grace laughing and decided to take a look at what was happening. "Usually, the security would alert me that he was about to come," Grace said. "Blanket immediately stopped. The kids looked frightened." She said she knew that Michael was furious, and she knew he would fire her. The Rwandan-born nanny confirmed that Michael often fired her when he thought they were becoming too fond of her. Michael told her: "Whenever the children got too attached to you, I would send you away." The glamorous 42-year-old said the children hated the masks they were forced to wear while in public. She said she would deliberately lose them so that the children did not have to wear them. She lost the masks or forgot to pack them at any opportunity. Grace had ties to the black militant organization, the Nation of Islam. She knew its controversial leader, Louis Farrakhan, whom she enlisted for help in running Michael's affairs. Michael appointed Leonard Muhammad (Nation of Islam Chief of Staff) as business manager. Michael rented his most recent residence from the Nation of Islam. Grace told later about the Nation of Islam: "They would inflate prices. They were telling him it cost $100,000 (£60,000) a month to rent a mansion when other similar properties would cost only $25,000 (£15,000) a month." She said Michael was clueless about money. "Once he got a $1 million (£600,000) job in Japan," she said. Grace also added: "He only received $200,000 (£120,000) after all his people took their share."

Deepak Chopra, friend of both Grace and Michael wrote an article and placed it on his website. It was called: "A Tribute to My Friend." Deepak's article was also published on Huffingtonpost.com the following morning after Michael's death. He wrote: "Michael's reluctance to grow up was another part of the paradox. My children adored him, and in return he responded in a childlike way. He declared often, as former child stars do, that he was robbed of his childhood. Considering the monstrously exaggerated value our society places on celebrity, which was showered on Michael without stint, the public was callous to his very real personal pain. It became another tawdry piece of the tabloid Jacko, pictured as a weird changeling and as something far more sinister. It's not my place to comment on the troubles Michael fell heir to from the past and then amplified by his misguided choices in life. He was surrounded by enablers, including a shameful plethora of M.D.s in Los Angeles and elsewhere who supplied him with prescription drugs. As many times as he would candidly confess that he had a problem, the conversation always ended with a deflection and denial. As I write this paragraph, the reports of drug abuse are spreading across the cable news channels. The instant I heard of his death this afternoon, I had a sinking feeling that prescription drugs would play a key part."

Grace Rwaramba, who worked for Michael for more then 17 years, had all the answers. She started in his office, and looked after Michael's three children for many years after his sexual abuse trial. Recently, the troubled *Thriller* singer sacked her because he was jealous of her closeness to his children. Michael's long serving nanny claimed he was a diluted, drug addict wreck who was preyed upon for cash by members of Nation of Islam. Grace talked to journalist Daphne Barak about her life with Michael and revealed the grim secrets of her former employer's life just before flying from London to Los Angeles to assist the family after his death. She said: "Michael, in recent months, had become dirty and unkempt." She also claimed: "He initially mistakenly thought he had only signed up to perform 10 concerts at the O2 arena in London, not the grueling series of 50 he had actually contracted to do." Grace had been the mystery woman in Michael's life for years. She said: "I took these babies in my arm on the first day of their life. They are my babies." Grace desperately attempted to contact the children after she heard Michael died suddenly.

She told Daphne that Michael's children would regard her as their mother.

The journalist experienced an extraordinary insight into how the family of Michael and the Nation of Islam dealt with the vacuum left by his death. Her experiences were published on Timesonline.co.uk in the week following Michael's death. Katherine, Michael's mother, contacted Grace from his house at Friday morning. She wanted to know where Michael's money was. Katherine said, "Grace, the children are crying. They are asking about you. They can't believe that their father died. Grace, you remember Michael used to hide cash at the house. I am here. Where can it be?" Grace told her to look at the garbage bags and under the carpets. "These are places were Michael normally puts his money," she said and asked if she could talk to the children. Katherine explained her they were sleeping. She was surprised because she just heard Katherine saying they were crying. Grace told Times Online's reporter Daphne Barak: "She never let me speak to them." But then Katherine said: "Grace, where are you? Come. I will pick you up from the airport. She sounded so strong. So strong!" A few hours later Grace tried again to talk to Paris, Prince and Blanket after begging a brother from the Nation of Islam at Michael's house but the answer was no. Grace was expected to be contacted by the coroner as soon as she arrived home in Los Angeles. Grace had unraveled the bizarre nomadic life running around the world with Michael and his kids.

She told Daphne: "We had no cash flow. When Paris had her birthday this April, I wanted to buy balloons, things, to make a happy birthday. There was no money in the house. I had to put everything on my personal credit card. I brought people to clean the house. The room of the kids needed to be cleaned. But they weren't paid."

Grace knew Michael was not only a good father but also a drug addict. At one point she confessed: "I was pumping out his stomach after he took too many drugs." She tried to call Michael many times since the last winter because she was afraid the children were not being taken care of, but Michael refused to talk to her. He even changed his phone number a few times. Grace told that Michael took a mixture of pills. Grace: "He always ate too little and mixed too much. He always mixed so much of it. There was one period that it was so bad that I didn't let the children see him." She also claimed Michael was furious with her for getting his mother and sister Janet to help. Grace told Daphne: "We tried to do an intervention. It was me, Janet, his mother. I co-ordinated it. He was so angry with me. He screamed at me, 'You betrayed my trust. You called them behind my back.'" Grace told him: "Michael, I didn't betray your trust. I try to help you. But he didn't want to listen. That was one of the times he let me go."

After Grace heard the shocking news about Michael's death, she called Deepak Chopra. Deepak introduced her to Michael when she was eighteen years old and became close friends with Grace. Grace was since her childhood a big fan of Michael and kept an eye on Michael for Deepak. She even would call him whenever Michael was down or running too close to the edge. The two both knew what was going on with Michael and his, as seemed ever lasting, addiction. Deepak wrote in an article: "How heartbreaking for Grace that no one's protective instincts and genuine love could avert this tragic day. An hour ago she was sobbing on the telephone from London. As a result, I couldn't help but write this brief remembrance in sadness. But when the shock subsides and a thousand public voices recount Michael's brilliant, joyous, embattled, enigmatic, bizarre trajectory, I hope the word 'joyous' is the one that will rise from the ashes and shine as he once did." Deepak remembered that Michael once told his son: "I don't want to go out like Marlon Brando. I want to go out like Elvis."

Grace however feared that the Jacksons will blame her for his drug-taking. Michael the superstar, wasn't able to borrow money from anybody. Grace told Times Online also: "Suddenly I can't remember now how it came, he received some money. Instead of buying a small house, so that we won't go from one hotel to another, or stay with friends, he told me, 'Grace, you have to go immediately to Florence to buy antiques.' He wanted me to spend $ 1.6 million (£1 million)." Grace also told journalist Daphne Barak that she was dismissed for a final time in December last year. Previously she was sacked after she called in Michael's mother Katherine and his sister Janet in an attempt to persuade him to deal with his drug addiction, but Michael wouldn't listen.

Michael's autopsy was completed Friday. The L.A. County Coroner said there was no trauma to the star's body and "no indication of foul play." The L.A. County Coroner also said that Michael had been taking "some prescription medications." The cause of death was deferred because additional testing, including toxicology and other tests, is needed. "It will take 4-6 weeks to complete," the L.A. County Coroner said.

Tracy Klujian, who briefly served as a personal trainer to Mr. Jackson's former accountant, said on MSNBC, the morning after Michael's death: "Michael's death has left a permanent hole in my soul. Michael Jackson's passing is a tragedy for millions of his fans around the world. But to those of us who knew someone who sort of knew him, it's even more painful."

NyMag.com said in an article by Erica Orden: "Just how much will one pay for a piece of the departed King of Pop? We're about to find out. Less than 24 hours after Michael Jackson's death comes the first posthumous auction of assorted bits and pieces of Jackson memorabilia, as today Julien's Auctions hosts its Summer Sale, including 21 items from Michael Jackson's career and personal life. The sale, scheduled to take place at Planet Hollywood in Las Vegas, isn't limited to Jackson ephemera — the catalogue lists over 900 items culled from numerous celebrities, including Marilyn Monroe and Elvis Presley — but there are some gems from Jackson's past. Items on the block include handwritten lyrics to *Bad* (estimate: $500 to $700), a drawing by Jackson of an adolescent boy (estimate: $1,500 to $2,000), and a pearl-and-Swarovski-crystal-studded shirt from the Jacksons' Victory tour (estimate: $1,000 to $1,500). The *Bad* lyrics and the shirt are both from the collection of David Gest. The executive director of Julien's, Martin Nolan told to reporters: "We do not want to be seen as capitalizing on a tragedy. We're just focusing on the positive side of this, which is giving people the chance to see these items. They weren't really the focus of the sale before, but now they'll take center stage. After peoples' demise, their valuables go up, and he had such a loyal fan base that I would expect that would be the case here."

The Associated Press reported: "A crystal-studded shirt worn on stage by Michael Jackson: $52,500. A young Jackson's painting of Mickey Mouse: $25,000. Owning a piece of a pop icon who died before his time: Priceless. Or, at least, very expensive. Twenty-one items once owned by Jackson sold at auction Friday for a total of $205,000, dwarfing the auction house's early conservative estimate of $6,000 for the collection.

The estimate was made before Jackson died unexpectedly Thursday at a Los Angeles hospital. On Friday, the items took on new meaning, and likely new value, as collectors and a few fans gathered at the Planet Hollywood hotel-casino with the hope of walking away with a piece of the late King of Pop."

According to the article, which was also published on Foxnews.com, "The items for sale Friday came from a collection owned by David Gest, the producer and promoter once married to Liza Minnelli. Jackson introduced the couple and was best man at their wedding. Among the lot were handwritten lyrics of Jackson's hit song *Bad*, an album cover signed by each member of the Jackson 5, and a handwritten note from Jackson to an unidentified "Greg." "Thanks for a magic moment in my life, I hope it was the same for you, please come visit me at Neverland," the undated note reads. "Lets hope this is the beginning of a lovy friendship and never lose your boyish spirit its imortal." The note sold for $18,750 to an unidentified bidder on the phone. The annual two-day celebrity sale was scheduled for months and promoted mainly for its large number of Elvis Presley and Marilyn Monroe items. Julien Auctions chief executive Darren Julien said he worried some would accuse him of profiting from Jackson's death. "I thought about pulling the lots, but we have people bidding from all over the world," he said. "Everything we did was to honor Michael Jackson."

Leading U.S. civil rights campaigner and friend of Jackson, The Reverend Al Sharpton, told Sky News: "As a friend of Michael's for the past 35 years, I call on people from around the world to pray for him and his family." The singer Cher said: "I'm having a million different reactions I didn't expect I would feel. He was a great singer. God gives you certain gifts and this child was just an extraordinary child touched by this ability. He could sing like nobody else and he was able to connect with people."

Sir Howard Stringer, Chairman, CEO and President, Sony Corporation, commented on Michael's passing: "Michael Jackson was a brilliant troubadour for his generation, a genius whose music reflected the passion and creativity of an era. His artistry and magnetism changed the music landscape forever. We have been profoundly affected by his originality, creativity and amazing body of work. The entire Sony family extends our deepest condolences to his family and to the millions of fans around the world who loved him." Rolf Schmidt-Holtz, CEO, Sony Music Entertainment, said: "Michael Jackson's unsurpassed artistry and beloved music brought joy to every corner of the world. We join today with his millions of fans in expressing our profound sadness and we offer our deepest condolences to his family and loved ones. It was a true privilege for all of us in the Sony Music family to work with one of the most talented superstars in the history of music. We will miss him greatly." Martin Bandier, Chairman & CEO of Sony/ATV Music Publishing, said: "Michael was the kind of amazing talent that comes along once in a lifetime. He was an incredible recording artist, an insightful businessman, an unmatched performer, and a true icon. To all of us at Sony/ATV Music Publishing, he was also a trusted and passionate partner, who was very proud of our accomplishments. He will be dearly missed. We wish his children and entire family our deepest condolences."

The singer Justin Timberlake said: "I can't find the words right now to express how deeply saddened I am by Michael's passing. We have lost a genius and a true ambassador of not only pop music, but of all music. He has been an inspiration to multiple generations, and I will always cherish the moments I shared with him on stage and all of the things I learned about music from him and the time we spent together. My heart goes out to his family and loved ones."

The United States House of Representatives observed a moment of silence in memory of Michael Jackson. You can read the transcript of the moment's introduction in the Congressional Record, dated June 26, 2009. The commemoration was lead by Representatives Jesse Jackson Jr. and Diane Watson. June 26, 2009 MOMENT OF SILENCE IN TRIBUTE TO MICHAEL JACKSON.

(Ms. Watson asked and was given permission to address the House for 1 minute.) Ms. Watson: "Madam Speaker, we rise to pay a 1-minute tribute to a star that shot high into the sky and now remains there. We would like all of those to join us who would like to take a moment to remember Michael Jackson, so Members may come and join us here at the mike. I would just like to say to our House of Representatives, to the country and to the world, a young man has left Earth but now resides in the stars. He was a talented, multi-talented person who entertained the world with his dynamic portrayals, the songs that he had written, and his style of dancing. We think that it is appropriate to say that we pay tribute to the culture that he has left behind, his legacy. I would like now to ask my colleague, Mr. JACKSON, if he would close out, and all those who stand with us send our condolences, our heartfelt sorrow to his family, his friends, and to his millions of fans throughout the world. Mr. JACKSON of Illinois. Madam Speaker, if there is a God, and I believe there is, and that God distributes grace and mercy and talent to all of his children, on August 29, 1958, he visited Gary, Indiana, and touched a young man with an abundance of his blessings. With that gift, Michael Joe Jackson would touch and change the world. His heart couldn't get any bigger, and yesterday, it arrested. I come to the floor today on behalf of a generation to thank God for letting all of us live in his generation and in his era. With that, Madam Speaker, we would ask Members to please stand for a moment of silence."

Lisa Marie Presley, Michael's ex wife wrote an emotional and most revealing letter on her My Space page. The message mysteriously disappeared one day after it was published. But Lisa Marie's message went all around the globe. Lisa Marie wrote that Michael knew he wouldn't become a old man. She did know he used drugs, and she had tried to talk with him about his drugs problem. Her statement was called: *He Knew.*

"Years ago Michael and I were having a deep conversation about life in general. I can't recall the exact subject matter but he may have been questioning me about the circumstances of my Fathers Death. At some point he paused, he stared at me very intensely and he stated with an almost calm certainty, 'I am afraid that I am going to end up like him, the way he did.' I promptly tried to deter him from the idea, at which point he just shrugged his shoulders and nodded almost matter of fact as if to let me know, he knew what he knew and that was kind of that. 14 years later I am sitting here watching on the news an ambulance leaves the driveway of his home, the big gates, the crowds outside the gates, the coverage, the crowds outside the hospital, the Cause of death and what may have led up to it and the memory of this conversation hit me, as did the unstoppable tears. A predicted ending by him, by loved ones and by me, but what I didn't predict was how much it was going to hurt when it finally happened. The person I failed to help is being transferred right now to the LA County Coroners office for his Autopsy.

"All of my indifference and detachment that I worked so hard to achieve over the years has just gone into the bowels of hell and right now I am gutted. I am going to say now what I have never said before because I want the truth out there for once. Our relationship was not "a sham" as is being reported in the press. It was an unusual relationship yes, where two unusual people who did not live or know a 'Normal life' found a connection, perhaps with some suspect timing on his part. Nonetheless, I do believe he loved me as much as he could love anyone and I loved him very much. I wanted to "save him." I wanted to save him from the inevitable which is what has just happened. His family and his loved ones also wanted to save him from this as well but didn't know how and this was 14 years ago.

"We all worried that this would be the outcome then. At that time, In trying to save him, I almost lost myself. He was an incredibly dynamic force and power that was not to be underestimated. When he used it for something good, It was the best and when he used it for something bad, It was really, REALLY bad. Mediocrity was not a concept that would even for a second enter Michael Jackson's being or actions. I became very ill and emotionally/spiritually exhausted in my quest to save him from certain self-destructive behavior and from the awful vampires and leeches he would always manage to magnetize around him. I was in over my head while trying. I had my children to care for, I had to make a decision. The hardest decision I have ever had to make, which was to walk away and let his fate have him, even though I desperately loved him and tried to stop or reverse it somehow.

"After the Divorce, I spent a few years obsessing about him and what I could have done different, in regret. Then I spent some angry years at the whole situation. At some point, I truly became Indifferent, until now. As I sit here overwhelmed with sadness, reflection and confusion at what was my biggest failure to date, watching on the news almost play by play The exact Scenario I saw happen on August 16th, 1977 happening again right now with Michael (A sight I never wanted to see again) just as he predicted, I am truly, truly gutted. Any ill experience or words I have felt towards him in the past has just died inside of me along with him. He was an amazing person and I am lucky to have gotten as close to him as I did and to have had the many experiences and years that we had together.

"I desperately hope that he can be relieved from his pain, pressure and turmoil now. He deserves to be free from all of that and I hope he is in a better place or will be. I also hope that anyone else who feels they have failed to help him can be set free because he hopefully finally is. The World is in shock but somehow he knew exactly how his fate would be played out some day more than anyone else knew, and he was right. I really needed to say this right now, thanks for listening. ~LMP (Lisa Marie Presley)"

Movie magician Steven Spielberg compared Michael to the greatest singers and dancers in American history. He released his statement about the death of Michael Jackson exclusively to Entertainment Weekly: "Just as there will never be another Fred Astaire or Chuck Berry or Elvis Presley, there will never be anyone comparable to Michael Jackson. His talent, his wonderment and his mystery make him legend."

Stuart Backerman, Michael's publicist from 2002 to 2004, talked openly to journalist John

Mackie of The Vancouver Sun, the day after Michael died. He was on the operating table when Michael died. He told the Vancouver Sun: "He had significant asset base, and royalties coming in, but because of his crazy profligate shopping habits and unfettered spending, he spent more than he was bringing in, and had a tremendous burn rate of several million dollars a month running Neverland, shopping and going crazy, flying people all over the world. He kept borrowing against his asset base, and put himself in a deep cash flow situation." He also told John Mackie: "If Michael had wanted to liquidate his stake in the Beatles catalog, minus all his debts, he would have been left with whatever, $100 million, $200 million. Who knows exactly how much, but he wouldn't have been poor. But he didn't want to do that, because he had an emotional attachment [to the Beatles catalog]." According to The Vancouver Sun, Stuart was in the hospital when he received the terrible news about Michael. He said: "I was literally on the operating table when I heard the nurses outside. Michael Jackson has been rushed to the hospital! He had a cardiac arrest and may die! I'm like freaking out, but basically I was given this shot [of anaesthetic]. I had the surgery and woke up. The first thing I asked was 'What's happening with Michael?' And unfortunately the news was that he had passed away." Stuart knew about Michael's health. He told John Mackie the day after Michael died: "Even in 2001 he could barely do two sets of 20 minutes at that Madison Square Garden [Motown] celebration. Since then he hasn't really practiced. I've heard from very, very good sources, in fact it's been confirmed as I understand it, that at 11:30 a.m. yesterday he was given an injection of Demerol. Because he used Demerol following the Pepsi commercial and the burning of his hair and the scalding of his scalp, Demerol.

Yesterday at 11:30 a.m. he was injected with Demerol. So I would say between that, the pressure he's been under trying to practice and rehearse and get in shape after all the years of doing nothing and all the other stresses that I've mentioned, it created almost a lethal cocktail of situations that put him over the edge and taxed his heart to the degree that he couldn't handle it." Stuart explained to John that Michael wanted to be a businessman, "He didn't want to perform anymore. The stress of doing it, was going against the grain of his soul. The reason he hired me and other people was that he wanted to reposition his life. He wanted to go into owning animation studios, maybe doing choreography, being a businessman. He didn't want to perform. He wanted to be a businessman, and he saw the Beatles catalog as the culmination [of his business acumen]. And it was one of the greatest business decisions of all time, particularly for a celebrity. So for him to give that up, liquidate it, pay off his debts and then have whatever he had left, would be a real blow to his ego. And more importantly, a blow to his acumen. When you have too much money, it's very, very dangerous." He also told The Vancouver Sun: "You see all these young teen [stars], the Britney Spears and Lindsay Lohans who have made a couple of million bucks. They don't know what to do with it and they get themselves in trouble. Michael was no different, only the numbers were larger, with more zeroes."

Dame Elizabeth Taylor twittered on June 19th, at 11.29 a.m.: "Life without earrings is empty!," followed by several messages to her friend Arnie (Dr. Arnold Klein). Around 5.04 p.m. she published another message on Twitter, "Somebody I care for very much sent the following note to me with flowers and I wanted to share it with you," At 5.06 p.m. Dame Elizabeth received a message, "Dearest Elizabeth, You make the sun shine, the clouds move and the world spin. So many people love you and so do I. Love Always." Three days later Liz wrote at 1:56 p.m. "I will never be able to thank my dear friend, Dr. Arnold Klein enough for the stunning drawing by Matisse" Two minutes later she wrote: "Dear Arnie, What have you been up to since you've been back? Twitter me back. All my love, Elizabeth," 1:58 p.m., June 22nd. A few days later after she discovered Michael died, she wrote 4 messages within 5 minutes, and she was shocked. Dame Elizabeth Taylor expressed her grief over the death of her dear friend Michael in heartbreaking statements, "My heart ... my mind ... are broken. I loved Michael with all my soul and I can't imagine life without him. We had so much in common and we had such loving fun together. I was packing up my clothes to go to London for his opening when I heard the news. I still can't believe it. I don't want to believe it. It can't be so. He will live in my heart forever but it's not enough. My life feels so empty. I don't think anyone knew how much we loved each other. The purest most giving love I've ever known. Oh God! I'm going to miss him." Only a few minutes later: "I can't yet imagine life without him. But I guess with God's help... I'll learn. I keep looking at the photo he gave me of himself, which says, 'To my true love Elizabeth, I love you forever.' And, I will love HIM forever."

    Usher expressed his extreme sorrow over the sudden death of Michael. Usher who once said, 'I study legends because I want to be a legend. Frank Sinatra, Fred Estaire, Michael Jackson. That's who inspires me,' expressed his grief in a statement. It read: "This loss has deeply saddened me. It is with a heavy heart I composed this statement; May God cover you, Michael. We all lift your name up in prayer. I pray for the entire

Jackson family, particularly Michael's mother, children and all his fans that loved him so much. I would not be the artist, performer and philanthropist I am today without the influence of Michael. I have great admiration and respect for him, and I'm so thankful I had the opportunity to meet and perform with such a great entertainer, who in so many ways transcended the culture. He broke barriers, he changed radio formats! With music, he made it possible for people like Oprah Winfrey and Barack Obama to impact the mainstream world. His legacy is unparalleled. Michael Jackson will never be forgotten." The actor Joe Pesci told Fox News: "He was a fun kid and did so much. He always reinvented himself time and time again and certainly was a great entertainer and dancer and great to watch with all that energy. He was excited about getting back to the stage. He was downhearted for a while and I think he finally got himself up." Chris Brown said in his statement: "Michael Jackson is the reason why I do music and why I am an entertainer. I am devastated by this great loss, and I will continue to be humbled and inspired by his legacy. My prayers are with his family. Michael will be deeply missed, but never forgotten. He's the greatest, the best ever. No one will ever be better." Chris, who is from Virginia, performed a tribute to the late singer at the MTV *Video Music Awards* in 2008. He was dressed in a replica of Michael's *Thriller* jacket. Corey Feldman, a former child star, who was a close friend of Michael, wrote on his website: "I come to you today with great sadness, acknowledging the loss of the greatest entertainer in the history of mankind. For me he was more than that, he was my idol, he was a role model, he was someone to cry to when my childhood was unbearable, he was a brother, he was a dear friend. I am trembling and shaking at the moment and it is very hard to type. I am filled with tremendous sadness and remorse. All I choose to remember from this point is the good times we shared and what an inspiration he was to me and the rest of the world. Nobody will ever be able to do what Michael Jackson has done in this industry, and he was so close to doing it all again. I am truly, and deeply sorry for all of the heartbroken fans and supporters worldwide. I think I am still in shock. So I must end this now."

Was the stress of the upcoming concert the cause of Michael's cardiac arrest? Michael was being sued in America and this could have been a key factor in his sad and untimely death. Michael trained a few days for his *This Is It* tour in the United Kingdom, which was to be held in the O2 Arena in July. Lou Ferrigno, the original Hulk, had been working with Michael to help in train for the shows. Lou trained with Jackson years ago, when he was much younger and fitter. He insisted Michael left him in no doubt that he was ready for his headline-grabbing comeback in London. He said: "He was great. I trained him on and off for 15 years and when I saw him a few months ago, the way he moved - I'd never seen him look better. He moved convinced me that he was going to make the biggest come back in history." Lou remembered Michael "never" said anything about being in pain. Lou said: "As a matter of fact sometimes he would be dancing, showing me the moves, between the sets, our exercising, and he convinced me, I said, 'This guy can pull it off'. When I saw him he was not frail." The actor told his last training session with Michael was at the end of May before commitments took Lou out of California. He further said: "Michael showed no sign of drug use."

People were wondering if Michael had tried to do more than his body would allow. Was it all finally too much for him? Was Michael's addiction to Demerol the true cause of his fatal end? Did the doctor do it? Dr. Murray was most probably in heavy debt. For sure he was insured under and on the concert promoter's payroll. Confirmation of Michael's addiction to painkillers could most likely be the cause of death. Reports are starting to point the finger at Demerol. It's believed Michael has taken too large of a dose. The sensitive Mariah Carey posted on her Twitter: "No artist will ever take his place. His star will shine forever." A journalist said: "There is something unsettling in this passing and we are going to get to the bottom of it." Many questions were regarding the doctor who was apparently in over his head financially. Madonna announced: "I can't stop crying over the sad news. I have always admired Michael Jackson. The world has lost one of the greats, but his music will live on forever! My heart goes out to his three children and other members of his family. God bless." Demi Moore, wife of Ashton Kutcher, said: "I am greatly saddened for the loss of both Farrah Fawcett and Michael Jackson. Especially for their children!" Quincy Jones wrote on Twitter: "I am absolutely devastated at this tragic and unexpected news. For Michael to be taken away from us so suddenly at such a young age, I just don't have the words. Divinity brought our souls together on The Wiz and allowed us to do what we were able to throughout the 80's. To this day, the music we created together on *Off The Wall*, *Thriller* and *Bad* is played in every corner of the world and the reason for that is because he had it all, talent, grace, professionalism and dedication. He was the consummate entertainer and his contributions and legacy will be felt upon the world forever." California Governor and Terminator star Arnold Schwarzenegger said: "The world has lost one of the most influential and iconic figures in the music industry. Michael was a pop phenomenon who never stopped pushing the envelope of creativity." Whitney Houston who happened to have had a lot of problems herself stated: "I am full of grief." Ex-Fugees rapper Wyclef Jean wrote on his Twitter page: "He lives forever in my heart. I will never forget the day he came to see me in the studio and I played him music. R.I.P. to Michael Jackson my music god. Some lost Elvis Presley and we lost Michael Jackson... I cried today because Michael Jackson was a Father that we all lost!"

Britney heard the news while she was shopping. When she returned at her house, she was in shock. Britney Spears: "I was so excited to see his show in London. We were going to be on tour in Europe at the same time and I was going to fly in to see him. He has been an inspiration throughout my entire life and I'm devastated he's gone!" Eddie Van Halen, who played guitar on Jackson's *Beat It*, told TMZ: "I am really shocked; as I'm sure the world is, to hear the news. I had the pleasure of working with Michael on *Beat It* back in '83, one of my fondest memories in my career. Michael will be missed and may he rest in peace." A Gossiboo Staff Writer wrote: "Michael Jackson may be gone, but his legend will live on. It is killing me inside to post this at the moment as I can not stop crying at how many moments in life Michael Jackson's music has touched my heart. He will and is always the King of Pop, a True irreplaceable talent that our world will always miss. A great friend of mine introduced me to Michael when I was a young child. He has been in my life within 6-degrees of separation. She is gone now and so is he, but his life will be one to always celebrate as there will NEVER be another MICHAEL JACKSON in our time or in history. Like Elvis, Michael is unforgettable."

Singer and songwriter Barry Manilow expressed his shock and grief over the death of pop icon Michael Jackson in a statement to ET. Barry Manilow stated: "It doesn't seem possible. How could Michael Jackson not be with us? This experience is surreal. He was one of the most gifted and original talents the world has ever known. He inspired a generation of young people and amazed the rest of the world. There has never been anyone like him. There will never be another Michael Jackson. I can't wrap my mind around this terrible news." Michael's friend and singer Dionne Warwick said: "We have lost an icon in our industry and my heartfelt condolences go out to his family and children in this hour of sorrow that they are now going through. He will live on in my memory and most definitely through the music he shared with so many." Pharrell Williams said: "It's the end of an era, but Michael will be remembered forever. R.I.P." One of Michael's closest friends, Elizabeth Taylor, who was preparing to fly to London for his upcoming shows, and had expressed her feelings on Twitter was said by her reps to be "too devastated" to issue any official statement. "He was an extraordinary talent and a truly great international star," John Landis told the Los Angeles Times: "He was an extraordinary talent and a truly great international star. He had a troubled and complicated life and despite his gifts, remains a tragic figure. My wife, Deborah, and I will always have great affection for him."

New shocking evidence showed that the doctor's car was around the back of the house and nobody knew it was there. Police took the car away and was looking for the doctor who was with Michael just before he died. It is further to believe that the family will benefit from Michael's estate. His estate could be well supported to go beyond just paying off all creditors, because, there will no longer be personal spending. Michael's musical catalog alone is worth millions and since he has past he is possibly worth more dead than he was alive. One thing we all know for sure, that Michael's legacy will live on and enjoyed around the world.

The Guardian wrote on Saturday, June, 27: "Doctors hires lawyer as Jacksons hire pathologist." The article read: "The doctor who was with Michael Jackson when he died has hired a notoriously aggressive lawyer and is insisting he has done nothing wrong as the singer's death appeared to open rifts between his family and other players in his complicated life. The lawyer, Matt Alford, described on his own website as an "intimidating bad ass" who goes about his work "with a scorched-earth mentality", went on television with an impassioned defense of his client, Conrad Murray, underlining that he was just a witness and not a suspect. Los Angeles police issued a brief statement after talking to Dr. Murray on Saturday, saying he had been cooperative and provided "information which will aid the investigation."

According to Dr. Murray's lawyer the doctor found Michael in his bed with a faint pulse, but he wasn't breathing anymore. The lawyer said Dr. Murray immediately began administering CPR. An official postmortem failed to determine the cause of death. It was said toxicology tests could take four to six weeks. Michael's family hired a private pathologist to conduct a second postmortem examination over the weekend. They said that on the tape of the emergency call requesting an ambulance, Dr. Murray was described as "pumping" Michael on a bed and not on the floor or another hard surface. The family questioned whether the doctor had carried out resuscitation attempts properly.

According to sources familiar with the case, a private pathologist completed a second autopsy on Michael's body after his body has been released to the family. This was believed to be taking place in Los Angeles last night. Los Angeles Times wrote: "The second autopsy came a day after an initial examination by the LA County coroner's office did not immediately determine a cause of death. Officials said additional lab tests, including a toxicology screen, were required to uncover why the 50-year-old pop star went into cardiac arrest in his rented Holmby Hills mansion Thursday."

The Rev. Jesse Jackson, who visited Michael's family Friday, said in a Good Morning America interview that his relatives had a host of questions about the circumstances of his death. He indicated the key area of concern had to do with Jackson's personal physician, Dr. Conrad Murray, who was by his side when he stopped breathing. Jesse Jackson said: "When did the doctor come? What did he do? Did he inject him? If so, with what? Was he on the scene twice? Before and then reaction to? Did he use the Demerol? It's a very powerful drug. Was he injected once? Was he injected twice?" Former medical examiners said that families often opt for a second autopsy. "They either distrust officials or they'd like a second opinion to be assured of the cause of death," they said. Michael Baden, chief forensic pathologist for the New York State Police and former chief medical examiner for New York City said: "One of the immediate benefits of getting a second autopsy is giving the family a chance for answers before the official autopsy results are released by the county." He further said: "Certainly, the family can get more information more quickly than waiting for the first autopsy. A private pathologist can get results from a private lab in a week or two. He also said: "The reason an official autopsy can take four to six weeks to complete is that officials are proceeding with a methodology to provide a chain of evidence that will be admissible in court, and that takes a little bit of time."

The Sun wrote that a source close to the Jackson entourage had told them: "Michael's family and fans will be horrified when they realize the appalling state he was in. He was skin and bone, his hair had fallen out and had been eating nothing but pills when he died. Injection marks all over his body and the disfigurement caused by years of plastic surgery show he'd been in terminal decline for years." Michael's father Joe Jackson predicted his son's tragic death would increase Michael's legend. As police confirmed Dr. Murray is "not a suspect", an emotional Joe said: "Michael was the biggest superstar in the world and in history. He was loved by everybody, whether poor or wealthy." Another family member said: "His doctors and the hangers-on stood by as he self-destructed. Somebody is going to have to pay."

Linda Rivera from New York, said: "The doctors responsible for prescribing the drugs and the enablers who surrounded Michael are guilty of enormous abuse. They should not be allowed to get away with it. Prescription DRUGS and over the counter drugs ARE DANGEROUS! Every year, many thousands of people in America die from taking prescription drugs (taking them correctly!) There are extremely dangerous side effects with every drug. The so-called "cure" is far worse and far more dangerous than the actual illness." Someone from Houston wrote: "Michael needed more positive people around him, not just those with their hand's on his check book, someone who truly had a heart." JS, Hollis from New Hampshire wrote a moving note saying, "Sad to see a legend in our time go. I would love to see him on tour." Bill from London stated: "I was on Prozac for six months but it was only 5mg, 20mg seems a very high dose."

According to leading pharmacist David Pruce, of the Royal Pharmaceutical Society, "The cocktail of drugs being taken by Michael Jackson at the time of his death was highly unusual and potentially dangerous." He told the Daily Mail: "The mix is highly unusual and not something I would ever expect to see and would not recommend. The article read: "The singer was taking a combination of antidepressants, anxiety pills, painkillers and stimulants, which would have left him listless and unresponsive. Some have been associated with serious side effects, including breathing problems and mood swings." David Pruce said the combination of the drugs could be dangerous: "The additive side effects, the side effects of the drugs in combination together, could be potentially dangerous if not monitored closely. Painkillers can cause breathing problems and, in high doses, can stop people breathing altogether. The other drugs would reduce his responsiveness and make him drowsy and difficult to wake. It would be possible to see this prescription combination in the United Kingdom but it certainly would not be desirable. It's a very odd list."

Each drug was being prescribed in low to moderate 'normal' doses, despite the fact that the combination was rare. It is understood that Michael was being injected twice a day with the morphine-related painkiller Demerol. Demerol is called Pethidine in the United Kingdom and is usually given to women in childbirth. Michael also received, according to Daily Mail, twice-a-day 3mg doses of the powerful narcotic Dilaudid, along with further injections of the painkiller Vistaril. The article said: "He was also taking 250mg a day of the anxiety drug Xanax, which is similar to Valium, along with 20mg of anti-depressant Prozac and

100mg of Zoloft. Jackson was also taking the anti-indigestion drug Prilosec. An 'upper', the stimulant Ritalin normally given to children to treat Attention Deficit Hyperactivity Disorder, was also prescribed in 10mg doses."

Martin Bashir remembered Michael: "I think the world has now lost the greatest entertainer it's probably ever known. It is very sad." But the same man conducted a series of interviews with the world acclaimed King of Pop that would soon after it was aired cause further scrutiny towards Michael. Michael was in 1993 already embroiled in another scandal centering around child molestation claims that dated back to the early '90s. It was good friend and spoon bender, Uri Geller, who recommended the pop star to the ITV journalist. Why Martin had to bring up and prioritize upon Michael's child molestation claims? Was it an attempt to show Michael in a damaging light? Martin well ignored Michael's good words. For some people, Martin Bashir has Michael's blood on his hands. People stated: "When you kill someone's spirit, it's only a matter of time before the body gives up." Others announced: "Bashir is a very unethical journalist and ABC should fire him. He twisted the interview to fit his intention to bring down Michael Jackson. It seemed as if he enjoys bringing down African-Americans; he did the same with Marion Jones." Some others said: "In his zeal to establish himself as a notable journalist, he sacrificed Michael, a loving human being, like a lamb to the slaughter. Now in death he pays him homage? Has he no decency?" Others questioned his subjective style: "Everyone who viewed Bashir's interview will forever remember his 'subjective' style of journalism and goal to prove a point. Who paid him to do this?? That was not true journalism."

Michael was emotional attached to others in need. His kindness has always been turned into something weird, strange, odd. Michael felt often very lonely, and he even told reporters many times he had no real friends. His constant loss of trust in people disillusioned him with anyone close-by. Michael surrounded himself with people who were using him and was paranoid about people using him. This part of Michael, Martin Bashir didn't understand. The legendary artist wanted to show the world how to share and love each other. Martin Bashir decided to give a "completely distorted view of Michael, just to fuel his own want for fame." This man who has been called an unethical parasite, "wanted to achieve greatness for himself by trying to bring down a man who spent all his life helping people." The first and final parts of the documentary are able to be viewed on YouTube.com. ITV Productions Limited made copyright claims for the rest of the show. Even in these clips you see how ruthless and heartless Martin Bashir is and a strong sense of sensationalism is revealed.

Many stars couldn't believe the news when they heard of Michael's sudden demise. Jaime Foxx reflected on Michael's massive impact on pop music. Jamie told the TV show Extra: "You cannot say enough about what he has given to us musically and culturally. We take for granted people like him. All he wanted to do was give us great music, and that's what he did. Every single day was dedicated to us."

"Can Michael Jackson's demons be explained?", wrote BBC News Magazine on Saturday morning, two days after Michael's death. "Michael Jackson, who has died at 50, is known to have been a man who struggled with a host of inner demons," the article says. Peter Sharp, chartered psychologist at the British Psychological

Society talked to BBC News: "Violence occasioned by a parent on a child leaves lasting psychological and physical impact. Young people in receipt of physical violence have difficulty forming and maintaining long-term relationships." He added: "They're 'anxious-avoidant', which means they will often take on what they know they can be successful in, therefore avoid challenges outside their comfort zones and may try to provide their worth by excelling and over-excelling in one particular area. If that person thinks that to have affirmation and validity, they need to be successful at something, there is a risk that this is the only thing about them they define as worthy."

Peter Congdon, a psychologist who works with extremely intelligent or gifted children said: "It's well known that the best preparation for growing up is to live fully as a child. Parents of clever or talented children shouldn't forget this. Accelerated mental development for example, can slow down social and mental growth, and the result can be a lop-sided and maladjusted individual."

Jay Belsky, director of the Institute for the Study of Children, Families and Social Issues at Birkbeck College, University of College London told BBC: "With a gift, the issue becomes, 'Am I loved because I sing and dance or because I'm worthy of being loved?' I think the child figures that out, not necessarily in a conscious way but does it register? Certainly. Children vary in their sensitivity to things, and you might think of Michael Jackson as one who benefited from being impressionable. You might think of him as a kid who was highly malleable for better or worse. Better in the sense that he could take advantage of the musical lessons and dance lessons and that kind of guidance, where for another kid it might be water off a duck's back. But this same quality may have counted against him when he took alleged comments about his appearance to heart." But big families can multiply sibling rivalries. "You can have a healthy sibling rivalry in which the older child is someone who you can compete with and reach for and as you struggle to do so, he or she is encouraging you and enabling you. But if the sibling is demeaning and bullying, then what could be wonderfully facilitating can be destructive. A child with an older sibling can be inspired by his or her accomplishments in music, dancing or basketball, for example, the child may want to be like that or better," the psychology professor said.

During an interview with police, Dr. Conrad Murray told Los Angeles Police Department detectives: "I have given the intravenously administered drug to my client hours before he passed." A senior investigator said that Dr. Conrad Murray made the revelation during an informal police interview, without his lawyer present. The singer's doctor also told cops his hiding place with Michael's secret stash of potentially deadly drugs. Dr. Conrad Murray told officers in the morning on Saturday, June 27, that the stash of drugs was hidden in his closet at Michael's home. The Daily Star quoted the investigator as saying: "It was almost by accident that he said it." Cops discovered Propofol and other drugs, an IV line and three tanks of oxygen in Michael's bedroom. 15 more oxygen tanks were found during a search at Michael's mansion. Initially, cops had failed to find the cache in Michael's Los Angeles home, but the information the doctor had given the LAPD, on the Saturday after Michael's death triggered another broader search warrant. After the doctor had spoken, cops immediately sought a second search warrant, and found the hoard, including Propofol, in a cupboard in the guest room after the weekend. When the LAPD returned to Michael's house, they discovered 'various drugs' secretly stashed in a closet of the guest room where Dr. Murray was staying. "The drugs were concealed, they weren't obvious," a law enforcement source said.

It's been said Dr. Conrad Murray allegedly hooked Michael up to an IV drip of the drug, and either wasn't paying attention, left the room when the singer's heart stopped beating, or fell asleep. TMZ reported that there was no EKG machine or pulse oximeter found in Jackson's home, though those machines are usually used to monitor the pulse of a patient being administered Propofol.

The Texas Medical Board found out information about the father of Dr. Murray, 56, Dr. Rawle Andrews. Dr. Murray's late biological dad met his son for the first time when Conrad was 25. It has emerged that the father of Michael's doctor Conrad Murray had been disciplined for over-subscribing addictive drugs. Dr. Murray knew of the disciplinary action against him. Dr. Andrews had been found to have prescribed controlled substances with 'addictive potential' to two patients. That went on for extended periods in the 1990s 'without adequate indication'. Included among the four pain-relieving drugs was Stadol, which is similar to Demerol, a powerful drug also prescribed to Michael. Because Michael's personal physician injected Michael with strong anesthetic Propofol, police officials think the drug took the singer to his end. An official said Dr. Conrad Murray regularly pumped the King of Pop with Propofol to help him falling asleep, a practice not meant for the drug's intended use. Michael who reportedly suffered insomnia had asked the doctor to help him stop his drugs habits. Dr. Murray's attorney Ed Chernoff insisted the medic did not administer any drug that contributed to Michael's death.

But sources predicted that Michael's death could result in manslaughter or even murder charges. The Sun quoted a case insider as saying: "Michael Jackson was a walking drug store when he died - he never stood a chance." The insider said: "The body can build up extreme tolerances to huge doses of drugs but eventually it overloads and just shuts down. That is what happened to Michael." The source added: "There is increasing talk of manslaughter charges if it can be shown he was given drugs without proper regard for his safety." Police Chief William Bratton is waiting for the final toxicology reports. He said: "Based on those, we will have an idea what we are dealing with. Are we dealing with a homicide or are we dealing with accidental overdose?"

A spokesman for promoter AEG said: "Full ticket refund information and procedures will be released early next week." Ticketmaster's website went into meltdown. I a message on its phone line customers were told, to 'await communication.' Fans who bought from sites such as Ticketmaster and See Tickets, or secondary retailers Viagogo and Seatwave will get a full refund.

The Kent mansion into which Michael Jackson was due to move the weekend after his death stayed empty. Speculation was growing that fears over the upheaval of relocating from the United Stated to United Kingdom might have contributed to Michael's sudden death. Michael was suffering extreme stress because of performing for the first time in eight years. The Foxbury Manor near Orpington which Michael Jackson was going to rent until February for $1.7 million (£1 million) was personally selected by Michael after visiting it secretly around the time of his press conference in London on March 5. The property's owner, businessman Osman Ertosun, his wife and two children were preparing to stay elsewhere for a year. The Grade II-listed mansion is among the largest private properties in Greater London. An army of tradesmen renovated the house for weeks to suit Michael's extraordinary tastes. Features also included fairground rides, a bowling alley and an 8ft security fence around the sprawling eight-acre grounds. Michael himself hired top interior designers to stamp his personality on the suites intended for him and his children. One child room had a *Star Wars* theme. A neighbor said he noticed already an increase in security while Michael was staying there shortly. The neighbor was told by a policeman he would not tell the exact date Michael would arrive, but urged them to stay quiet. The house that originally featured 32 bedrooms was recently renovated and it now has 11 massive suites, including a music room, cinema and indoor swimming pool. The house, surrounded by woods and a lake, was build in 1875 by David Brandon, Queen Victorias favorite architect. The main bedroom is said to cover 1,800 sqft.. Mr. Ertosun, 42, a chairman of Excelcare, a company that owns 32 care and nursing homes across South-East England bought the house in January 2004.

The world was united in grief as millions mourned the famous pop legend. Thousands gathered outside the Los Angeles hospital where he died. In Gary, Indiana, people laid flowers and stood outside the house where Michael was born. Others descended on Michael's home to leave flowers and letters of condolence. Commuters in New York's Times Square looked shocked as news of the tragedy was displayed on giant TV screens hanging high above the streets. In France, the unofficial Princess Diana shrine in central Paris was turned over to Michael. In Berlin, fans gathered outside the Kaiser Wilhelm Memorial Church while others signed a book of condolence at the city's Madame Tussauds. In Munich, Germany, candles were left burning outside the main cathedral and in Amsterdam, the Netherlands, people went to the Dam square to sing and pray together. Across Asia, stunned fans, Michael's most passionate supporters, woke to the sad news. Japan was likely to be mourning for some time because Michael was a "true superstar". Fans from China wept and signed books of condolence in cities including Shanghai. An elaborate sand sculpture on a beach in Puri, was a tribute from fans from India. Former South African President Nelson Mandela, for whom Jackson sang in 1998, issued a message through his foundation. It said Michael's death would be felt worldwide. Grieving fans from Russia laid flowers and all kind of messages outside the Unites States embassy in Moscow.

Usher, admirer of Michael, told reporters of Time Magazine about his feelings when he heard Michael died: "I was shooting a Macy's commercial and me and Martha Stewart were standing side by side taking a picture, and I remember looking over to her and I said: "They said that Michael had an incident, a cardiac arrest," and she and I were both in denial. No, that's just some fabricated story that they came up with. We kind of shrugged it off. I went, and I turned on CNN, and they said he had experienced issues of cardiac arrest. And I knew this was very serious. I had an engagement in Paris, and as I boarded my plane, I didn't know what to think. By the time I landed, there was his family releasing a statement. Man, I lost it. I cried myself to sleep. This man, he meant so much to me as an entertainer; as an individual, he taught me so much, even though he didn't know it. Michael Jackson was the first African American to sing to a crossover audience. I do feel like without Michael Jackson, MTV would not be on the map. It would not be what it is today. This is bigger than the loss of Elvis."

Stevie Wonder, friend of Michael said in Time Magazine's Special about Michael Jackson: "I first met Michael when I was in Detroit. He came to Motown, and they were talking about this boy from Gary, Indiana, and the Jackson 5, and everyone was excited. He was a little boy then. He would always come into the studio curious about how I worked and what I did. 'How do you do that?', 'Why do you do that?' I think he understood clearly from seeing various people do the music scene that it definitely took work. He must have been around 9 or 10 then, and I definitely felt that he would be someone. You heard the voice, and all he could do was grow. And that's what he did. I remember playing air hockey one time, and we were going back and forth. I play air hockey on the side as opposed to the end of the table because it's more accessible for me to really understand what's happening. He said, 'Oh, you're cheating'. And I said, 'Aw, I'm not cheating, come on.' And we went on and on for hours, just playing air hockey and being silly. He had a childlike heart. And that was very, very impressive to me. At the end of the day, we're all human beings, and for those who can't see that it is possible for a man who's an adult to have a childlike spirit, it doesn't mean that they're weird, it doesn't mean they're a freak or whatever ridiculous things people say. We have all kinds of people in the world. The most important thing is that your heart is in a good place."

According to AmericanHeart.org, American Heart Association, Inc., the AHA Recommendation regarding cardiac arrest: "The American Heart Association urges the public to be prepared for cardiac emergencies: Know the warning signs of cardiac arrest. During cardiac arrest a victim loses consciousness, stops normal breathing and loses pulse and blood pressure. Call 911 immediately to access the emergency medical system if you see any cardiac arrest warning signs. Give cardiopulmonary resuscitation (CPR) to help keep the cardiac arrest victim alive until emergency help arrives. CPR keeps blood and oxygen flowing to the heart and brain until defibrillation can be administered."

Pietra Thornton from Los Angeles wrote on the internet: "Michael Jackson suffered from an autoimmune disease better known as LUPUS or S.L.E. I too suffer from this incurable, debilitating illness and have been battling it for the past 8+ years. I am involved with Lupus LA & am aware of Michael's Lupus due to that involvement. Persons suffering with Lupus are often plagued by a flurry of ill effects. Predominantly large numbers of young people (age 20-50) battling Lupus often undergo arterial, vascular abnormalities, excessive blood clotting often calling for drugs such as Cumadin which are blood thinners. People with Lupus often have the Anticoagulate syndrome wherein "sticky blood", often the culprit in premature cases of heart disease leading to heart attacks and sudden pulmonary embolisms, astronomical cases leading to death are indicative of a classic Lupus patient. Based on the fact that Michael was beginning to get more involved in Lupus fundraisers desiring to assist in raising Lupus awareness... indicative of his own dwindling health.

Ian Halperin, a journalist who wrote a book about Michael's life said, just before the pop singer died, in an article on Mail Online: "I had more than a glimpse of the real Michael; as an award-winning freelance journalist and film-maker, I spent more than five years inside his camp. Many in his entourage spoke frankly to me and that made it possible for me to write authoritatively last

December that Michael had six months to live, a claim that, at the time, his official spokesman, Dr. Tohme Tohme, called a complete fabrication. The singer, he told the world, was in fine health. Six months and one day later, Jackson was dead. Some liked to snigger at his public image, and it is true that flamboyant clothes and bizarre make-up made for a comic grotesque; yet without them, his appearance was distressing; with skin blemishes, thinning hair and discolored fingernails." Ian Halperin, who's book is probably not well accepted by all members of the Jackson family stated: "I had established beyond doubt, for example, that Jackson relied on an extensive collection of wigs to hide his greying hair." Ian who admitted, "I had started my investigation convinced that Jackson was guilty. By the end, I no longer believed that," could not find a single shred of evidence suggesting that Michael had ever molested any child. He wrote: "But I found significant evidence demonstrating that most, if not all, of his accusers lacked credibility and were motivated primarily by money."

He further confessed: "He was also playing a truly dangerous game. It is clear to me that Michael was homosexual and that his taste was for young men, albeit not as young as Jordan Chandler or Gavin Arvizo. In the course of my investigations, I spoke to two of his gay lovers, one a Hollywood waiter, the other an aspiring actor. The waiter had remained friends, perhaps more, with the singer until his death last week. He had served Jackson at a restaurant, Jackson made his interest plain and the two slept together the following night. According to the waiter, Jackson fell in love." Real names of these by Ian so called "lovers" were not given. People have called Ian Halperin, the award winning journalist, a liar. Others said they didn't even wanted to see the book after seeing reactions about the book on the internet. Ian's book *Unmasked: The Final Years of Michael Jackson* was published right after Michael's death. It is still for sale.

The Jackson family spoke for the first time of their devastation at his 'tragic' death and were considering whether to hold an official public memorial service.

The Heal the World Foundation (HTWF) is a universal charity organization designed to improve the condition of all mankind. According to the website of Heal the World Foundation: "We fight to rescue the world's most vulnerable: the children, elderly and animals from privation, abuse and exploitation. We address the most urgent global problems of the day, problems like hunger, homelessness and the moral decay of mankind." Heal The World Foundation made a moving and emotional statement after Michael's death. It said: "A Message from the HTWF President To Mr. Jackson's beloved fans and all those who have written,

"Please forgive me if my writing is poor, I won't be eloquent, as I've not yet had the opportunity to process this tragedy and I am not myself, nor are we prepared to answer all of you personally yet, so please accept this as a group response, for the time.

"This is Melissa Johnson and I am one of many, who have been helping to develop the initiatives of HTWF and doing its work since 1993. I cry along side the whole world and my heart is broken in two. My prayers go out to the family, his precious children and all those who I know are hurting from the loss of him on Earth. There is a void in the air we all breath, as it no longer is shared with a man of extraordinary value to the world. You all knew and loved him most for his music, but my small part in his life and knowledge of him was not as a pop legend, but a legend for change and a force for good and charity, a side of him, even in his death, is rarely talked about. His rare love and devotion to the helpless, the downtrodden, the innocent and the world's most needy is why I grieve today. They lost their greatest advocate. Mr. Jackson was not a perfect man, but I know he strived to become the best version of himself and was surrounded by those that would not let him serve and love the world with the vigor he desired. Over the years, I fell in love, not with a superstar or a pop icon as the world did, but with a miracle, a masterpeace of 'love and service', that was the blue print for the future of HTWF.

"I learned of a work and a plan that I believed Mr. Jackson could actually make happen, saving millions of lives, not merely results for the worlds most needy, but a shift in the way that people treat each other. From indifference to concern, from inaction to action, from selfishness to service. He was pure in heart and he loved humanity with a passion I had never witnessed in any other human being and likely will never see again. It was not manufactured love, like a politician who puts on a face for people, it was pure, innocent and simple. He was full of love and he fought the world's disapproval boldly, to hold on to his child-like qualities and inner beauty. I believe he WAS a king, but not merely of POP, a king in character, the royal blood of an honorable and God-like man, flowed through his body and he was good at levels most of us could never attain ourselves. I believed that Mr. Jackson would DO what he said he would do and change peoples minds and their hearts. Then the whole world. Not through music alone, but with a clearly defined plan and devotion to carry it out. Starting a movement with his fans and eventually a world of well indented people, people who were fed up with the environment they had created for themselves.

"He wanted to be remembered as one of the worlds greatest contributors and instruments for good, along side Gandhi and Mother Theresa, Mandela and Martin Luther King Jr. He just wanted to love us, all of us and in 1992 he founded Heal The World Foundation, then in 1993, the first false allegations hit and year after year, until his death, every time he tried to serve and love us, there was some rapacious person there to slow him, cripple him and destroy any chance for his good works. How many genuinely abused children were NOT helped in the last decade because Mr. Jackson's name, charity and good work was damaged so severely.

"Accused of abusing the VERY children he set out to RESCUE and HEAL. Corey Feldman once said, calling Mr. Jackson a child abuser is like calling Santa Claus a thief! I believe the world will come to know as I have always known, that Mr. Jackson would never hurt any child and did have a propensity to love children especially, but love them as he loved his very own. How could he not? He said many times, that a child's heart is not judgmental or unkind, its boldly honest and wholesome, not crude and manipulative as he came to experience with adults in his life. How many Millions of lives would have been saved if we had protected our beloved ambassadors of peace, goodwill and charity. Living Legends for good, like Mr. Jackson and Princess Diana?

"How much more GOOD could they have done? The loss of Mr. Jackson is not to Mr. Jackson, he is in Paradise and is ok now, the loss is to humanity, to the most vulnerable and the sick, to the abused children and forgotten child in all of us. We needed him, he didn't need us. The whole world loses a teacher, a leader and an example of good character and we will never know how much he could have taught us. Mr. Jackson is gone now and It is unclear if the Jackson Family will want to continue his charity work and his humanitarian legacy and in what manner. The staff at HTWF only ask that the public be patient with us and allow the family time to grieve as we wait for the direction they would have us go.

"HTWF belongs to God first and then to Mr. Jackson, as God's instrument for miracles and good to the world and we must all be respectful and wait for the family to come up for air, before and IF we can move forward on Mr. Jackson's behalf. Many have asked what we plan to do and I don't know yet, we are left at the mercy of God and the Jackson family have a heavy burden to bare, but I do know personally, I won't let the adversary take me out, before I accomplish the things that God has prepared for me and I leave the world a lot better off, than the way I entered it.

"My prayers are with you all and I ask that your prayers be with the family, his precious children and finally myself, that I be given the strength to do right always, in God's purposes and in the magic and glory of HTWF. As Mr. Jackson loved his fans so deeply, I have seen clearly why, as I cannot express the joy you all have brought to my life. Your beauty, your loyalty, your love for others.

My deep gratitude and love to you all,
Melissa Johnson
President
Heal the World Foundation

An American website claimed detectives are also planning to speak to Michael's aide Dr. Tohme Tohme about an 'alleged indirect connection' between the prescription drugs in Michael's house and the pop star's death. Londell McMillan, Jackson family attorney voiced the family's concerns over Michael's personal physician, who was in his bedroom when the singer fell into cardiac arrest. He told relatives are "deeply troubled with the circumstances surrounding" the pop star's death last week. Michael's doctor, who said Michael was not breathing when he discovered him in his bedroom, claimed he had a faint pulse. McMillan said on Monday's Today: "It's been well documented that Michael was receiving medical care on the bed as opposed to on the floor."

Edward Chernoff, attorney for Dr. Murray, told Dateline on Sunday night that Dr. Murray gave Michael gentle chest compressions on his bed due to his frail condition. Edward Chernoff stated: "He was a frail man. He didn't like to drink or eat. He wasn't exactly healthy." About the CPR he said: "He [Doctor Murray] had one hand behind his back and he was compressing with the other hand. He was compressing hard enough that the doctor knew he was pumping blood throughout the system." Chernoff told Dateline that Dr. Murray certainly wasn't prescribing or administering drugs like Demerol and Oxycontin to Michael Jackson. "Now, if toxicology comes back and shows those drugs in his system, it will be a surprise to us," he said. Edward Chernoff had even more revealing news. He told the press: "It took Dr. Conrad Murray a half-hour to call 911 after finding Michael unconscious. He didn't immediately make the call from his cell phone because he didn't know the exact address of Michael's mansion." His rented mansion is in one of the most famous streets in the country, in Beverly Hills, just above Sunset Blvd. Dr. Murray's attorney also said: "Dr. Murray eventually got someone in the house to make the call."

AEG informed fans that they have from July 1 until August 14 to request either the refund or the souvenir ticket at MichaelJacksonLive.com. The refund will include all service charges as well. AEG President and CEO Randy Phillips said in an announcement of the refund policy: "The world lost a kind soul who just happened to be the greatest entertainer the world has ever known. Since he loved his fans in life, it is incumbent upon us to treat them with the same reverence and respect after his death." The show promoter also announced that the fans who paid to attend the *This Is It* show can either get fully reimbursed for their purchase or receive a keepsake copy of the ticket, which features graphics inspired and designed by Michael himself.

Billboard reported that if it is revealed that Michael died of a preexisting condition or of a drug overdose, AEG Live could be liable for any loss. This includes the estimated $30 million the company sunk into the elaborate production, the cost of refunding the tickets to fans and the $10 million it reportedly fronted Michael and his entourage. The first of the *This Is It* shows was scheduled to take place on July 13. The series would have earned millions.

The 2009 BET Awards were dedicated to Michael Jackson. The awards were dedicated to the life, legacy and legend of the music and entertainment icon. Michael has had a significant impact on the Black Entertainment Television (BET) network. Janet Jackson made a brief appearance on stage during the 2009 BET Awards in Los Angeles. The 43-year-old sister of Michael honored her older brother during the ceremony. Michael's influences, innovations and contributions have been well recognized in the music world. Michael Jackson was the first artist inducted into the *BET Walk of Fame* in 1995. Father Joe Jackson appeared also at the BET Awards and was seated front row center with Rev. Al Sharpton.

Janet said: "My entire family wanted to be here tonight but it was just too painful, so they elected me to speak to all of you. I'm going to keep it very short. To you, Michael is an icon. To us, Michael is family. And he will forever live in all of our hearts. On behalf of my family, and myself, thank you for all of your love. Thank you for all of your support. We miss him so much. Thank you so much." The awards were hosted by Oscar-winning actor and rapper Jamie Foxx. Both Jamie Foxx and Ne-Yo performed emotional tributes to Michael Jackson singing the Jackson Five hit *I'll Be There*. Singer Beyonce sang a version of *Ave Maria* in his honor, while other tributes came from American R&B band New Edition. They sang a medley of Jackson Five hits including *I Want You Back* and *ABC*, complete with the classic dance moves. Singer Keri Hilson channeled Jackson in a black suit with white socks and black shades.

The Times wrote: "Back on top: Jackson legacy grows. With deep sadness etched in her face and tears welling in her eyes, Michael Jackson's younger sister Janet made her first public appearance since his death, joining a star-studded tribute to the King of Pop at the Black Entertainment Television awards in Los Angeles overnight." Singer Alicia Keys urged people to remember Michael in a "respectful, positive way". Alicia said: "We miss him and we love him and we just feel devastated." Hip-hop mogul Sean Diddy Combs, who labeled Michael "the greatest artist of all time" said: "He's one of the reasons why Barack Obama is president."

People.com found out what Michael's chimpanzee Bubbles is doing. They wrote an article about the chimp, who is now 26 years old. It said: "With all the discussion surrounding the shocking death of Michael Jackson, people have wondered whatever happened to his beloved chimpanzee Bubbles. It turns out, the chimp is alive and well and monkeying around in a Florida primate sanctuary." Sanctuary director Patti Ragan told People.com: "He's a very sweet and nice chimp, he really is. I've seen him go to the drinking fountain, start to take a sip of water and then, when he hears one of the younger ones coming, he'll step back and let them have a sip." Before Michael adopted Bubbles in the '80s, he was born at a facility in Texas that breeds primates for medical testing. Since 2005, after Michael's former animal trainer stopped working with primates, Bubbles lived in Ragan's sanctuary.

A rep for Michael contacted the facility when Michael heard Bubbles moved to the sanctuary. Michael wanted to come and visit his former buddy but he never showed up. Bubbles now weighs 160 lbs. His facial features have also changed. Patti told People.com: "That pink baby face of his has disappeared. He still has a lot of fleshy color in his face. But he's a huge guy now and that probably is going to surprise a lot of people." According to People.com Bubbles hasn't been told of his former owner's recent death. "We haven't said anything to him yet," Patti said. "He's been his usual self, interacting with friends, eating well, taking cover when it rains," she added.

TMZ reported Michael never filed legal papers to adopt his children, Michael Jr., Paris, and Prince Michael II. Legal experts told TMZ Michael would be presumed the father but it's not conclusive by any means. Questions are raising why Michael never formally adopt. Michael believed no third party would try and claim custody. And Michael never thought Debbie Rowe would mount a custody challenge.

Justin Timberlake has performed with the King of Pop, including a 'NSYNC duet with Jackson at the 2001 MTV Video Music Awards held at the

Metropolitan Opera House at Lincoln Center in New York City. He has been heavily influenced by Michael, and also wore a fedora and glove. Justin showed off Jackson-esque dance moves in his *Cry Me a River* video. He told MTV United Kingdom: "The thing about Michael is the memories. I'm lucky enough to have memories, actually, physically, with him on stage and off." The outpouring of emotion for Michael from friends and fans is, "a testament to how big a deal it is, obviously, because he's created so many cultural photos in people's minds with his music that he was and always will be the King of Pop. To create the things that he created with his music is untouchable. He opened the minds of the world to be able to do that through his music... [it's] a feat not accomplished by many people, maybe only a handful of people. I don't think anyone ever did it like him. He opened the minds of people about music. He opened the minds of people about culture. Even if it was this much in your conscious, he helped with segregation. His music did that and not a lot of people can say that. Michael was the baddest!"

Co-star in "The Wiz", Diana Ross told MTV News in a statement. "I can't stop crying; this is too sudden and shocking. I am unable to imagine this. My heart is hurting. I am in prayer for his kids and the family."

Quincy Jones wrote in a blog for the Los Angeles Times: "[Michael] was so shy he'd sit down and sing behind the couch with his back to me while I sat there with my hands over my eyes with the lights off." He added: "There will be a lot written about what came next in Michael's life, but for me all of that is just noise. I promise you in 50, 75, 100 years, what will be remembered is the music." He concluded with the words that it was not an accident that almost three decades later, no matter where he would go in the world, in every club and karaoke bar, like clockwork, you hear *Billie Jean*, *Beat It*, *Wanna Be Startin' Somethin'*, *Rock With You*, and *Thriller*. Quincy Jones sent his condolences and love to the family. Quincy, 76, who called Michael his "little brother", told reporters: "The relationship between a producer and an artist is one of love and tremendous trust. He's my little brother that's gone. I'd never in my wildest nightmares dream he'd leave before me."

Donald Trump reacted on Michael's mystery death to Time Magazine: "Michael Jackson kept a home in one of Trump's buildings in New York City. He was a very good friend of mine. He was an amazing guy, but beyond all else, he was the greatest entertainer I've ever known. He had magic. He was a genius. He was also a really good person, and when you got to know him, you realized how smart he was. He was brilliant. We were at the Trump Taj Mahal in Atlantic City. There were thousands of people literally crushing us. We had 20 bodyguards, but it was really dangerous. He dropped to his knees and started crawling to the exit. He did it so routinely, I thought he fell. And I said, "Michael, is it always like this?" He goes, "Yeah, this is nothing. Japan is much worse." Donald also said: "Now, Michael wasn't the same Michael for the last 10 years. He was not well. He had a lot of problems, a lot of difficulties. But Michael in his prime, there's never been anybody like him. His life was different than anybody I've ever known. But he had a very rough 10 years. He was embarrassed by it. He was embarrassed by what was happening to him. But he's not going to be remembered for the last 10 years; he's going to be remembered for the first 35 years."

The Reverend Al Sharpton led a memorial, on Tuesday, June 30, for Michael Jackson at

Harlem's Apollo Theater. Thousands of fans had lined up early in the morning. It opened its doors at 2 o'clock in the afternoon. Al Sharpton explained earlier from his office: "The Apollo has always been the symbol for black music and, later on, popular music because as black music expanded, American popular music became greatly grounded in the black music tradition. No one was responsible for that more than Michael Jackson."

He further said: "I said, 'We need to do a memorial in New York and give the people in New York an opportunity to express their love for Michael, similar to when we brought James Brown's body to the Apollo.' Michael was a part of Amateur Night at the Apollo, Michael in 2002 came back and performed at the Apollo for the Democratic National Committee. At 5.26 Eastern time, which was the time Michael was announced dead, I will call for a silent prayer to remember Michael five days after the exact moment of the announcement [of his death]. I will give a eulogy for this community and what he meant to us." Sharpton also said that, "the love for Michael in the black community is immense despite the talk in some media that African-Americans had become ambivalent about him over the years." The Reverend continued: "What mainstream media is doing is catching up with black support of Michael. Blacks never abandoned Michael. When Michael had the problem with his catalog, he came to Harlem and we marched with Michael. When Michael was indicted with the molestation case, black people stood by him, all the civil-rights leaders, and were criticized for being there. We never abandoned Michael. What is interesting now [is that] in his death, they're discovering our support for Michael. When everyone abandoned Michael, it was his family there and his base community. It's fitting the Apollo has the first big memorial for him because we were the ones that never left Michael. We were proud of him wherever he went, whatever changes he went through. We understood his success was our success. Michael Jackson represents to us something we understand. When the whole world turned on Michael, we never turned on Michael."

He also felt no one supported Michael more than his family. He addressed father Joe Jackson's controversial statements on the BET Awards red carpet a few days before. The Reverend said, explaining the press conference he held with Joe earlier, "Joe wanted to thank the fans for all the love, and he felt there had been some distortion that he was trying to promote a record when he did the BET red carpet. But my position is, whether one thinks what he said on the red carpet was appropriate or not, Joe Jackson is the head of that family and he stood by [Michael] during his trial. Look at the footage, Joe and Katherine walked him in and out of that courtroom. To say he doesn't care about his son is absurd. When it looked like all was lost, that family stood by him."

Sources said: "Michael will not be buried at his former California residence, Neverland Ranch, despite the wishes of members of his family." The Los Angeles Times said that even though Gov. Arnold Schwarzenegger had agreed to help overcome state obstacles to the plan, it has been dropped as unfeasible because of legal restrictions.

Not even a week after Michael died, police found a dangerous and potent drug used for surgical anesthesia in his house. The extremely powerful drug, called Propofol, is used to put people under anesthesia before surgery. The drug is only available to medical personnel and can't be properly prescribed for home use. Propofol can only be administered with an IV. Propofol burns and Lidocaine, also a drug, is used to reduce the pain that comes with the Propofol injection. Lidocaine was found near Michael's body when doctors and police arrived on June 25. A side-effect of Propofol is cardiac arrest, when it is taken in combination with narcotic painkillers. Propofol is so powerful it could have stopped Michael's heart on its own. The drug is inappropriate and reckless for home use. The doctor that facilitated it for Michael could be prosecuted for manslaughter when it is proven it caused his death.

Brooke Shields was 13 when she first met Michael. The two 'instantly became friends', mainly because sexual tension was off the table. "Nothing was jaded about him," the now 44-year-old actress told Rolling Stone magazine for a special commemorative issue about Michael. Brooke describes her young self as 'the most celebrated virgin ever' at a time when women "wanted to throw themselves at (Jackson) and feel like they were going to teach him." They met unfortunately only a few times. Brooke said that as Michael grew up, "the more asexual he became to me." But he was curious about Brooke's early relationships. "He was like a little kid who talked about the bases, what first base was, what second base was," Brooke said. "It sounded very odd to the outside, I can imagine, but to the inside, to someone who's never really left his bubble, you can understand how he would be curious." Brooke said she last saw Michael in 1991, 18 years ago, at Elizabeth Taylor's most recent wedding. "We snuck in and took pictures of ourselves next to her dress," she recalled. "We always seemed to revert to being little kids." Brooke was going to speak at Michael's memorial service a few days later.

We do not know much about Michael's sex life. Lisa Marie had stated before that their marriage was very sexual in the first year, and then the flame faded at the end. But with Michael trying to stop his addiction to drugs for years it is to believed the pair never ended up in one bed together, except for the video clip *You are Not Alone* where they are both barely naked. Michael was always shy when it came to talking about his sexuality. When Oprah asked him if he was a virgin, he told her: "I am a gentleman and I wouldn't say." This was after the time he was seeing Brooke Shields. He always felt embarrassed when the issue of sex came up.

Michael 's run on the charts is not over because Billboard reported that on the first two days of the sales week for music retailers, more than 110,000 copies of his albums were sold. That means he again dominate the catalog sales chart next week. The most popular title was *Thriller*, with 44,000 copies sold in the United States, followed by *The Essential Michael Jackson* and *Number Ones*. Those albums, in the reverse order, were Michael's most popular last week. Michael sold a total of 422,000 albums and 2.3 million single tracks online, breaking several records.

Entertainer Dick Clark said: "Of all the thousands of entertainers I have worked with, Michael was the most outstanding. Many have tried and will try to copy him, but his talent will never be matched. He was truly one-of-a-kind." R. Kelly, who wrote *Hold My Hand*, the Akon-produced Michael Jackson track that leaked last year, says Michael never lost his passion. "He was the King of Pop, the biggest to ever do it, and the one thing you never lose whether known by the whole world or just 10 people, is your love for music," R. Kelly said. "That never goes away, and it never went away for him amidst his troubles." Akon last spoke to Michael three months before he died. "He would always tell me to eat right and ask me if I was exercising and drinking water," he said. "He'd always stress you had to take care of yourself before you can go off and do anything else."

Michael was working on two albums at the time of his death; one in the pop area and another that would consist of instrumental classical compositions. Michael was working on the pop album with songwriter Claude Kelly and Akon. Akon said Michael was motivated by the ticket sales for his performances. Akon: "He said, 'My fans are still there. They still love me. They're alive.' His kids are like his first priority, and they had never seen him perform live. He was trying to create the most incredible show for his kids."

Composer David Michael Frank who had worked with Michael on a 1989 TV tribute to Sammy Davis Jr. received a call from Michael's assistant two months ago about collaborating for a new music production. Frank met Michael a few times the last weeks. "He seemed totally healthy, not frail, and gave me a firm handshake when we met. He seemed in good health, had a good voice and was in good spirits," he said. "He was very skinny, but from what I knew, he was always thin. He was also taller than I pictured, but he might have been wearing some platform shoes. And he was impeccably dressed." Michael invited Frank to his home in Los Angeles' Holmby Hills. He told the composer he was working on an instrumental album of classical music and asked for help with orchestration. David Michael was surprised and impressed by Michael's knowledge of classical music. "He had two demos of two pieces he'd written, but they weren't complete," he said. "For one of them, he had a whole section of it done in his head. He had not recorded it. He hummed it to me as I sat at the keyboard in his pool house and we figured out the chords, I guess this recording I made is the only copy that exists of this music."

Weeks later, Michael called to see how the work was progressing on the orchestrations. David Michael: "He mentioned more instrumental music of his he wanted to record, including one jazz piece. I hope one day his family will decide to record this music as a tribute and show the world the depth of his artistry."

Despite his frail appearance, everyone who worked with Michael said his voice was in fine form. A keyboardist who worked together with Michael as a musical director of the *Bad* tour, Greg Phillinganes, said Michael sounded as good as he ever did. "He still had a good voice and never had a problem singing. There were questions about him being able to pull off the tour on the choreography side, but sources working with him told me he was dancing all the time, every day, and was very focused, excited and committed to making this tour the best it could be."

AEG Live, the concert promoter for Michael Jackson's aborted concert tour, acknowledged that they had "in excess of 100" hours of footage of the performers rehearsals and life behind the scenes. "Including from the final rehearsal on Wednesday night, the evening before Michael died," the promoter said. He also said the company was still considering what to do with this vast store of valuable footage, but acknowledged that a movie was one thing under consideration.

According to several people close to the defunct concert tour, Michael's last rehearsal at the Staples Center on Wednesday, the evening of his death, could be released as the performer's last album singing his greatest hits. This rehearsal was also recorded in multi-camera, high-definition video and multi-track audio. The recordings were made as part of concert promotion company AEG Live's deal with Michael. The deal included a plan to produce both an album and DVD of what

Jackson had called his "final performance" tour, titled *This Is It*. One AEG official boasted to a colleague that they had, "a live album in the can." Press reports have said that AEG Live stands to lose tens of millions of dollars from the unexpected cancellation of Jackson's 50-date London tour. The audio and video release of Michael's last performances would undoubtedly sell millions of units worldwide.

Jermaine Jackson said on NBC's Today show that he and Michael's three children saw Michael's dead body. Jermaine previously had said about his brother Michael: "I don't know how people are going to take this, but I wish it was me." Jermaine Jackson added: "I would like to see Neverland Ranch as my brother's final resting place. He went too soon. I wanted to be there for him. I was there and he was sort of like molded. Things he couldn't say, I would say them. During the trials, during everything," he said. Jermaine told that when he rushed to UCLA Medical Center, "I wanted to see Michael, and I wanted to see my brother, and see him there lifeless and breathless was very emotional for me, but I held myself together, because I know he's very much alive."

Record producer Quincy Jones had revealed he didn't not believe Michael was suffering from Vitiligo, a condition which changed the color of his skin. He believes Michael wanted to alter his appearance. Quincy told Details magazine: "I don't believe in any of that bulls**t, no. No. Never. I've been around junkies and stuff all my life. I've heard every excuse. It's like smokers, 'I only smoke when I drink' and all that stuff. But it's bulls**t. You're justifying something that's destructive to your existence. But when somebody's hell-bent on it, you can't stop 'em. What his face turned into is ridiculous. Chemical peels and all of it. And I don't understand it. But he obviously didn't want to be black. You see his kids?" Quincy also told: "He'd come up with, 'Man, I promise you I have this disease,' and so forth, and 'I have a blister on my lungs,' and all that kind of bulls**t. It's hard, because Michael's a Virgo, man, he's very set in his ways. You can't talk him out of it. I'm just a musician and a record producer. I'm not a psychiatrist. I don't understand all that stuff. We all got problems." According to Details magazine Quincy used to worry Michael was out of touch with reality, and "wanted him to sing songs about love and human emotion to try to help him." Quincy said about the song *Ben*: "I just wanted to hear him deal with a romantic relationship with a human being rather than a rat. I'm saying that facetiously, but it's true. I saw him at the Oscars very emotional about *Ben* and I wanted to hear him get in touch with a real human relationship. *She's Out of My Life* from *Off the Wall* was written by Tommy Bahler from a very bad ending to a marriage. So it was very real. I was saving it for Sinatra. But I gave it to Michael. And Michael cried during every take, and I left the tears in."

The idea to name his last tour, "This Is It" came from Michael. On July 21, 2002, he received a package from Miami, send by one of his doctors. The doctor wrote: "Dear MJ. Hi and how are you, I am not sure if you received my package earlier, so I am sending it again (!). **It's a 5–7 day program that offers you the solution**. Buprinex is the potent narcotic I told you about last week. It is just like the D but better. I have everything ready, **This is it**. Do it before your second chapter, You are the best you are **an ICON** and you belong to the TOPS. '**U aint seen Nothin yet**'. Let's do it as soon as possible, read the attached and call me."

The letter was send from the 'Center For Regenerative Medicine' in Miami, Florida. Michael send a thank note to the responsible doctor, doctor

Dr. Alimorad Farshchian. The little note was published on the doctor's website, but was removed after Michael's death. It said: "Dear Dr. Farshchian. April. 2001. Thank you, You are god sent. Michael Jackson." The letter to Michael included information on how to use the medications: "As with any medical procedure, there are some risks and potential problems. If patients do not follow through with instructions, do not attend clitic, or take more medicine then intended, then there could potentially be problems with overdose and accidents." It also said: "I believe strongly that patients should be on Naltrexone therapy for at least twelve months. **This prevents them from relapsing back to narcotic use** and gives the patients a chance to start making changes in their lives and building up a support program. I highly recommend oral Naltrexone for the balance of 12 months. Studies show that there have been patients who have died following periods of abstinence from narcotics. This appears to be caused by lack of tolerance following a period of abstinence. Naltrexone is extremely good at making people abstinent but when the Naltrexone wears off, patients have a very low tolerance. It is extremely easy for them to use too much Demerol and have an overdose which can be fatal. Patients need to understand this clearly and be extremely careful if they do relapse back to narcotic use."

Dr. Alimorad Farshchian M.D. limited his practice in 2001 to Non-surgical Orthopedics and Sports Medicine. In 2003, Dr. Alimorad Farshchian, who is happily married with 2 children, was honored to be chosen as doctor of the year for 2003 by United States Republican Congressional Committee's Physician Advisory Board. Dr. Alimorad Farshchian believes that Naltrexone therapy should be given for 12 months because this gives the patient a change to have their brain physically recover from the damage from the narcotics. It also gives the patient an excellent change to begin on the road to recovery. Michael wrote on a piece of paper that was found in 2003: "Buprenex, synthetic Demeroll. Buprenex does the same as Demerol, the only difference is you can not become an addict on Buprenex."

According to the family lawyer, Brian Oxman, Michael was taking 40 prescription pills a day during his 2005 abuse trial. He insists the King of Pop was taking huge amounts of strong painkiller Vicodin as Michael fought allegations of child abuse. Brian told newspaper The Sun the lengthy court battle took its toll on Michael, who reportedly became addicted to the painkiller. Brian said: "During Michael's court trial he was taking 40 Vicodin a day, and this may have even increased. It's an insane amount of drugs to be given, and to be taken." In the months before his untimely death Brian told Michael he was concerned about his dependency on pills, including prescription painkillers and anti-anxiety drugs. "I did warn him about the drugs, but I am sorry I didn't warn him enough. I am going to wait until I get the toxicology report, and if his death has something to do with drugs, I am prepared to name names of doctors who prescribed them," he told The Sun.

Different doctors described drugs like Alprazolam to Michael. It is reported that Dr. Arnold Klein and Dr. William Vanvalin both described Alprazolam in 1 mg and 2 mg to Michael in 2002, both under the name of Frank Tyson. This medicine is a Benzodiazepine used to treat anxiety, nervousness and panic disorder. It may also be used to treat other conditions as determined by your doctor. Possible side effects of Alprazolam that may go away during treatment include excessive daytime drowsiness, unusual weakness, dizziness, lightheadedness, headache, clumsiness or unsteadiness. Xanax, prescribed to Michael in the summer of 2002 under the name of Manuel Rivera, has possible side effects such as drowsiness, incoordination, headache, fatique, change in sex drive, change in appetite, change in weight, difficulty urinating or stomach upset may occur the first few days as your body adjusts to the medication. Other side effects are pounding/irregular heartbeat, skin rash, changes in vision, slurred speech or behavioral changes.

Attorney Thomas Arthur Mesereau, Jr. talked after Michael's death to some reporters about his trial with Michael and about Michael's death. The taped interview, recorded on the street of Los Angeles was shown on TMZ's website: "Drugs were not the issue in the criminal case," Thomas said. "We were very lucky, fortunate, God was with us, the jury was with us. That's all I was there for." The attorney didn't know much about the evidence in Michael's last case. He told reporters: "You've got to investigate, you've got to find real evidence. If they [the doctors] oversubscribed medication, if they tried to unable him, if they tried to manipulate him, they should be prosecuted. When I represented Michael, I sat with him 5 days a week, for 5 months on the trial. He was always lucid, very consciousness, just very articulate. I never had any sense that he was over-medicated, never." When asked about Michael's pajamas, he said: "The fact of the matter is, he hurt his back that morning and went to the hospital. I told the judge what was going on. He wanted him there in 45 minutes, or he was going to put him in jail, and then bail. I said to Michael: 'You come to court right now, whatever you are wearing, OK.' That was MY idea, that is my fault. He wanted to go home and change, but I wanted him there right away, cause I didn't want him in jail. So I am responsible for that." When asked by a reporter why so many doctors were part of his life at that time, Thomas said: "I really don't know, I was there to defend him in a criminal case. I made very clear, when I came into the case, that I was there for one purpose. To protect him an win his freedom. I really wasn't involved in his business affairs, I wasn't involved in his music business." Thomas told Inside Edition he believed the two-year investigation and trial on child molestation charges may have contributed to Michael's death. "I think the poor soul may have just not fully recovered from leaving Neverland," he said on the syndicated show. "He lost weight, his cheeks became sunken in. His eyes became heavy. He was terrified. I always saw him as lucid, articulate and coherent. Never did I think he was under medication or a dangerous drug."

Miami born director and producer Brett Ratner, best known for his films such as *The Family Man*, *After the Sunset*, *Red Dragon*, the *Rush Hour* series, and *X-Men: The Last Stand*, was a few years ago best friends with Michael. His statement was published at MTV.com saying: "Michael was not only a great friend, but a true inspiration in my life. I will never forget his kindness to me, and his beautiful heart. He was the best father and truly loved his children. I will miss him." Brett said in a statement before his death: "I know that people looked at Michael and thought he was strange, but to me, he was fascinating. He was the most inspirational person in my life. His one dream was to cure all the sick children in the world. And when I'd say, 'Isn't that impossible?' Michael would just start to cry. He was very emotional about things that moved him. I guess you'd have to say he was a pure innocent in a world that wasn't so innocent anymore."

The Daily Express however, believed that Michael was not so innocent anymore. Cops searched Michael's home and found a bottle of the heroin substitute methadone, according to a new report. On July 3, The Daily Express expressed in an article: "The *Thriller* hitmaker's rented property in Holmby Hills, California was awash with prescription drugs, including six other types of super-strength painkillers, a batch of sedatives, and potent sleeping pills. A total of 20 different kinds of prescription medication were recovered from the property after Jackson died last Thursday (25 June 2009), but the revelation that methadone was among them will stun fans. The green liquid is used to help wean junkies off heroin by mimicking the effects of the drug and easing withdrawal symptoms. And in a shocking new development, police in Los Angeles are reportedly considering launching a manslaughter investigation amid fears aides obtained medication for Jackson without any regard for his safety."

Sources told tabloid The Sun: "The Jackson mansion was more like a drugstore than someone's home. Powerful narcotic painkillers of all kinds were found. There was no reasonable excuse for them all being there. Police want to know whether the other people named on the medicine labels really needed the drugs prescribed to them and will be speaking to the doctors involved. Officers are looking very seriously at the people surrounding Michael Jackson and whether they behaved responsibly."

It was told that despite his enormous addiction to painkillers, Michael wanted to have more children. He even tried to buy Octomum's babies over the telephone. Michael loved his own children so much that the singer insisted on taking his three children with him while he trotted the globe, photographer Ian Barkley said. "Michael ensured every hotel he stayed at was made super-safe so that the chances of his kids falling ill or injuring themselves were lessened as much as possible," he told reporters. The Daily Express quoted Ian Barkley as having told Eonline.com: "His kids totally love their dad and he was extremely protective over them. Even when we were just around his staff, he was protective. We would baby-proof everywhere, like really expensive suites. They would tape up every corner with cardboard and make sure the kids couldn't hurt themselves, and they were very strict on what the kids would eat to make sure they didn't have allergies. To some it was odd, but under the circumstances it was understandable." The photographer who followed Michael from 2002 until 2005 also revealed to Sunday Mirror that Michael had a secret girlfriend who his children called "mom". Ian said: "Grace loved Michael and he loved her, it was an open secret among staff." The loyal nanny, who lately revealed Michael hid cash in black bags under carpets at his Los Angeles mansion, and who also had a short-lived romance with Michael's older brother Jermaine in the early Nineties, became a dominant figure in the family's lives. A source was saying: "Everything was done Grace's way." Ian told The Daily Express he believes the children should live with his nanny rather than Michael's mother, who has temporary custody. Ian said: "Though I love Michael's mum Katherine, she is 79 and if she passes on, the best place for the kids to go would be to Grace. She really raised them. She was with them day in and day out. She really loved them and they adored her as they would a mother." About the relationship between Michael and Grace, Ian said: "The romance was well-known among staff but it was made very clear to them that this was not something that should become part of the public domain. But the difference between Grace and other women in Michael's life was that she had absolutely no interest in fame. It was something she actively avoided and Michael was determined to keep her and their relationship out of the public gaze."

Michael's former head of security in United Kingdom, Matt Fiddes revealed Michael had a secret lover, a woman. He refused to tell her name. Matt, 30 years old, who knew Michael since the 1990s, said: "The family were aware that there was someone special in his life who he loved and adored and had his ups and downs with." According to Sunday Mirror the nanny was said, "to have wielded so much power in the Jackson household that she controlled all access to the singer, even deciding which family members could speak to him." The Sunday Mirror also stated: "Grace was introduced to Jacko by his former spokesman Dr. Tohme R. Tohme in 1991. She started out as a secretary before working her way up to become the most important woman in the superstar's life. In 1999 she was picked to care for Jackson's oldest kids following his divorce from second wife Debbie Rowe." It was rumored Michael and Grace had secretly married. This was denied by Grace. She is still legally married to first husband Stacey Adair.

The Sun revealed that Matt, who is dad-of-five, told them that Michael would spend hours holed up in hotel rooms watching his DVD collection of The Simpsons, in which he famously provided the voice for a character in one episode. According to the Sun, the singer would also listen over and over again to Britney Spears. Meanwhile he would barely eat. Matt spoke with The Sun about Michael's 2003 trip to London and said: "We had a suite at a top hotel. His doctor was there and in the evening he would make me double lock my hotel room door, which was right next to where Michael was. He would come in and clearly make sure I was out of the way while he was in the room with Michael. Then I would go and check on him again. He would be drowsy and out of it. He would manage to walk to his bedroom and fall asleep on the bed, but then he would not wake up until two or three in the afternoon."

Recalling the London Zoo trip, Matt said almost with with tears in his eyes: "Michael had been sedated the night before and just wouldn't wake up. Uri went into his room, and was screaming at Michael. We were worried. We were shaking him, saying: 'Come on, wake up.' Uri was saying: 'What are you doing? Have you taken something?' Then he came round drowsy, and said he was jetlagged. He came round, but not enough to take him to the zoo. Uri had to make up an excuse for him." Matt also said packages full of prescription drugs arrived at Michael's hotel from the United States marked for "Mr Sterling". Matt revealed that other aliases included "Jack London" and "Omar Arnold". Matt and friend Uri Geller routinely swept Michael's room of syringes and needles. They tried to protect Michael from his own medics.

According to The Sun, disgusted Matt said that the cocktail of drugs left Michael so weak he regularly slept for days at a time and missed important business meetings. Matt said: "The doctors would change every few months, but there was always one there who would often claim just to be a friend. It went two ways with what they did with Michael. Either he'd be totally sedated or they'd give him something which would make him incredibly high. When that happened he would chant or be very overexcitable. He had clearly been given some kind of amphetamine-based prescription medication. That concerned the heck out of me. If you give someone a sedative and then they take an upper, your heart doesn't know where to go. But none of his aides questioned it. If you did that you were thrown out from the court of 'yes' men surrounding him. He was totally and utterly isolated and he lived on scraps.

"He'd only eat a quarter of a normal meal. He had a small frame but getting him to eat was a big deal, one meal a day and you were lucky. Me and his friends used to literally sit him down and say, 'You eat that'." Michael had called Matt to say: "I will not end up like Elvis. I'm going to work hard for a few years, retire, live good and spend the time with my children. I don't want to perform into old age." Matt who worked for free for Michael said: "I've been close to Michael's brother Jermaine for years. We tried everything to get Michael away from these leeches and we just couldn't do it." Uri Geller agreed: "I didn't live with Michael, but like Matt, the things I did witness were simply horrifying, and destroyed my hope for his future. I feel this could have been avoided. I tried to do my best and we were very close friends, but I was unable to save him, I did not live with him or travel with him recently so I would try to talk to Michael whenever I could and ask him to get help, to help himself and heal himself before something bad happened."

Some people described Michael as 'an anesthesia addict.' Even when it was not medically necessary, Michael would be sedated. He would be put under for acne treatment, Botox, collagen injections and cosmetic surgery. Michael told his doctors he was afraid of hypodermic needles. During and after his minor outpatient procedures, Michael would get controlled substances, such as Demerol.

For Michael's memorial event, a online lottery had been launched in which the singer's fans could win tickets to his memorial, which was to be held in Los Angeles' Staples Center, the place where Michael has been rehearsing for his upcoming London comeback shows. The memorial was scheduled for Tuesday, July 7. Tim Leiweke from the Staples Center said: "It is the family's wish to create a service and celebration that all of Michael's fans around the world can be part of." People could enter the draw at Staplescenter.com, which saw 17,500 tickets be randomly given out. 11,000 fans received seats inside the arena, with another 6,500 allowed to watch on screens in the nearby Nokia Theatre. The service was also broadcast worldwide on TV and the internet. It has been claimed as many as 700,000 people would flock to the arena on that day.

In London Madonna took time out of her show to honor the late singer. Her emotional tribute to Michael Jackson during her concert at London's O2, just days before the King of Pop was due to appear at the same venue, started with a huge picture of Michael as a child being beamed above the stage. The Material Girl performed a 90 second dedication to Michael halfway through her gig. Madonna stepped back to be with her backing dancers while a Michael impersonator, wearing a sequined jacket, black hat and trademark white glove, moonwalked across the stage to a short melody of Michael's greatest hits, including *Billie Jean* and *Wanna Be Startin' Somethin'*. Madonna told the crowd: "To one of the greatest performers the world has ever known, Michael Jackson." Many people said the short performance was the highlight of the show.

Hulk star Lou Ferrigno told reporters that Michael was most probably killed by the weight of his massive debts. Lou said the only reason Michael was going back on stage was to clear his debts. He said: "He was under tremendous stress, so much I think it killed him. He was $400 million in debt. In the past, he had backed out of doing live shows but this time he was under the gun. The debts put a huge strain on him." Michael met Lou through a mutual pal in 1995. Lou recalled: "Our friend had a bunch of guests over. Michael was there and I was introduced to him. The friend had a gym and I walked over to it and Michael kept staring at me. He was acting really shy. Eventually we got talking. Michael needed to get ready for his *HIStory World Tour*, so I told him to train with me. He came to my house in Santa Monica and that's how I became a close friend. He was great, a nice guy, really sweet. He was self-conscious about people staring at him, people touching him, wanting a piece of him. But he let his guard down when he was with me. There was no show."

The Mirror quoted Lou saying: "He had undergone a five-hour medical in February and had passed with flying colors, but he wanted to be fitter. So I would go to his house with an inflatable exercise ball and 3lb dumbbells. He did not like the dumbbells. He said he didn't want big shoulders and big muscles like me. I laughed and said, 'Michael, there's no way you will get big shoulders from 3lb dumbbells.' He ate only one meal a day, always in the evening. He'd wake up and not have anything for the whole day, and when he did eat it was always vegetarian. He wore whatever he put on first thing. So if he put pajamas on he would wear pajamas for the rest of the day. But it was always with a suit jacket, that was the Michael Jackson signature. Sometimes when we worked out he would take his jacket off and he looked lean and motivated. I was with him until the end of May and he was fine. There was no sign of drug use and his flexibility was improving. That was important as he was a little tight in certain areas. He hadn't danced for so long."

Michael always liked to work out while listening to music. The legendary dancer even taught the Incredible Hulk the Moonwalk. Lou said: "We talked, had conversations about life and different things. There was no security, no bodyguards, nobody around. He didn't want anyone around when he worked out. We took regular breaks and he would show me his dance moves. They were awesome. He was doing part of his routine. He was still in great shape dance-wise. He was still as good as 15 years ago. Michael taught me the Moonwalk. I'm sworn to secrecy though, I can't give the secrets away." Michael seemed in good spirits, despite his financial problems," according to Lou. "He was very happy. He used to be lonely when I first saw him but he was very happy because he had his children. I made him laugh a lot and he was a real prankster. He was always playing jokes on me. He used to call me and pretend he was someone called Omar. He would pretend to be my stalker. He would talk on the phone in a disguised voice, real deep, saying things like, 'I know where you live' or, 'I know what you're doing'. I said, 'Michael, I think this is you' but he kept denying it. One time he came to an action-hero convention I was doing and he was dressed as some kind of monster. He had a full monster-style face mask on and nobody knew it was Michael. He came up to the table and was making weird noises. I just figured it was some guy who was into Star Trek, but afterwards I found out it was Michael Jackson. He wanted to disguise himself so that he could walk around and not be recognized. He was a child that never grew up," Lou said. According to the Mirror, Lou claimed that he and Michael had similar, angry childhoods. He said: "We had similar fathers. When we were growing up, we had a lot of pain and anger. He did not have a chance to make friends and became very self-conscious. He eventually overcame that. His escape was music, mine was to become a body-building champion. That's why we were so good together, he got to be a kid again. That's also why he created Neverland. It was not just for children to visit, he wanted his own Disneyland. He wanted to have fun, but wanted to do it away from the cameras."

Lou saw Michael three weeks before Michael died, when he was doing some shows on the East Coast. He said. "We were meant to get together a few more times before he went to England but then I heard on the news that he had passed on. I felt terrible, I was shocked. I thought it was a joke. It felt like a tremendous loss. It almost felt to me like 9/11. It shook the whole world, Michael Jackson just dropping dead." Lou believes the memorial is going to be huge at the Staples Center when the world remembers Michael. "The memorial is going to be huge. Maybe bigger than Princess Di's," he said.

TMZ reported, *Jackson Docs Can Run, But Can't Hide*. In the article we read how law enforcement officials combed through medical records to determine who supplied and administered the anesthesia Propofol and other drugs, to Michael Jackson. TMZ staff said: "It's no secret -- especially in a celebrity town like L.A. -- some doctor's use pseudonyms for celebrity patients and sometimes their medical charts somehow get 'lost'. But we've learned most doctors leave an indelible footprint when it comes to treating patients. Many doctors -- especially ones with big practices -- use medical software systems from MD Systems, NexTech and other companies. These companies provide the software that makes it easy to input billing data. Doctors typically input the patient's name, billing amount, type of treatment, type of drugs prescribed and administered, and date of service. Here's the thing -- that data cannot be deleted from the server. The system allows doctors to add other data like medical charts, and those things can be deleted. But if someone deletes that info, the software shows the name of the user who did it and the date it was done. Bottom line -- the basic billing information will not go away."

Dr. Allan Metzger, a doctor who has treated Michael Jackson for many years was reprimanded by the Medical Board of California for writing fraudulent prescriptions for Michael's sister, Janet. Dr. Allan Metzger received a public letter of reprimand in September, 2000. The letter stated, "You engaged in fraudulent medical practice based on prescriptions written for an international entertainer, using a false/fictitious name." Dr. Metzger said the entertainer was Janet Jackson. Dr. Metzger traveled with Michael during his *HIStory Tour* in 1996, and even videotaped Michael's wedding to Debbie Rowe. Dr. Metzger wrote prescriptions for Janet using the name of her private chef, Ricardo Macchi. The prescriptions were for diuretics. Janet was going on tour and wanted to guard against the disease hepatitis B, so Dr. Metzger wrote a prescription for a hepatitis B injection. The name on the prescription was Ricardo Macchi, again the name of her private chef. Dr. Metzger once told TMZ: "I had done this for Janet for her anonymity." Ricardo Macchi sued Dr. Metzger, but the suit was dropped and no money was paid out. Dr. Metzger admitted, "I have not treated Michael Jackson for many years." He talked on the phone over the years, giving him medical advice but he couldn't tell he prescribed medications: "I am not at liberty to discuss Michael's medical care." The doctor also admitted he talked with Michael two months before he died. They talked about the tour, nutrition, hydration and his children. He added: "I have nothing to do with this tragedy with Michael. I have not prescribed any medication in relation to what happened to him."

Standing in front of the American Legion in Wantagh, congressman Pete King told people we should be honoring the men and women of the Armed Forces, and not a 'pedophile' and 'child molester' like Michael Jackson. Even he was given airtime on television. In a bombshell report, Biographer Stacy Brown, who claims to be Michael's closest confidant for 26 years, said Michael Jackson was hooked on heroin for at least 13 years. "He was shooting heroin into his fingertips, toenails and chest. He was taking painkillers too but I don't think he knew just how dangerous it was," Stacy wrote.

As many as a million people were expected to come to downtown Los Angeles for the Michael Jackson memorial on Tuesday. Someone who worked for British Airways said: "There has been a 'huge influx' of reservations in the last few days by people from England trying to make their way to the memorial. We expect to sell out all the flights by the end of the day." The LAPD was trying to talk people who didn't have tickets out of coming. Assistant Chief Jim McDonnell told the public: "People who aren't lucky enough to win the drawing for tickets to the memorial should just stay home and watch it on TV." He also said: "The LAPD is working with the Jackson family on a 'private family function' at the Forest Lawn cemetery.

Tickets to the memorial were up for grabs over the weekend via an online lottery system. The demand for tickets was so great that the website crashed when half a million people tried to access it in the first 24 hours. The televised concert which was going to be held on July 7, was expected to attract a global audience of millions of people. The family had initially planned a funeral procession from the morgue to Michael's 2800-acre Neverland Ranch, where a viewing of the body would be open to the public.

According to his close friend Christian Audigier, Michael was an emotional individual. He told Michael never grew up. Christian Audigier, fashion designer, told Now in an exclusive interview: "He was like a big kid, you know. And he was a great father, he was all about his kids. The last time I saw him, we spent time with his kids for about an hour and, afterwards, we had dinner. He was always dancing and chatting and laughing. The designer told Now: "I was on my way to Paris and I was just about to board the plane and I heard on CNN that he had had a heart attack. And when I arrived in France, I found out that Michael had passed away. I was just too shocked and sad." His good friend Michael stayed in his house in Los Angeles where he died but Christian wasn't able to go his funeral. He told Now Magazine in the United Kingdom about his concern regarding Michael's children: "I hope they're going to be be OK. I think they are going to live with his mum Katherine for now. I want to try to stay in touch with them as I always saw them quite frequently whenever I would visit Michael." Christian spoke to Now's reporter Alexandra Wenman at his fine wine and champagne launch party at London club Movida on 1 July, only a few days after the tragic news of Michael's death. When Christian saw footage of him walking beside the late singer at one of his fashion shows on a large screen behind him, he told Alexandra: "Oh my God, it's very hard to see that. This was an amazing time in my life. I met Michael 4 years ago at a party and I liked him immediately. We became very close friends. I will miss him greatly."

VH1 published a MTV News Report, written by Gil Kaufman. The article said: "The public memorial service for Michael Jackson at Los Angeles' Staples Center on Tuesday will feature some of the late singer's closest collaborators, friends and fans paying tribute to the King of Pop. Among the stars expected to appear (and possibly perform) at the public event — which will take place after a private memorial earlier in the morning — are Jennifer Hudson, Mariah Carey, Stevie Wonder, Usher, John Mayer, Lionel Richie and Motown founder Berry Gordy, according to a statement from a spokesperson for the Jackson family." Gil wrote: "The list does not specify which of the attendees will perform, but Carey is reportedly slated to reprise her famous cover of the Jackson song *I'll Be There* at the public ceremony and CNN has reported that Oscar-winning actress/singer Hudson will also sing at the event. Wonder was a contemporary of Jackson's on the Motown label in the late 1960s and early 1970s, Usher has often stated how influential Jackson was on his career, and Mayer performed the iconic guitar solo in *Beat It* on *Fall Out Boy's 2008* cover of the song."

Other confirmed participants in the tribute to Michael are Motown legend Smokey Robinson, Jackson family friend the Reverend Al Sharpton, Brooke Shields, the Andrae Crouch Choir, Lakers icon Magic Johnson, Los Angeles Lakers star Kobe Bryant, Martin Luther King III, and Shaheen Jafargholi who toured as a young Michael Jackson in the *Thriller Live* show and sang *Who's Loving You*, from the Jackson 5, on the show *Britain's Got Talent*. A statement, given by a Jackson spokesman, said the lineup was preliminary and subject to change, but noted that no further information would be released regarding the program before the event on Tuesday.

Todd Leopold of CNN wrote: "Jackson spectacle likely a world event. Will Michael Jackson stop the world?" Todd's article on CNN started with the words that, "thousands are expected to swamp Los Angeles, California, to mourn him Tuesday at the Staples Center, and the accompanying media crush will be enormous. The tribute to the King of Pop at Harlem's Apollo Theater earlier this week drew coverage from all over the world, along with a public turnout in the thousands. Given the feverish interest in all things Jackson, the Los Angeles memorial could be one of the most-viewed events of all time." Todd quoted Toni Fitzgerald, of Media Life, who said in an e-mail interview, "This will obviously be a huge media event, and with Web streams of the funeral, it may be impossible to say for sure how many people watched once all is said and done, because there's still no comprehensive way to measure Web viewing." She also observed: "Jackson's death came up in just about every conversation I had from Thursday to Sunday, and yet only 5 million people tuned in to some of those broadcast specials. I expect you'll see very big tune-ins on the cable news networks and on BET, if they cover it; they had huge numbers for their BET Awards focused on Jackson over the weekend. With the celebrity factor thrown into the funeral, who'll be there, who'll talk, I would guess tens of millions in the U.S. will watch it on TV." Todd revealed in his article: "A handful of events have earned the kind of worldwide coverage to put the world on pause, if only for a moment. The numbers are easily exaggerated, nobody knows how many people are watching in groups or in public places, and the Web has complicated matters further. But in a multichannel, satellite TV, computer-and-cell phone world, the Jackson memorial could have an audience in the hundreds of millions." TV critic Ed

Bark of UncleBarky.com recalled in the article: "The 1963 assassination of John F. Kennedy had the nation locked in a trance for two or three days." According to CNN, "The world audience for the Apollo 11 moon landing has been estimated in the hundreds of millions." The BBC estimated 2.5 billion people watched the funeral of Princess Diana in 1997. Ken Tucker from Time Warner's Entertainment Weekly, said: "You have to go back to the Beatles, the death of John Lennon perhaps, and the death of Elvis Presley to find a comparable figure in, not just pop music, but pop culture. And Jackson so self-consciously turned himself into not just an American pop icon but a global pop icon. I think this does have worldwide implications and interest."

According to CNN, "the circumstances of Michael's death have led to comparisons with Presley's in 1977, but in terms of coverage, the two can't compare. The news wasn't even the top story on CBS' Evening News, Bark recalled, and there certainly wasn't wall-to-wall nationwide live coverage of his funeral. A public viewing drew about 30,000 fans; the funeral, two days after his death, was held in Graceland's living room." Ed Bark said there are parallels, at least in terms of coverage, with the Kennedy assassination. He told CNN: "These days it's so much harder to get a bulk audience on any given venue the way the [broadcast networks] did back then, but still the enormity [of the event], it's the syndicated tabloid shows, and TMZ and all the cable networks devoting lots of attention to it, [and] the broadcast networks can't seem to do enough specials in prime time. I do think it's comparative but in a very different way." CNN's article also said: "The sorts of events that have attracted the largest mass audiences have been scheduled entertainment or sports programs. Sixty percent of

America watched the 1983 M*A*S*H finale; more than half watched the 1980 Who Shot J.R. episode of Dallas and the 1977 Roots conclusion. The Beatles' first appearance on The Ed Sullivan Show in 1964 drew about 45 percent of the country. The Super Bowl is routinely the year's most watched program, with audiences north of 80 million, about 40 percent of United States television households."

According to other news sources, "The King of Pop Michael Jackson, whose funeral is slated for Tuesday morning, will be buried without his brain. The singer's brain has been taken out for neurological tests." A source from the coroner's office told, according to The Sunday Mirror, that removing the brain was, "the only way to carry out the tests." He said: "The tissue has to be examined. I can't tell you how long that is going to take." The test results could play a crucial role in criminal investigations into the star's death. The tests can only be done until the brain has sufficiently hardened. Results are expected to show up any past drug or alcohol abuse, or overdoses the star may have suffered. State attorney general Jerry Brown has ordered an investigation after six of Michael's doctors now face being quizzed by the Drug Enforcement Agency. A spokesman for Brown said: "If there has been abuses, charges will follow." According to Daily Mail, "Jackson's family doesn't want to postpone the funeral. They have decided to bury him without his brain."

Chapter 6
The Memorial

Tuesday, July 7, at 8 o'clock in the morning, singer Usher stood at the glass doors outside Staples Center in Los Angeles and told the thousands of fans: "We are aware of your sorrow! We are aware of your pain! And we are aware of your joy!" People came early that morning and gathered for Michael Jackson's Memorial Service in Los Angeles. They were instructed how to line up. Fans could leave their flowers and "gifts" on a table outside the arena. Usher said: "It is our pleasure, it is our privilege to welcome you." Before a galaxy of stars, Michael's loved ones, thousands of fans and other friends paid tribute to the pop legend. Inside, the stage that had been build in the arena had double podiums and double drum sets. Photos of a young Michael were shown on a screen and Michael's hit *Rock With You* was playing softly on a speaker. Jesse Jackson was the first celeb to hit the row of press stand-ups.

An hour later, Smokey Robinson talked to Spike Lee in front of the stage. A few minutes later the entire Kardashian family arrived, followed by Larry King and his wife, both in all black. The couple was escorted inside Staples Center. Jesse Jackson arrived in an Escalade with a group of people, and Louis Farrakhan arrived with an entourage of 15. Elizabeth Berkley was present as were Diddy, director Tyler Perry, director Brett Ratner, and others who were once friends of Michael. The majority of The King of Pop's so-called "friends" who spoke at his public memorial barely knew him. According to US magazine, "friends" such as Brooke Shields and Corey Feldman haven't seen or spoken to Michael in years. Brooke Shields was a teenager when she met Michael in the 80s. The last time Brooke saw Michael was at Elizabeth Taylor's wedding 18 years ago. Corey, who arrived late, dressed-up as Michael Jackson, wiped some tears from under his dark sunglasses and said he felt drained by Michael's death. The last time he spoke to Michael was a few years ago after they had a falling out. But also Michael's lifelong friends such as Diana Ross, who met Michael when he was still a kid, was a no-show. Also deeply missed was the legendary actress Elizabeth Taylor, who wished to avoid the Hollywood "whoopla". And Quincy Jones told Entertainment Tonight he wouldn't be attending the late King of Pop's funeral. "I won't go to any more funerals as long as I live. I can't handle it," he said.

The two-hour long tribute was a deeply emotional and public outpouring of grief, but also a musical celebration. Two hours before the ceremony began, it was said that Michael's body would be transported to the arena, either by hearse or chopper from L.A.'s Forest Lawn Cemetery, where a private ceremony for Michael's family was held earlier in the morning. 17,500 tickets (11,000 for Staples Center and 6,500 at the Nokia Theatre) were distributed freely to fans by lottery. Online prices were reportedly as high as $2,000. Some fans waited by the main entrance of the Staples Center and others stood at the rear driveway to await the arrival of Michael's hearse. When the wagon arrived, at 9:45 a.m., the golden casket covered in red roses was clearly visible through a window. Diff'rent Strokes star Todd Bridges told US: "I knew him, that's why it's special to be here. He was the greatest superstar, and I knew him every since I was a little kid, for many, many years, you know? I'm here to honor him." Seated with her mother and father, Nicky Hilton told US: "Michael was a good family friend. This is a part of history." Outside the Staples Center people were writing messages on big white walls, to express their feelings. Not much later an announcer said: "Ladies and gentlemen, please take your seats. The service will begin very, very shortly." Inside the arena, fans and mourners were handed a free 14-page color program with photographs of Michael from all phases of his career and personalized testimonials from Michael's friends, brothers and sisters. La Toya's comment reads, "You've done your work here, Michael. You've entertained us for decades and there's nothing else that you can prove or accomplish here on earth. Mike. I love you deeply (sic) and I can't wait to see you perform again. Keep the magic going!!!" Tito Jackson's comment reads, "My brother developed a shoe that showed resistance to gravity. What a man!" Barbara Walters was present, and so were Rev. Al Sharpton, Magic Johnson, Mike Tyson, John Mayer, Dionne Warwick and Kobe Bryant.

After a brief delay, the legendary Smokey Robinson kicked off the Michael Jackson memorial by reading statements from Diana Ross and Nelson Mandela. In the beginning moments of the memorial service, the first of many fans shouted, "We love you, Michael!"

Then, it was mostly silence and Smokey read his first messages of condolences by one of Michael's greatest friends, Diana Ross. The Motown diva, named by Michael in his will as an alternative guardian to his children, said she had chosen to mourn privately: "I want you to know that even though I'm not there at the Staples Center, I'm there in my heart. I decided to pause and be silent. This feels right for me. Michael was a personal love of mine, a treasured part of my world, part of the fabric of my life in a way that I can't seem to find words to express. Michael wanted me to be there for his children, and I will be there if they ever need me. I hope today brings closure for all those who loved him. Thank you, Katherine and Joe, for sharing your son with the world, and with me. I send my love and condolences to the Jackson family." - Diana Ross.

Smokey Robinson read the tribute from former South African president Nelson Mandela: "Michael was a giant and a legend in the music industry. And we mourn with the millions of fans worldwide. We had great admiration for his talent and that he was able to triumph over tragedy on so many occasions in his life. My wife and I, our family, our friends, send you our condolences during this time of mourning. Be strong, Nelson Mandela."

Usher who probably rehearsed for his performance, arrived late wearing a yellow rose. He kissed Brooke Shields shortly on the cheek before he sat down. Jesse Jackson and Al Sharpton exchanged greetings while other guests took their seats. Most of the guests were in traditional funeral wear, but surprisingly, many were wearing all white, including some of Michael's family members.

Following Smokey's tribute, there was a lengthy gap in proceedings, before a Gospel choir took to the stage. The choir singing *We're going to see the King* launched an emotional public memorial event, as thousands of fans bade farewell to the beloved singer. They sang *Soon and Very*

Soon, featuring the refrain *We are going to see the King*. Chris Tucker entered as the choir was singing while others were taking photographs silently.

    Then the singer's red rose-covered casket was wheeled into the front and center of the stage. The golden casket was rolled out by Michael's brothers acting as pallbearers, each of them wearing a single, sequined glove. There was a standing ovation as Michael's family entered the arena and took their seats. The choir sang "Hallelujah! Hallelujah! ...."

    Pastor Lucious W. Smith of the Friendship Baptist Church in Pasadena gave the invocation: "Good morning and welcome, my name is Pastor Lucious Smith and I'm proud to call the Jackson family my friends. To millions around the world Michael Jackson was an idol, a hero, even a king, but first and foremost this man before us today was our brother, our son, our father and our friend. Michael Jackson was and always shall be a beloved part of the Jackson family and the family of man. And so today we gather those who know and love Michael best and those who came to know and love him through his good works. We come together in this space where only days ago Michael sang, and danced and brought his joy as only he could. We come together and we remember the time. We remember this man by celebrating his life and all of the love that he brought to our own lives for half a century. Our hearts are heavy today because this man, this brother, this son, this father and this friend is gone far too soon. But as long as we remember our time with him, the truth is he is never really gone at all. As long as we remember him, he will be there forever to comfort us. In his very beautiful and very human heart Michael Jackson wanted nothing more than to give love to the world. To share of his singular talent and his soul and perhaps beloved back in return through his words, his music and his countless good deeds, Michael did so much to try and heal our world. And so for the Jackson family and for all who grieve his loss everywhere in our world, may this moment of remembrance, a moment of healing, a moment of music and a moment of love bring comfort to those who loved our friend. God Bless you."

Mariah Carey had the difficult task of being the first performer on stage. Mariah wore a black, low-cut gown by Jenny Packham and began her fragile rendition of the Jackson 5 ballad, *I'll Be There*, joined by her *MTV Unplugged* duet partner Trey Lorenz. Images of the Jackson 5 flashed on the big screen behind them. Mariah described only one day after the event how hard it was for her to sing on the memorial. Seeing Michael's casket made it difficult for her to get through the performance. When her voice cracked in the first few moments of her cover of the Jackson 5, she felt like she disappointed everyone. Maria told Today: "I feel a little bit like I let everybody down, but I really did try and it was difficult. But you know what I think? It was a true and honest emotional moment." Mariah also took to her Twitter to share her disappointment over her performance with her fans. Mariah: "Trying to sing today was basically impossible for me. I could barely keep myself from crying." She apologized for the performance. She tweeted: "I'm sorry that I wasn't able to pull it together and really do it right, but I was literally choked up when I saw him there in front of me. One thing I know is, we will never really have to say goodbye to MJ. His legacy lives on through his music and the millions of people he inspired with his timeless music. He will be forever in our hearts."

Rapper-turned actress-turned singer, Queen Latifah, one of the many celebrities that paid tribute to Michael Jackson, delivered a eulogy to Michael and said: "I never actually got to meet him. My [business] partner met him because we managed 'Naughty by Nature' and they did a remix with him. He thought I had beautiful cheekbones." She called Michael 'the biggest star on Earth', and told the crowd how much she loved and admired the King of Pop. "Somehow, when Michael Jackson sang, when he danced, you never felt distance. You felt like you were right there... I loved him all my life... Michael was the biggest star on earth," she said. Veteran poet and writer Maya Angelou paid tribute to Michael in an eulogy read by Queen Latifah. Maya wrote the poem especially for the occasion and was called "We Had Him".

Queen Latifah read: "Beloveds, now we know that we know nothing, now that our bright and shining star can slip away from our fingertips like a puff of summer wind. Without notice, our dear love can escape our doting embrace. Sing our songs among the stars and walk our dances across the face of the moon. In the instant that Michael is gone, we know nothing. No clocks can tell time. No oceans can rush our tides with the abrupt absence of our treasure. Though we are many, each of us is achingly alone, piercingly alone. Only when we confess our confusion can we remember that he was a gift to us and we did have him. He came to us from the creator, trailing creativity in abundance. Despite the anguish, his life was sheathed in mother love, family love, and survived and did more than that. He thrived with passion and compassion, humor and style. We had him whether we know who he was or did not know, he was ours and we were his. We had him, beautiful, delighting our eyes. His hat, aslant over his brow, and took a pose on his toes for all of us. And we laughed and stomped our feet for him. We were enchanted with his passion because he held nothing. He gave us all he had been given. Today in Tokyo, beneath the Eiffel Tower, in Ghana's Black Star Square, in Johannesburg and Pittsburgh, in Birmingham, Alabama, and Birmingham, England. We are missing Michael. But we do know we had him, and we are the world."

Fans were deeply moved and expressed their feelings on blogs on the internet. Some reacted on ibtimes.com. Diana: "What a beautiful sentiment. Maya Angelou's poem paints a thousand pictures. We did have him. Thank you for reminding us of what a gift we were truly given when Michael entered our world. I don't think any other words could have done him such justice. I feel that the world really is a darker place without our shining star. May he finally live as we would never let him. Peacefully. Thank you, Michael. You will be missed." A Michael Jackson fan wrote after the memorial: "Michael Jackson was one of the best artists of our time. He was an inspiration to us all and he will never be forgotten. No matter how bad the media portrayed him, we all know he was just an innocent lost child inside trying to break free from normality because he wanted to be different, original and unique. No one can hurt him now. He gave to the world with his charities and music and asked for nothing in return. He was the boy that didn't want to grow up. I feel honored and privileged to have heard his music during my time and feel sorry for the next generation of people to grow up without getting the chance to watch a legend perform but can only log on to something like YouTube and watch his past performances while we grew up watching them LIVE. There will be no one as good, as great, as awesome as him. Thank you Michael for sharing your talent. I still can't do the moonwalk but I'll never stop trying. Just like you. =)."

Gerry stated a few days after the memorial, in a written reaction (edited shorter): "If ever a man was given a memorial fit for a King, it was Michael, as he fully deserved. The accolades, the protectiveness, the loyalty, the out-pour of love, the defenses of him, the intense devotion had me crying from word one to the very end. I could not get a grip. I couldn't have planned any moment better myself. The emotion, the gifts of words offered, Maya Angelou's beautiful poem and depth of kindness and loyalty in having it presented on her behalf was so much more than I could endure, and I am NOT a crier. I have grieved for this man for so so many years because of all he has endured and suffered being an abused child myself and full-well knowing the aftermath of that kind of childhood and now the man is where God intended, within the gates of total love and acceptance and freedom. I always wished he was my lil brother so I could be a part of his support system and someone to hug him and say to him, "I understand, Mikey."

Barb wrote, 8 days after the memorial: "It has been three weeks and I am still heart-broken. If only you could have known how many people truly cared about you and loved you. Not everyone believes the trash that has been written and said about you. You truly are a special gift, blessed by God with immense talent and compassion. My heart aches for your pain and sadness in your life. It is unfortunate that it seems you were surrounded by people who did not really care about you and only took from you whatever they could. There are so many who would have freely surrounded you with love and support and maybe you would have been a little less lonely. I pray that you are with Jesus now where you are fully understood and loved unconditionally. Thank you for all you gave. I love you and miss you."

Forever Fan wrote: "I know that in life one thing is guaranteed, and that is death. I also know that we have each been placed on this earth for bigger reason. I'm only 24 years old and was not on earth when Michael was a mega star, but regardless, he had impact. God blessed him with the gift to heal the world via his talent to not only entertain but to take us on journey to a better place where we are united as one and nothing separates us. That's why to me he will always and 'yes always' remain King of Pop. No matter where you go in the world, if its the richest or the poorest, everyone knows Michael. No matter who you ask, old or young, everyone knows Michael. So thank you for blessing us with one of you're many angels on earth. Michael, I truly hope that you can rest in peace and that for once in you're life they will put you to rest! Maya Angelou to me is another Angel on earth, she could have not said it better. We had you and we are the world!"

Liane wrote: "We had him and did not appreciate what we had. It's a shame he is gone from us down here forever but heaven will receive a gift back. Thank you Michael for sharing your gift and thank you God for bringing angels down among us to delight! Michael let your sweet spirit forever reign and may you rest in sweet eternal peace. I admire you and love you eternally! Never ever will you be forgotten, your twinkling eyes and your big smile will forever be in our hearts. MJ forever!"

Alicia: "I, too, am still heartbroken, and feel enormously sad that he was so lonely and sad and taken advantage of in his life. He was such a gift to us, and many of us humans exploited it, for which I am truly sorry. I am sure he knows, now that he walks with God, that he was so loved. That is all that gives me solace right now. Thank you Maya Angelou for your beautiful poem that was so perfect for Michael. And thank you Michael, I will love and miss you forever, and always remember."

    Tiffany age 11, "Maya Angelou's poem: "We Had Him" was so beautiful. Her poem relates a lot to Michael in real life. This poem has meaning with every single word. Michael made singing and dancing fun no matter how hard it was. Michael had lots of passion and even more compassion. In the part: "In the instant Michael is gone, we know nothing. No clocks can tell our time. No oceans can rush our tides with the abrupt absence of our treasure." It has a lot of meaning because when Michael the shining star is gone, the whole world froze, the clocks stopped ticking and the Earth stopped rotating. Also in "walk our dances across the face of the moon" reminds me of his classic "moonwalk". It's true. Michael gave the world all of his talents in singing and dance. He kept nothing to himself. One of his dances he dances on his toes and Maya knew that and took Michael's performing life into her poem. This makes the poem like an autobiography and a poem of him. His father isn't Joe Jackson. His father is God. Michael was only raised by the Jackson's but Maya knew that truly he is Michael God. Even though some people truly adored Michael, he still left their loving care. That part was to me and maybe some others was the most meaningful part. Even though Michael is gone his soul, spirit, music and passion lives forever. The newspaper reporters cannot say any horrible lies about him now because he is resting with the moon and the stars. Michael was our gift. No one can replace this gift. Michael is something that comes only once in a lifetime. Even though we are many, Maya made us remember that everyone can feel very lonely in this big world now. In the last four sentences: "Today in Tokyo, beneath the Eiffel Tower, in Ghana's Black Star Square... We are missing Michael. But we do know we had him and we are the world." To me that just summarizes that everywhere in the world everyone is missing Michael. And, the world that Michael healed is missing him. Long live your spirit Michael. How Maya can think of this meaningful poem might always be a mystery to me."

Winsy expressed her feelings: "The shining star that shined from the west to the east from 'north, we had him indeed, we never known till he was gone! But still he will always be in our hearts forever and will always be the star shining trough our souls! Love you MJ. The world have lost the precious gift of all!" Jane's message said: "I cried - so beautiful - Maya Angelou's poem is perfect for Michael Jackson. And we are missing him. Everywhere."

Essel wrote: "All the world shall crave for Michael Jackson's presence; Now in living memory we see his absence. *HIStory* shall tell, retell and foretell how we all leaned to care about others."

And Sidney wrote the morning after the service: "Thank you Maya for this beautiful poem and for reminding us that he truly was our shining star. WE HAD HIM and we will always have him in our heart and in our mind. I love you Michael and I thank you for being you and giving us the best days of our lives. R.I.P."

The Associated Press wrote: "It was not spectacular, extravagant or bizarre. There were songs and tears but little dancing. Instead, Michael Jackson's memorial was a sombre, spiritual ceremony that reached back for the essence of the man. Singer, dancer, superstar, humanitarian: That was how the some 20,000 people gathered inside Los Angeles Staples Center arena on Tuesday, and untold millions watching around the world, remembered Jackson, whose immense talents almost drowned beneath the spectacle of his life and fame."

The Los Angeles Times reporters Geoff Boucher and Cara Mia DiMassa wrote: "Music legends, sports figures, and civil rights leaders paid tribute to Michael Jackson today during an emotional, song-filled service at Staples Center that was part polished entertainment, part revival meeting. Jackson was praised as a music pioneer and a barrier-breaking cultural figure, who the Rev. Al Sharpton said paved the way for other black entertainers to reach superstardom." Celebrityviplounge.com reporters said: "The Michael Jackson memorial has brought celebrities out to pay tribute to the man who inspired them in their own musical careers. Michael Jackson's coffin was brought to the Staples Center and is being placed at the front of the stage where big name musicians will sing above him." Rolling Stone reporter Steve Appleford wrote: "At their best, the brief musical performances were like a flipside to the renowned Motown 25th anniversary show in 1983, where Jackson first unveiled his 'moonwalk'. It was less a simple celebration of a musical legacy than a glimpse at the depth of feeling within that lineage of pop music. It brought out the best in Tuesday's performers. Even Lionel Richie put away the smooth loverman ballads and turned up the gospel on a rousing *Jesus Is Love*."

Motown Founder Berry Gordy told the audience, "Michael was like a son to me," and concluded him, "the greatest entertainer who ever lived." Berry, who was responsible for many of Michael's hits, said: "He was driven by his hunger to learn to constantly top himself to be the best. He was the consummate student. He studied the greats and became greater. He raised the bar and then broke the bar. His talent and creativity thrust him and entertainment into another stratosphere. The Motown family mourns the death of our friend and brother Michael Jackson who was like a son to me. Our deep condolences go out to all his family, his parents; Joe, Katherine, his beautiful children, his sisters and brothers and his nieces and nephews. Michael Jackson was 10 years old when he and his brothers auditioned for me in Motown in Detroit that July day in 1968, and blew us all away. The Jackson 5 were just amazing, and little Michael's performance was way beyond his years. This little kid had an incredible knowingness about him. He sang with such feeling and inspiration. Michael had a quality that I couldn't completely understand but we all knew he was special. Aside from singing and dancing like James Brown and Jackie Wilson, he sung a Smokey Robinson song called *Who's Lovin' You*. He sang it with the sadness and passion of a man who'd been living the blues and heartbreak his whole life. And as great as Smokey sang it, I thought Michael was better. I went to Smokey and said, "hey man I think he got you on that one." Smokey said, "me too." That was Motown. Motown was built on love and competition and sometimes the competition got in the way of the love but the love always won out. We competed on everything." Barry explained they had a baseball game every week, the Jacksons vs. the Gordy's. He said: "Unfortunately for us, Tito and Jackie were big homerun hitters. They would knock the ball out of the park. But then so was my son Barry and I'm not going to tell you who won most of the games, but I will tell you that the Gordy's cried a lot. And even though little Michael was the catchers for the Jackson's and missed a lot of balls, we still cried a lot. But we swam and we joked and we played games and when Michael performed his songs you could feel the hipness in his soul because that's what he loved to do. Michael inspired me so much that for days I walked around humming a bright little happy tune with him in mind... then I put a group together and we came up with 4 hit records for them, *I Want You Back*, *ABC*, *The Love You Save* and *I'll Be There*. The Jackson 5 was the only group in history to have their first 4 records go to number 1. In 1983, the brothers reunited and returned to do Motown 25th anniversary show. After a high powered dazzling melody of their songs Michael took the stage alone and made pop history. From the first beat of *Billie Jean*, I was mesmerized. And when he did his iconic moonwalk, I was shocked. It was magic. Michael Jackson went into orbit, and never came down. At 10 years old, he had passion. He had passion to be the greatest entertainer in the world and he was willing to work as hard to do whatever it took to become what he indeed became, the undisputed King of Pop, the world over. What kid wouldn't give his right arm to fulfill his wildest childhood dreams? Michael loved it all, every moment on stage, every moment in rehearsal. Michael loved creating what have never been done before. He loved everything and everybody, especially his fans. I must say though that he did have two personalities. Off stage he was shy, soft spoken and childlike, but when he took the stage in front of his screaming fans he turned into another person. A master, a take no prisoner show man. It was like kill or be killed. I mean Michael was awesome, totally in charge. In fact, the more I think about Michael Jackson, the more I think, 'The King of Pop is not big enough for him. I think he is simply the greatest entertainer that ever lived.' Michael, thank you for the joy. Thank you for the love. You will live in my heart forever. I love you."

After some videos of Michael, which were shown on a big screen, Stevie Wonder performed, sitting at a grand piano. He sadly told the crowd, "This is a moment I wish I didn't live to see coming. But as much as I can say that we mean it,

I do know that God is good... Michael, I love you, and I've told you that many times." Stevie sang a heartbreaking *Never Dreamed You'd Leave in Summer*, adding the line: "Michael, why didn't you stay?"

Kobe Bryant and Magic Johnson, took the stage and gave moving speeches at Michael Jackson's memorial. Kobe Bryant described Michael's goodwill: "You all know that nobody ever gave on stage like Michael Jackson, but Michael was also a true humanitarian who gave just as much off stage as he did on the stage. Michael and his family came from humble roots and Michael always cared very deeply for those in need. And beyond all of his records that he wrote as a recording artist, Michael even made the Guinness Book of World Records for most charities supported by a pop star. Because he gave so much for so many of us, for so long, Michael Jackson will be with us forever."

Magic Johnson recalled appearing in Michael's video for *Remember the Time*. He told he went to Michael's house to discuss ideas: "I met Jackie Jackson about 30 years ago and he was a season ticket holder for the Lakers as well as his brother Marlon. Jackie and I became friends and he began to invite me out to their home. Then I got to know the brothers and the sisters and his incredible mother and father. We love to play with fire crackers and just have fun. And Barry, just like you lost to the Jackson's in softball, so did I. And we had some incredible times together. Then Jackie invited me to go on tour with the brothers and then I got to see the genius of Michael Jackson. He was so incredible; he always had command of not only the band, his brothers but also the audience. I truly believe that Michael made me a better point guard and basketball player as I watched him, be so great, and be the greatest entertainer ever. From there, Michel called me one day and said, "I want to talk to you about being in a video *Remember the Time*." But I had to double check with Jackie to make sure it was really Michael because I was scared to death to go over to his house because this was my idol, he was everything to me. So I went over to his house to have dinner. The chef came out and said what would you like, I said some grilled chicken. So as we begin to talk about the video and what he wanted me to do, the chef brought me out the grilled chicken but he brought Michael out a bucket of Kentucky Fried Chicken. And I went crazy, like wait a minute, 'Michael you eat Kentucky Fried Chicken?' That made my day. That was the greatest moment of my life. We had such a good time sitting on the floor eating that bucket of Kentucky Fried Chicken, and I want to say this, 'This is a celebration of his life, of his legacy'. I want to thank Michael for opening up so many doors for African Americans to be on day time shows, late night shows. He allowed Kobe and I to have our jerseys in people's homes across the world because he was already there. And he opened all those doors for us. His three children will have the most incredible grandmother that God has put on this earth, to take care of them. Michael's three children will have incredible uncles and aunts to take care of them as well, and they will have plenty of cousins to play with. So may God continue to bless this incredible family. We say that we're praying for you, remain strong. We want to thank the city of Los Angeles for putting this on, AEG for putting it on as well, and may God continue to bless you Michael."

Oscar-winner Jennifer Hudson, visibly pregnant in a beautiful white gown, sang a soaring rendition of Michael's hit *Will You Be There* while dancers circled around her slowly. She never met Michael Jackson. Neither has John Mayer.

The Rev. Al Sharpton made a rousing speech. He told the congregation: "Michael brought Blacks, Whites, Asians and Latinos together. All over the world today people are gathered in love visions, to celebrate the life of a man that taught the world how to love. People may be wondering why there is such an emotional outburst. But you would have to understand the journey of Michael, to understand what he meant to all of us. For these that sit here as the Jackson family, a mother and father with 9 children, who rose from a working class family in Gary, Indiana. They had nothing but a dream; no one believed in those days that these kinds of dreams could come true. But they keep on believing and Michael never let the world turn him around from his dreams. I first met Michael around 1970, Black Expo, Chicago, Illinois. Reverend Jesse Jackson who stood by this family till now. And from that day as a cute kid, to this moment, he never gave up dreaming. It was that dream, that changed culture, all over the world. When Michael started, it was a different world. But because Michael kept going, because he didn't accept limitations, because he refused to let people decide his boundaries. He opened up the whole world. In the music world, he put on one glove, pulled his pants up and broke down the color curtain. When now our videos are shown and magazines put us on the cover, it was Michael Jackson that brought Blacks and Whites and Asians and Latinos together. It was Michael Jackson that made us sing *We Are The World*, and feed the hungry, long before Live Aid. Because Michael Jackson kept going, he created a comfort level where people that felt they were separate, became interconnected with his music. And it was that comfort level, that kids from Japan and Ghana and France and Iowa and Pennsylvania got comfortable enough with each other so later it wasn't strange to us, to watch Oprah on television. It wasn't strange to watch Tiger Woods' golf. Those young kids grew up from being teenage comfortable fans of Michael, to being 40 years old and being comfortable to vote for a person of color to be the president of the United States of America. Michael did that! Michael made us love each other. Michael taught us to stand with each other. There are those that like to dig around mess, but millions around the world we're going to uphold his message. It's not about mess; it's about his love message. As you climb up steep mountains sometimes you scar your knee. Sometimes you break the skin but don't focus on the scars, focus on the journey. Michael beat them. Michael rose to the top. He out sang his cynics. He out danced his doubters. He outperformed the pessimists. Every time he got knocked down he got back up. Every time you counted him out he came back in. Michael never stopped! Michael never stopped! Michael never stopped!" He received a standing ovation for his words.

He continued: "I want to say to Mrs. Jackson and Joe Jackson, his sisters and brothers; we thank you for giving us someone that taught us love, someone that taught us hope. We want to thank you because we know he was your dream too. We know that your heart is broken; I know you have some comforts from a letter from the President of the United States and Nelson Mandela but this was your child, this was your brother, this was your cousin. Nothing will fill your hearts loss, but I hope the love that people have shown, will make you know he didn't live in vain. I want his three children to know: [there] was nothing strange about your Daddy. It was strange what your Daddy had to deal with." The crowd cheered and gave a standing ovation. Rev. Al Sharpton continued saying: "But he dealt with it anyway. He dealt with it for us. So some came today, Mrs. Jackson, to say good bye to Michael; I came to say thank you. Thank you because you never stopped. Thank you because you never gave up. Thank you because you never gave out. Thank you because you tore down our divisions. Thank you because you irradiated barriers. Thank you because you gave us hope. Thank you Michael! Thank you Michael! Thank you Michael!" His speech prompted again a standing ovation, with Michael's daughter Paris among the first to stand.

After Rev. Al Sharpton spoke to the public, John Mayer mesmerized the audience as he played the guitar. He first rolled out a pair of vintage amps and had brought his Stratocaster guitar for his instrumental version of *Human Nature*. After he got off stage, John was shown embracing members of the Jackson family. John Mayer was later interviewed by Larry King on CNN. He told Larry King he had never met Michael personally but admired him and was influenced by his work, as were so many of his generation.

An emotional Brooke Shields told of happy times they shared as teens and young adults, even once sneaking a peak at Liz Taylor's wedding dress while the actress slept nearby. "Michael was one of a kind. I was thinking back to when we met and the many times that we spent together and whenever we were out together and there would be a picture taken there would be a caption of some kind and the caption usually said something like 'an odd couple' or 'an unlikely pair' but to us it was the most natural and easiest of friendships. I was 13 when we met and from that day on our friendship grew. Michael always knew he could count on me to support him or be his date and that we would have fun no matter where we were. We had a bond and maybe it was because we both understood what it was like to be in the spotlight at a very young age. I used to tease him and I'd say: 'You know... I started when I was 11 months old, you're a slacker. You were what, 5?' Both of us needed to be adults very early. But when we were together, we were two little kids having fun. We never collaborated together, we never performed together, or danced on the same stage although he did try in vain one night to unsuccessfully teach me the moonwalk and he just basically just shook his head and crossed his arms at my attempt.

"We never filmed a video or recorded a song, but what we did do was laugh. It was a competition to see who can make the other one laugh more or be sillier. Michael loved to laugh. His heart would just burst out of him when he was laughing. He adored it when I did silly imitations or told him stories about my life. MJ's laugh was the sweetest and purest [laugh] of anyone's I had ever known. His sense of humor was delightful and he was very mischievous. I remember it was the night before Elizabeth Taylor's wedding and he had called me prior and asked if I would join him, he didn't want to be alone for all the festivities. And it was the night before the big day and Michael and I tried to sneak in to get the first peak of the dress and we were just giggling like crazy and we almost passed out in hysterics when we realized that Elizabeth was actually asleep in the bed. We thought she was in an entirely different room. And we had to laugh and sneak out and then at the point of the wedding when there was the first dance basically we had to joke that we were the mother and father of the bride. Yes it may have seemed very odd to the outside, but we made it fun and we made it real.

"When he started wearing the glove, I was like what's up with the glove? I was like look if you're going to hold my hand it better be the non gloved one because sequence really hurts me...it digs in. He would just shake his head and he would just smile. He loved to be teased. Seeing him smile made you feel like everything was going to be alright. To the outside world, Michael was a genius with unchallenged ability. To the people who were lucky enough to know him personally he was caring and funny, honest, pure, non-jaded and he was a lover of life. He cared so deeply for his family and his friends and his fans. He was often referred to as the King but the Michael I knew always reminded me more of *The Little Prince.* Thinking of him now I'd like to share a passage from the book: What moves me so deeply about this sleeping little prince is his loyalty to a flower-- the image of a rose shining within him like the flame within a lamp, even when he's asleep... And I realized he was even more fragile than I thought. Lamps must be protected. A gust of wind can blow them out.

"Michael's sensitivity was even more extraordinary than his talent. And his true truth resided in his heart. As *The Little Prince* also said, 'Eyes are blind'. You have to look with the heart. What's most important is invisible. Michael saw everything with his heart. To his family, his brothers and sisters, Katherine, Joe and to his children, Prince, Paris, Blanket, my prayers are with you. Michael's favorite song was not one of the countless masterpieces that he gave us but it was a song that Charlie Chaplin wrote for the movie Modern Times. It's called *Smile.* There's a line in the song that says 'smile though your heart is aching.' Today, although our hearts are aching we need to look up where he is undoubtedly perched in a crescent moon and we need to smile," she said fighting back her tears after not seeing him in person for almost twenty years.

Michael's brother, who got Michael involved in the Nation of Islam performed Charlie Chaplin's *Smile*. It was Michael's favorite song, Brooke Shields said at the memorial service.

Smile, though your heart is aching
Smile, even though it's breaking
When there are clouds in the sky
You'll get by...

If you smile
With your fear and sorrow
Smile and maybe tomorrow

You'll find that life is still worthwhile
If you just...

Light up your face with sadness
Hide every trace of gladness
All through the year... will be ever so near
That's the time you must keep on trying

Smile, what's the use in crying
You'll find that life is still worthwhile
If you'll just...

Smile, though your heart is aching
Smile, even though it's breaking
When there are clouds in the sky
You'll get by...

If you smile
Through your fear and sorrow
Smile and maybe tomorrow
You'll find that life is still worthwhile
If you'll just Smile...

(Instrumental)

That's the time you must keep on trying
Smile, what's the use in crying
You'll find that life is still worthwhile
If you'll just Smile

(Original Music by Charlie Chaplin.
Original Lyrics by John Turner and
Geoffrey Parsons)

After Jermaine sang his emotional and own version of *Smile*, Jermaine took his flower boutonniere off his lapel, and tossed it on the coffin.

John Turner (real name James Phillips) and Geoffrey Parsons added lyrics to the original music by Charlie Chaplin, and it became a popular hit when Nat 'King' Cole recorded it. Michael's version of *Smile* appeared on 1995's *HIStory: Past, Present and Future, Book I*. On his *HIStory World Tour*, he dedicated *Smile* to Princess Diana. Michael admired Charlie Chaplin who was knighted by Queen Elizabeth II, and became Sir Charles Spencer Chaplin.

Charlie Chaplin and Michael had a lot in common. They both were composers, screenwriters, directors, choreographers and actors. Charlie Chaplin once said: "Laughter is the tonic, the relief, the surcease for pain." Like Michael, Charlie Chaplin also liked to act. "I remain just one thing, and one thing only, and that is a clown. It places me on a far higher plane than any politician," Charlie once said.

Martin Luther King III spoke. After quoting his father, he said: "Michael Jackson was truly the best." He continued: "First I must say to Mrs. Katherine Jackson, Mr. Joseph Jackson, the children of Michael Jackson, to Michael Jackson's brothers and sisters and the entire Jackson family, our prayers and condolences are constantly with you. My father once said that in life one must discover what their calling is, and when they do they must do their jobs so well that the living, the dead and the unborn could do them no better. He constantly taught us to become our best by stating that if you cannot be a pine on the top of the hill why just be a shrub in the valley, but be the best little shrub on the side of the road. Be a bush if you cannot be a tree. If you cannot be the highway just be a trail. If you cannot be the sun, just be a star. For it isn't by size that you win or you fail, you got to be the best of what you are. Michael Jackson was truly the best of what he was."

Martin Luther King Jr. also said that, "every time you're allowed to be a street sweeper you must sweep streets so well. In fact you must sweep streets like Beethoven composed music. Sweep streets he said, like Shakespeare wrote poetry. Sweep streets like Raphael painted pictures. Sweep streets so well that all the hosts of the heavens and earths would have to pause and say, here lived the great street sweeper that did his job well. On June 25th, because he was the best, I believe heaven and earth did pause indeed to say of Michael Joseph Jackson, here lived a great entertainer who did his job well."

Bernice King said: "To the Jackson family, being a part of a world renounced family who has also experienced a sudden death on more than one occasion; my prayer is that no one and nothing public, fact or fiction, true or rumored will separate you from the love God which is in Christ Jesus. Because ultimately at the end of the day it is only God's love that will anchor you, sustain you and move you to a higher ground far above the noise of life, there you will find the peace, comfort and joy to move forward to advance Michael's legacy. And for all of us it is apparent that like our father and mother, Martin and Coretta King, Michael's life and work was inspired by the love of God. Throughout the ages few are chosen from amongst us to use their gifts and talents to demonstrate God's love in an effort to bring the world together in true sister and brotherhood. Michael was such a one. He epitomized the words of our father that an individual hasn't started living until he can rise above the narrow confines of his individualistic concerns to the broader concerns of humanity. Michael was always concerned with others with humanity. And I want the world to know that despite being embroiled in accusations and persecutions, as a humanitarian he thought it not robbery to concern himself with one of this world's other greatest humanitarians, our mother, during her illness just three months before her death. In October, 2005, I was with mom when Michael called to say... and although she couldn't speak because of a debilitating stroke... she listened as he said to her that he had been praying on his knees everyday for her. That to him, she was America's true royalty and he wanted her to know if music was being played in her room because of its healing effect. My only wish is that he could have seen the glow on her face. If faces could smile as we know they do, that day Michael Jackson made our mother's face smile in spite of her condition. What an unforgettable moment. He was such a thoughtful and selfless man, full of the unconditional love of God and good works that touched and changed lives. He was indeed a shining light. Like our father Martin and in remembrance of Michael, may we all be inspired to go and let our lights shine. Rest in peace our brother Michael."

Sheila Jackson Lee honored Michael Jackson. She told the world: "I'm Congresswoman Sheila Jackson Lee and I hale from Houston Texas but I come to you on behalf of the many members of the United State's House of Representatives. I come to you on behalf of the Congressional Black Caucus chairwoman Barbara Lee, a Californian. And I come to you as every man and every woman for I cannot write music, or dance or sing but I do know an American story. To Mr. and Mrs. Jackson and his wonderful family of brothers and sisters and cousins, to Michael, Joseph, to Katherine and Paris, and to Prince, all of these wonderful, beautiful symbols of America. And I can tell you as a member of the United States Congress. We understand the Constitution. We understand Laws and we know that people are innocent until proven otherwise. That is what the Constitution stands for. So I mourn today, I come too to thank you. For many people don't understand the hearts of entertainers. They don't know how big their hearts are. They don't know how they heal the world on behalf of America. When we're at war, our icons like Michael sing about healing the world and so he called us into public service. It did not matter whether we were black or white. He even told us to beat it, beat the violence. He told us to look at yourself in the mirror because it meant that if you were going to make a difference look at the man or woman in the mirror. I come to you today to say thank you. Some of you come from all faiths and we respect that here in America. But there is a story whose theme is so symbolic of this young and beautiful man. I love the story of the Good Samaritan because it talks about those who walk by the diminished, the devastated and the poor. This was a broken and beaten man lying along a road. No one stopped except someone called the Samaritan. It could be in any faith. It's all about charity and love, and I call Michael Jackson the Good Samaritan. I call him Michael Jackson who cared and loved for the world. It bothered me, I grew up with him as all of us and so many did. And so what an honor and a privilege to see him up close. When he came to the United States Congress in my office and looked some 15 African ambassadors, representatives of heads of states. Sitting in an office listening to Michael Jackson talk about caring and fighting HIV Aids. They looked at him, he had a twinkle, they listened, he listened. What a miraculous experience to be able to listen and see Michael in action. You know there were words cast about but I wonder if anybody was on his shoulder when he walked into Walter Reed Hospital and he walked along the aisles and the rows in the hospital rooms. This was in the mist of the Iraq War, doctors stopped, nurses stopped, and individual soldiers who had lost limbs stopped and were in essence moved and touched as Michael was by his desire to come and thank them for their sacrifices. So don't tell me what an American story is all about; it is assault of the earth. With this family took the talent that God had given them and made it into a miraculous and wonderful story for America. I come today for you to recognize that the flag flies and the people who have spoken have spoken to the people's house. They recognize and they speak and those of us who serve in elected office we respond to the people. Michael fought for the tolerance of all people. In fact I am reminded although I speak in the tongues of all faith that Michael fought the good fight. He was someone who understood and I hope Mr. and Mrs. Jackson and the family will know that the Lord is our shepherd and we shall not want. Michael Jackson you got to know his story and it has not been told by all of what you've heard. He was someone who understood if he was burned, he built a burn unit. If a hospital needed beds, he built those beds. If they needed money for developing countries, Michael gave. If he was in

Namibia, he went to orphanages. Michael never stopped giving and he touched those whose lives could be reconstructed, because the king, yes the king, the King stopped and said I care about you."

She also said that, "congressional black caucus and members of the House of Representatives stopped, stopped, stopped and had a moment of silence for this wonderful legend and icon. And so to the family let me simply come and someone that wishes she was long lost Sheila Jackson Lee but I'll keep looking and seeing by coming to say to you that America appreciates and thanks you for Michael Jackson's life. For that reason we have introduced into the House of Representatives this resolution 600 that will be debated on the floor of the house that claims Michael Jackson as an American Legend and musical icon, a world humanitarian. Someone who will be honored forever and forever and forever and forever and forever (standing ovation). We are the world and we are better because Michael Joseph Jackson lived. On behalf of myself and the people who have spoken, Michael Jackson, I salute you."

"Sheila Jackson Lee Honors Michael Jackson, At Incredible Length," wrote Richard Connelly for Houstonpress.com. Richard continued saying: "Via The Hill's blog, we've learned of our own Sheila Jackson Lee's epic attempt to immortalize Michael Jackson. Amazingly, Lee's bill declaring the House of Representatives 'recognizes Michael Jackson as a global humanitarian and a noted leader in the fight against worldwide hunger and medical crises' is a bit, long-winded." Ed Zimmerman wrote on Hill.com the following: "Oddly enough, the legislation was referred to the House Foreign Affairs Committee. The full text of that resolution has been published, and it's long.

"The legislation lists Jackson's accomplishments in endless detail, from his number 1 hits to the details of his charity work. At the conclusion, the legislation resolves that Congress: (1) recognizes Michael Jackson as a global humanitarian and a noted leader in the fight against worldwide hunger and medical crises; and (2) celebrates Michael Jackson as an accomplished contributor to the worlds of arts and entertainment, scientific advances in the treatment of HIV/AIDS, and global food security. Jackson's death has been a controversial topic in Congress. The Congressional Black Caucus spearheaded a moment of silence for the late King of Pop, which some lawmakers found offensive. Today, Rep. Pete King (R-N.Y.) called Jackson a 'pervert' and a 'low-life.' Guess that's one vote against Jackson-Lee's resolution." The resolution can be found at the Library of Congress.

> Honoring an American legend and musical icon.
> (Introduced in House)
>
> HRES 600 IH1S
>
> 111th CONGRESS
>
> 1st Session
>
> H. RES. 600
> Honoring an American legend and musical icon.
>
> IN THE HOUSE OF REPRESENTATIVES
>
> June 26, 2009

Ms. JACKSON-LEE of Texas (for herself and Ms. WATSON) submitted the following resolution; which was referred to the Committee on Foreign Affairs

---

RESOLUTION

Honoring an American legend and musical icon.

Whereas Michael Jackson was not only an accomplished recording and performing artist, he was a noted humanitarian;

Whereas Michael Jackson began his stellar recording career as the featured member of *The Jackson 5*, which was the first act in recorded history to have their first four major label singles *I Want You Back*, *ABC*, *The Love You Save*, and *I'll Be There*, reached the top of the American charts;

Whereas the internationally recognized *Thriller* released in 1982, which became a smash hit yielded seven top-10 singles. The album sold 21 million copies in the United States and at least 27 million worldwide. It was a monumental moment in music history;

Whereas Michael Jackson was labeled *The King of Pop*, Jackson's music is internationally recognized and critically acclaimed;

Whereas Michael Jackson was one of the few artists to have been inducted into the Rock and Roll Hall of Fame twice;

Whereas in the early 1980s, Michael Jackson became a dominant figure in popular music and the first African-American entertainer to amass a strong crossover following on MTV. The popularity of his music videos airing on MTV, such as *Beat It*, *Billie Jean* and *Thriller* --widely credited with transforming the music video from a promotional tool into an art form-- helped bring the relatively new channel to fame;

Whereas, on January 10, 1984, Michael Jackson visited the unit for burn victims at Brotman-Memorial Hospital in Los Angeles, and demonstrated his concern with people suffering from grievous injuries;

Whereas, on April 9, 1984, David Smithee, a 14-year-old boy suffering from cystic fibroses was invited to Michael's home, in response to a dying request to meet Michael. David passed away 7 weeks later;

Whereas, on April 14, 1984, Michael Jackson was single handedly responsible for equipping a 19-bed-unit at Mount Sinai New York Medical Center. This center is now a critical part of the T.J. Martell Foundation for leukemia and cancer research;

Whereas, on July 5, 1984, during the Jackson's press conference at Tavern On The Green, Michael announced that his portion of the earnings from the *Victory Tour* would be donated to three charitable organizations: The United Negro College Fund, Camp Good Times, and the T.J. Martell Foundation; Whereas, on July 14, 1984, after the first concert of the *Victory Tour*, Michael met 8 terminally ill children backstage;

Whereas, on December 13, 1984, Michael visited the Brotman Memorial Hospital, where he had been treated when he was burned during the producing of a Pepsi commercial. He subsequently donated all the money he received from Pepsi, $1.5 million, to the Michael Jackson Burn Center for Children;

Whereas, on January 28, 1985 Michael and 44 other artists met to record *We Are The World*, written by Michael and Lionel Richie, a project devoted to fighting global hunger. The proceeds of this record were donated to the starving people in Africa;

Whereas in 1986, Michael set up the Michael Jackson UNCF Endowed Scholarship Fund. This $1.5 million fund is aimed toward assisting students majoring in performance art and communications, with money given each year to students attending a UNCF member college or university;

Whereas, on February 28, 1986, after having had a heart-transplant, 14-year-old Donna Ashlock from California received a call from Michael Jackson. He had heard that she was a fan. Michael invited Donna to his home following her recovery;

Whereas, on September 13, 1987, Michael supported a campaign against racism. He made every effort to publicly support NAACP, in the fight against discrimination of African-American artists;

Whereas in October 1987, at the end of his *Bad Tour*, Michael donated personal items to UNESCO for a charitable auction. The proceeds of his donation were allocated for the education of children in developing countries;

Whereas, on February 1, 1988, The Song *Man In the Mirror* entered the charts. The proceeds from the sales of this record went directly and exclusively to Camp Ronald McDonald for Good Times, a camp for children who suffer from Cancer;

Whereas, on March 1, 1988, at a press conference held by his sponsor Pepsi, Michael presented a $600,000 check to the United Negro College Fund;

Whereas on April 1988, Michael Jackson ensured that free tickets to three concerts in Atlanta, Georgia, were specifically set aside for the Make a Wish Foundation;

Whereas, on May 22, 1988, Michael visited cancer-stricken children in the Bambini-Gesu Children's Hospital in Rome. He signed autographs and gave away sweets and records to the young patients. He also announced his monetary donation of 100,000 pounds to the hospital;

Whereas, on July 16, 1988, Michael met the Prince of Wales and his wife Diana, where he donated 150,000 pounds for the Prince's Trust, and a check of 100,000 pounds for the children's hospital at Great Ormond Street;

Whereas, on July 20, 1988, Michael visited terminally ill children at Great Ormond Street Hospital. At a unit for less critical patients he stayed longer and to engage in story telling time with the children;

Whereas, on August 29, 1988, at his 30th birthday Michael performed a concert in Leeds, England, for the English charity organization *Give For Life*, an organization designed as an immunization charity for children. Michael presented a check for 65,000 pounds;

Whereas on January 1989, the proceeds of one of Michael's shows in Los Angeles were donated to Childhelp USA, the biggest charity organization against child abuse. In appreciation of the contributions of Michael, Childhelp of Southern California founded the Michael Jackson International Institute for Research On Child Abuse;

Whereas, on January 10, 1989, upon the winding down of his *Bad Tour*, Michael Jackson donated tickets for each concert to underprivileged children, and made contributions to hospitals, orphanages and charity organizations throughout each stop on his tour;

Whereas, on February 7, 1989, Michael visited the Cleveland Elementary School in Stockton, California, a site of playground violence where 5 children had been tragically killed and 39 had been wounded;

Whereas, on March 5, 1989, Michael invited 200 underprivileged children of the St. Vincent

Institute for Handicapped Children and of the organization Big Brothers and Big Sisters to the Circus Vargas in Santa Barbara. Following the event, the children were invited to his ranch to visit his private Zoo at Neverland Ranch;

Whereas in December 1991, Michael's office MJJ Productions donated more than 200 turkey dinners to needy families in Los Angeles;

Whereas in February 1992, within 11 days Michael covered 30,000 miles in Africa, to visit hospitals, orphanages, schools, churches, and institutions for mentally handicapped children;

Whereas, on February 3, 1992, at a press conference at the New York Radio City Music Hall, Michael announced that he is planning a new world tour, to raise funds for his new Heal The World Foundation. This Foundation was designed to support the fight against AIDS, Juvenile Diabetes, the Ronald McDonald Camp, and the Make A Wish Foundation;

Whereas, on May 6, 1992, Michael defrayed the funeral expenses for Ramon Sanchez, who was killed during the Los Angeles riots;

Whereas, on June 26, 1992, Michael presented the Mayor of Munich, Mr. Kronawitter, with a 40,000 DM check for the needy people of the city;

Whereas on July 1992, Michael donated 821,477,296 Lire to La Partita del Cuore (The Heart Match) in Rome and donated 120,000 DM to children's charities in Estonia and Latvia;

Whereas, on July 25, 1992, at his concert in Dublin, Ireland, Michael announced that he will give 400,000 pounds of the tour earnings to various charities;

Whereas in June 1993, Michael announced a donation of $1.25 million for children suffering as a result of the riots in Los Angeles;

Whereas on October 1993, Michael Jackson donated $100,000 to the Children's Defense Fund, the Children's Diabetes Foundation, the Atlanta Project, and the Boys and Girl Clubs of Newark, New Jersey;

Whereas on December 1993, in conjunction with the Gorbachev Foundation, Michael Jackson airlifted 60,000 doses of children's vaccines to Tblisi, Georgia;

Whereas in 1994, Michael donated $500,000 to Elizabeth Taylor's AIDS Foundation;

Whereas, on October 1, 1996, Michael donated the proceeds of his Tunisia concert to The National Solidarity Fund, a charity dedicated to fighting poverty;

Whereas, on December 9, 1996, during the *History Tour* visit in Manila, Michael visited a Children's Hospital, where he announced that a portion of his concert earnings will be donated to the renovation of the Hospital;

Whereas the *Millennium Issue* of the Guinness Book Of Records named Michael as the *Pop Star who supports the most charity organizations*;

Whereas in 2004, The African Ambassadors' Spouses Association, honored Michael Jackson for his worldwide humanitarian efforts, due to his fiscal contribution of more than $50 million to various charities, including many organizations that feed the hungry in Africa; and

Whereas we today mourn with and send our condolences to the children that Michael Jackson left behind: Prince Michael, Paris Michael, and Prince Michael II and his mother, father, brothers, and sisters: Now, therefore, be it."

Singer Usher, who broke down in tears on stage, had only met Michael once. He sat on a stool in dark shades as camera flashes filled the arena to sing *Gone Too Soon*, and soon walked down to the casket. Usher placed his hand on Michael's casket and photos of Jackson as a child flashed on the screen behind him. He became emotional. After Usher was finished with the song, he hugged Michael's brothers in the front row and broke into sobs. Usher then kneeled down to thank Katherine and Joe for their support and returned to his seat.

Britain's Got Talent star Shaheen Jafargholi sang *Who's Lovin' You* and said afterwards: "I love Michael Jackson. And, I tell you now, I just want to thank him so much for blessing me and every single individual on this earth, with his amazing music. And thank you very much, I love Michael Jackson." Shaheen Jafargholi was the day after the memorial CNN in Larry King Live. Larry King introduced Shaheen saying he had been invited by Michael for his upcoming tour. Larry said: "Shaheen was a big hit Tuesday." Shaheen, now only 12 years old, told Larry that Michael wanted him to perform in London. He told Larry: "Apparently he used to watch me on YouTube every day. He used to really like me." Larry asked Shaheen if he liked the idea of performing in the 'O2. Shaheen: "I just, when I first heard, I couldn't believe it. I mean, I was, to be honest, honored to be invited. When I found out I was in the 'O2 dates, that was amazing as well." Larry asked what did it feel like for Shaheen to perform at the memorial. Shaheen: "I just felt really honored, blessed, that I'd been given the opportunity and also just the chance to say good-bye to my idol and my hero in a way that no other person on earth ever could. I had a great opportunity. I'm really glad it happened." Larry told Shareen he had been sitting behind Berry Gordy, the famed founder of Motown. Larry said: "So I leaned over to him and I said, do you know this kid? And he said, 'I don't know who this is, but if I had a record company, I'd sign him tomorrow.' Do you have a recording contract?" Shaheen: "Not at the moment. I mean, we're waiting to see what's going to happen with me in the future. I mean, hopefully, you know, I'll be able to carry on singing basically just get better and progress."

Kenny Ortega took the stage after Shaheen and said: "My name is Kenny Ortega... Thank you, and I was Michael's partner in the creating and directing of many of his tours including *This Is It*. And Shaheen was invited by Michael to join him in London for the show so I just wanted to introduce him to everybody and to say thank you for coming all the way here to join us Shaheen.

"We were here, we were right here. A little less than a week ago and Michael was with us. And the band, and Michael Bearden, and the singers and the dancers and our choreographer Travis and our crew, we were all here and we were a family. This was our house. So when the Jackson family and Randy Philips asked Ken and I to help put together this memorial, we knew we had to do it here. We knew we had to invite the world to join us here in Michael's house. We were immediately surrounded by countless family, artists and friends and dear hearts that unconditionally made this day possible. As we came together as a team we knew we had to celebrate Michael's life through his music as well as commemorate his passing." Kenny Ortega, the director of Michael's comeback tour called Michael a "living legacy" before he introduced a group to sing *We Are the World*.

Children and additional celebs took the stage to sing *Heal the World*. Paris, Prince and Blanket sang along. Michael's daughter Paris sang together with singers Lionel Richie and Jennifer Hudson on stage and also Prince and Blanket sang along. According to WikiPedia: "In a 2001 Internet chat with fans, Jackson said "Heal the World" is the song he is most proud to have created. He also created the Heal the World Foundation, a charitable organization which was designed to improve the lives of children. The organization was also meant to teach children how to help others. This concept of 'betterment for all' would become a centerpiece for the *Dangerous World Tour*. In the documentary Living with Michael Jackson, Jackson said he created the song in his 'Giving Tree' at the Neverland Ranch. An ensemble performance of *We Are the World* and *Heal the World* closed Jackson's memorial service at the Staples Center in Los Angeles on July 7, 2009. The song was performed as rehearsed by Jackson at the venue just days earlier, in preparation for his planned *This Is It* tour in London.

The show ended with words from the Jackson family. Jermaine and his brother Marlon spoke and said: "Thank You," to all the fans and the guests for joining them in honoring their brother Michael. Paris put a tissue in her handbag, and leaned on Janet. Blanket stood in front of Janet, and Paris, who was standing in front of La Toya Jackson, took Blanket's hands.

Prince had his arm around Paris and she was holding Blanket. If there was any shocking moment, it came in the form of Michael's daughter, Paris Michael Katherine Jackson, who made her first public statement. She spoke after tributes from Michael's brothers, Jermaine and Marlon. Paris made clear she wanted to say something. She struggled slightly with adjusting the microphone to her height. But she couldn't find immediately words to speak.

"Speak up," said her aunt Janet Jackson sweetly, just as the little girl began to talk. She praised her fathers' life, and delivered a tearful statement to the Staples Center crowd. "Ever since I was born, Daddy has been the best father I could imagine," she said through sobs and dissolved into tears. She turned to lean on her aunt Janet but decided to say one last thing. "I just want to say I love him so much," she said and burst into tears. Paris' tearful goodbye humanized Michael in the eyes of millions of adoring fans across the globe, but also in the eyes of his own friends and family.

Michael's casket was rolled out by family members as *Man in the Mirror* played. Pastor Lucius Smith read a benediction and the memorial drawed to a close.

According to The Mirror, Michael's youngest son asked after the memorial his godfather Mark Lester a heartbreaking question, one that no child should ever have to ask: "Where's my daddy gone? On holiday?" The article said: "It was the moment that brought yet more tears to Mark Lester's eyes, after he had just said farewell to his friend Michael Jackson. The King of Pop's bewildered son Blanket looked at him and declared innocently that he thought his dad was simply away on holiday. Mark, godfather to all of Michael's children, told Hello! magazine he had the emotional conversation with Blanket right after the moving memorial service in Los Angeles. The 50-year-old former child actor said: "It is obvious to me that Blanket is still unsure about what exactly happened to his father. He added: "It was a rhetorical question and it broke my heart. Prince was taciturn, unusual for him, but he still had a hug." Mark Lester also said: "Paris gave me a tight hug and we just held each other for a while. We were both welling up. I told her that her dad would always lie in her heart and be remembered by at least half of the world. Paris replied: 'I'm just glad he is at peace.'" The Oliver star added: "She was disappointed my daughters weren't able to come to the memorial. She asked me, 'Can we come and stay with you at Christmas and I can bring the presents?' I was very touched and hope that can still be arranged. It's difficult to say until the custody arrangements have been finalized." According to the magazine, Mark was also planning to attend a second funeral, when Michael's body was finally laid to rest. He said: "Paris asked if I would bring my children, too. I know it would be a comfort to her as well as Prince and Blanket but I'm waiting on confirmation of a time and place."

The Rev. Al Sharpton said after the event: "There are those I feel in years to come, will try to distort him to his children, and not understand that the real challenges that Michael Jackson had to seriously face and did face and make a difference. And I thought it was very important to put in context for his children what he dealt with in history and what he was able to do."

CNN wrote: "For many watching, Paris' appearance marked a rare glimpse of a child who has spent most of her life shielded from the public. Born to two mothers -- Jackson's ex-wife Debbie Rowe and an unidentified woman who reportedly served as a surrogate -- Jackson's three children lived and traveled the world with him, their faces often covered by veils and masks when appearing in public. In its execution, the speech appeared to be a surprise to those on stage and off. Kenny Ortega told CNN's Campbell Brown: "It was a surprise they were there. All of us who know them were delighted they were strong enough to come and feel this love and great outpouring for their dad. We would've never expected that they had the strength. It was beautiful. Michael was so close with these beautiful children. Little Paris was his biggest fan... A little girl couldn't love her papa more."

According to Sydney Morning Herald, "As the ceremony ended, pallbearers carrying Jackson's golden casket swathed with red flowers emerged and loaded it into a black hearse, under the watchful eye of mourners and around 20 media helicopters hovering overhead. A motorcade of luxury vehicles then made a stately procession to the Staples Center, where family, friends and celebrities rubbed shoulders with ordinary fans who had won tickets via an online lottery. A bazaar of T-shirts, buttons, photos and other memorabilia sprouted in the blocks around the memorial. Movie theatres played the service live and people paused around the world to watch."

Rolling Stone's Steve Appleford said: "It was all tasteful and maybe too brief. But for all the shifts and apparent chaos reported in recent days, and all the changes in plans and venues, the memorial was strikingly well-staged at Staples, where Jackson spent his final weeks rehearsing for his planned 50 concerts at London's O2 Arena." Ex-spokesman of Michael, Stuart Backerman said: "It was very, very touching, and really it was an example of the good parent Michael was, because when I was at Neverland and with the kids, he really was a good loving father -- they had a fantastic relationship, and they were very close-knit. So to see Paris come on in such an emotional moment and obviously give her heart out to her father was very, very touching."

NYDailyNews.com reporters Joe Kemp and Rich Schapiro wrote the day after the memorial: "The two-hour ceremony inside Los Angeles' Staples Center was more subdued than spectacular, with little of the high drama that marked Jackson's remarkable life and sad death. There were somber speeches, soulful ballads and no shortage of superlatives. Usher broke down and Brooke Shields fought to keep her composure. Thunderous applause shook the packed coliseum when Motown Records founder Berry Gordy said Jackson's nickname didn't do him justice."

Meanwhile, the city of Los Angeles was begging for donations to cover the event's $1.4 million cost.

An ancient Brit praised Michael's popularity: "As an Ancient Brit, and a fan of MJ, I find it extremely saddening that a person with so much talent has had such a strife-torn life. Money and success do not go hand-in-hand with happiness and peace of mind. Michael gave so much of himself in his performances that it is inconceivable that there was so much mental torment behind the front. His popularity has soared since his demise. What a pity it deserted him when he needed it most. I still see before me a young man dancing as no other has danced, bewitching performances that were his trademark. His talent was overwhelming, unmatchable, and above all magical. One can only wish his soul peace now. But he will live on in our hearts and memories." Elites TV said: "Paris Jackson was the poignant conclusion to her father Michael's celebrated memorial service. At the same time, her few words served as a painful reminder of the conflicted legacy that, as some proclaim, the greatest entertainer of all time leaves behind in the wake of his sudden, tragic and mysterious death. In Michael Jackson's passing, this international icon casts as many if not more unanswered questions about the out of the ordinary life he led behind the curtain of his private stage."

The Rev. Al Sharpton said: "Michael Jackson made culture accept a person of color way before Tiger Woods, way before Oprah Winfrey, way before Barack Obama. Michael did with music what they later did in sports, and in politics and in television. No controversy will erase the historic impact." Many people have speculated that Paris Jackson's tearful speech at her late father's memorial was planned. Rev. Al Sharpton insisted it was impromptu. He told CNN's Larry King on

Tuesday night: "That touched everyone. And I think you couldn't script that. She's not reading a prompter. This is a young lady, in fact, if you saw it, they had really said they wanted Janet Jackson to speak. And Janet kind of brought her forward. And she spoke from the heart about her father. I think she's worried [about] the whole world [understanding] how human Michael Jackson was." The producer of the memorial, Ken Ehrlich, told CNN's Wolf Blitzer the day of the memorial: "A lot of the show was not scripted. Music was laid out, but most of the speakers really spoke from their heart, people who knew Michael well, and I think that's what gave the show its heart." Ken explained that the Jackson family told him, "we don't want to do a TV show, we want to do a memorial service." Ken said: "We hope you got the feeling you were watching a memorial service."

Michael's chef, Douglas Jones has claimed that he saw the star's personal physician, Dr. Conrad Murray, taking out oxygen tanks from his mansion. He told the National Enquirer after Michael's death: "On two separate occasions, I saw Dr. Murray pushing oxygen tanks through the kitchen and outside to the back of the house. The tanks were large, heavy-duty, four-foot green and silver tanks. Dr. Murray pushed the tanks through the kitchen where I was preparing lunch, and out the back door." He added: "I did watch what he did with them, but I thought it was odd, and in light of what I know now, it's obvious something was going on that was probably illegal." The chef revealed that he saw oxygen tanks stored on the premises. Oxygen is required to administer the anaesthetic Diprivan, and if what Douglas is saying is correct, it could prove devastating for Dr. Murray. His claims might add weight to the theory that Michael was being treated with a potentially deadly drug.

To some people Dr. Klein is just a creep. Why would a doctor be on television revealing any details about his patient's medical history? The esteemed doctor and supposed friend of Michael was on CNN television discussing his medical history with Larry King on Larry King Live, aired July 8, 2009. Dr. Arnold Klein has been dubbed "Dermatologist to the Stars." Dr. Klein is accredited with revolutionizing Botox with injectable fillers. The doctor is a board certified medical doctor, specializing in dermatology and cosmetic surgery. The interview is exclusive and reveals information about Michael's medical past. Patients are still protected under the health information privacy act (HIPA) even after they die. Dr. Arnie Klein talked with Larry about his friendship with Michael of almost 25 years and the loss that has left him devastated. Some people may disagree with Dr. Klein making some personal information public. Dr. Klein, professor of medicine and dermatology at UCLA, felt Michael's skin condition has been spoken about, but many people never believed the problems Michael was facing.

Larry King, host, said: "Tonight, a prime time exclusive -- Michael Jackson's doctor breaks his silence, answering the questions everyone wants answered." Larry asked how Michael and Dr. Klein met. Dr. Klein told Larry: "I met Michael because someone had brought him into my office. And they walked into the room with Michael. And I looked one... took one look at him and I said, 'you have lupus erythematosus'. Now, this was a long word." Larry: "Lupus?" Dr. Klein: "Lupus, yes. I mean, because he had red... a butterfly rash and he also had severe crusting you could see on the anterior portion of his scalp. I mean, I always am very visual. I'm a person who would look at the lips of Mona Lisa and not see her smile. I would see the lips." Dr. Klein told Larry that Michael came to visit him because of the problems he had with his skin. A very close friend of Michael had told him to go and visit a doctor. Dr. Klein: "And many people made fun of him."

Dr. Klein used to remember Michael tried to clean off his skin. He'd gone to these doctors that really hurt him very much. Dr. Klein said: "And he was exquisitely sensitive to pain." When Michael came in and Dr. Klein saw Michael's skin, he knew what Michael needed. "He had several things wrong with his skin." So the doctor said to Michael: "And you have thick crusting of your scalp, and you have some hair loss." Michael asked how he knew about all this. Dr. Klein: "I said, because it's the natural course of lupus. So I then did a biopsy. I diagnosed lupus. And then our relationship went from there."

Dr. Klein told Larry, he saw Michael a few days before he died: "He came to me because, basically, I was sort of rebuilding his face, because he had severe acne and scarring. He had scarring from having a lot of cosmetic surgery. And my expertise is, like it is with every one of my patients. My patients are my treasures. And I was rebuilding his face so he looked much more normal. And contrary to what people said, he could not take off his nose. His nose was attached. But it looked too small. And I just was trying to get him ready to do the concert, because in the way he looked in his face, he wanted it to be absolutely as perfect as it could be." Dr. Klein came onto the scene long after Michael had begun plastic surgery. Dr. Klein: "In fact, what I wanted to do is, you know, stop it, because I felt that, you know, we were losing body parts in the situation." Larry asked: "Do you know why, he was such a good-looking young man, why he even started the plastic surgery?" Dr. Klein: "I don't know because I can't definitively say. But I know that people made fun -- or family members -- of the size of his nose. He was very sensitive to that. And so he (was) doing cosmetic surgery." Dr. Klein told Larry: "Plastic surgery, it's unfortunate. If you want it done, there's someone who will do it."

Dr. Klein told Michael was dancing in his office, the last time he visited. He said: "He was in very good physical condition. He was dancing for my patients. He was very mentally aware when we saw him and he was in a very good mood, because he was very happy and..." Larry: "Was it good?" Dr. Klein: "It was a very, very happy mood." Larry asked if Dr. Klein was shocked when he died. Dr. Klein: "Oh, I sat and, I remember when I found out. I sat at my desk. For about five hours, I couldn't move, because I was very close to him. And it's not just because he's Michael Jackson, probably the most talented actor, or, excuse me, performer of our age. I mean when I lose anyone that I know I go, having lost my brother and my father when I was in medical school, I don't do well with death." When Larry asked Dr. Klein if he saw any evidence of needle marks that his body was riddled with, on this visit, Dr. Klein told Larry he did not examine his entire body. Dr. Klein: "I never saw needle marks on his body. I mean I never saw them. But I could tell you... but I didn't see a riddling of anything. People sound like he looked like he was made of, you know, there were holes in him. And there weren't anything like that. He wasn't emaciated. I mean, I know dancers because I've worked with dancers many times and dancers are very concerned about their weight. And so I knew that he always wanted to be thin. And I talked to him about eating enough and making sure he didn't over exercise, as some dancers, in order to remain thin, will over dance, in order to keep their weight down."

Larry wanted to know if Dr. Klein prescribed any pain killing medications. Dr. Klein said: "I mean I've some sedatives for, you know, when he had surgical procedures that were immense." He told Larry that Michael had a serious burn when he was burnt on the Pepsi commercial and was dealing with the severe hair loss when he contracted lupus. Dr. Klein: "So when you have to fix all these areas, you have to sedate him a little bit. But if you took all the pills I had given him in the last year at once, it wouldn't do anything to you."

Dr. Klein explained Larry how he, on occasion, gave Michael Demerol to sedate him: "And that was about the strongest medicine I ever used." Larry asked if Dr. Klein had worked with addicts. Dr. Klein said: "I wrote a book on heroin addiction. And I mean I think what's happening with drugs now is a disaster. I mean, when you look at the actor from the 'Batman' [movie]. I mean, look what happened to him." He added: "You have him. You have Michael. And the thing to remember from this, you have all these drugs now that they're being prescribed, the pills, like OxyContin, available on our high school campuses. And I think we have to do something about the ready availability of these drugs." Dr. King told Larry he knew, Michael at one time, had an addiction. Michael went to England and he withdrew that addiction at a secure setting, where he went off of drugs altogether. "And what I told Michael when I met him in this present situation when I was seeing him, that I had to keep reducing the dosage of what he was on, because he came to me with a huge tolerance level."

Dr. Klein is admitting he knew Michael was using drugs. Dr. Klein: "I mean, when you take drugs repeatedly, if you're..., unless you have something like a kidney stone for it, you may require some larger doses than normal. The other thing that you have to remember, when you're using certain drugs, you have what are called active intermediates. And what these are is, it takes a long time for the body to adjust. There are certain drugs, like they've been talking about Diprivan. It's a wonderful drug when used correctly." Larry: "It is. And it's used by anesthesiologists." Dr. Klein: "Right, because it's a very short-acting drug. It's very..., metabolized very quickly." Larry: "And you go to sleep." Dr. Klein: "You go to sleep and it's gotten rid of from the body very quickly." Larry asked Dr. Klein what would Diprivan be doing in someone's house? Dr. Klein: "I have no idea. And that's what doesn't make sense to me. And it's like anything I mean, it's the danger of all these substances that are available that people can get, because the very rich and the very poor, the very, well, the rich and the famous can buy anything they want to buy. I knew at one point that he was using Diprivan when he was on tour in Germany. And so he was using it, with an anesthesiologist, to go to sleep at night. And I told him he was absolutely insane. I said you have to understand that this drug, you can't repeatedly take. Because what happens with narcotics, no matter what you do, you build a tolerance to them."

Larry asked Dr. Klein if he is surprised that Diprivan was found in Michael's home, supposedly? Dr. Klein: "I am very shocked by it. But I have to tell you that it's not something that would be unheard of because I told him that this drug was very dangerous to use on a regular basis." He further added: "I spent half a year living with heroin addicts and writing a book about my experiences when I was in medical school, when I went to England after the death of my father and brother. And what I learned from experience is you couldn't really ever be assured that you're getting honest information from someone who is an addict." Larry: "Yes. Because they lie." Dr. Klein: "Well, they lie, because they want to procure medication."

It looks like almost everybody around Michael knew he was using some kind of drugs, but nobody took the responsibility to help him or talk about it. As we know now Michael refused any help. Larry asked Doctor Arnold Klein if he had seen any I.V. type equipment in Michael's house?" Dr. Klein said: "Never." Larry asked: "Did you ever see Diprivan in his home? Did you ever see it anywhere..." Dr. Klein: "No." Larry: "...associated with him?" Dr. Klein: "I mean I never did. And I also told him specifically the dangers of the Diprivan. The dangers of it being used by someone who is not an anesthesiologist."

The fact that friends of Michael knew he was on drugs would suggest that long time friend Dr. Klein knew his problems and maybe could have helped him. But instead Dr. Klein had no clue whether Michael was doing something wrong. Larry asked Dr. Klein if Michael had problems with sleeping. Dr. Klein: "Not that I knew of, except that once we went on tour with him. We were in Hawaii. He couldn't get to sleep. Me and my whole office went to sleep in the room with him. So I never knew that he had a problem with sleep until this whole tour came up or basically this problem with sleep at that time. I did know that he did certain, you know, local anesthesia. But this is not something we discussed repeatedly, except I just got shocked. He assured me he had stopped." Larry wanted to know more and asked: "And he never asked you to administer it, did he?" Dr. Klein: "No. I mean..." Larry: "And you wouldn't, I guess? That's an..." Dr. Klein: "It's not what I do."

Larry: "No, I know." Dr. Klein: "I'm a doctor. I'm a dermatologist."

Larry told Dr. Klein at least five doctors reportedly now were under investigation. He asked Dr. Klein if he has been contacted by any authorities, police or anyone? Dr. Klein: "The only thing I've done is I've turned my records, a long time ago, over to the medical examiner. I've not been contacted by the medical examiner." Larry: "Nothing with regard to this?" Dr. Klein: "No, sir." Larry: "Do you know anything about these doctors, supposedly?" Dr. Klein: "I know there are supposed doctors. I know there's various doctors who went on tour with him. I mean, I know there were a few doctors. I specifically don't remember their names. But I think they're going to review the records and go over specifically what happens. But you have to go back historically. What happened to Kanye West's mom? What happened to his mother? She died during surgery. How many people really have this problem when they have, you know, when they die during surgery, for whatever the reason is, whether or not they have liposuction. Then they sit around with a dead person and..." Larry: "Are there a lot of doctors practicing who shouldn't?" Dr. Klein: "Well, I don't want, that's..." Larry: "Would you guess?" Dr. Klein: "I would say there's certainly a large number of people. I don't think it's huge. But I'd say a significant number of doctors, where you really have to wonder what they're doing, because a lot of people have come into my field, which is mainly based in aesthetics, because I think it's the only place they belong, for untold reasons."

Larry also asked: "What is Vitiligo?" Dr. Klein: "It's a loss of pigment cells. For every 36 normal cells in your body, you have one pigment cell pumping pigment into them. Unfortunately, it's an autoimmune disease and lupus is an autoimmune disease. And they tend to go together, because you make antibodies against your pigment cells." Larry: "Did Michael have it?" Dr. Klein: "Absolutely. We biopsied." Larry: "What causes it?" Dr. Klein: "It's caused by your immune system and your immune system destroying your pigment cells." Larry: "Do black people have it more than white people?" Dr. Klein: "No. But it's just more visible on black people, because they have a dark skin. The other thing is, it certainly occurs with a family history. And I believe one of Michael's relatives did, in fact, have Vitiligo." Larry: "How bad was his?" Dr. Klein: "Oh, his was bad because he began to get a totally speckled look over his body. And he could..." Larry: "All over his body?" Dr. Klein: "All over his body, but on his face significantly; on his hands, which were very difficult to treat." Larry: "So let's clear up something. He was not someone desirous of being white?" Dr. Klein: "No. Michael was black. He was very proud of his black heritage. He changed the world for black people. We now have a black president." Larry: "So your decision there was he would go light?" Dr. Klein: "Well, yes, that's ultimately what the decision had to be, because there was too much Vitiligo to deal with and..." Larry: "Otherwise, he would have looked ridiculous?" Dr. Klein: "Well, you can't, he would have to wear heavy, heavy makeup on stage, which would be ridiculous. And he couldn't really go out in public without looking terribly peculiar."

Larry wanted to know if Michael still had hair. Dr. Klein: "He had lost a great deal of it. You forget this first fire..." Larry: "That was the Pepsi fire, right?" Dr. Klein: "Yes. But then what happened is he used a great deal of what are called tissue expanders in his scalp, which are balloons that grow up, blow up the scalp. And then what they do is they try to cut out the scar. Well, because he had lupus, what happened is every time they would do it, the bald spot would keep enlarging. So, I mean, he went through a lot of painful procedures with these tissue expanders until I put a stop to it. I said no more tissue expanders, because he had to wear a hat all the time and it was really painful for him." Larry: "So what would his..., without the hat, what would he look like?" Dr. Klein: "Well, he had a big raised ball on the top of his head because of this device. It would expand the tissue, which you cut out." Larry: "Did you see him one other time?" Dr. Klein: "Of course I did. But he would have a stretch back on the scar. I mean the scar would get worse after they removed it. And I had to put a stop to it. So I told Michael, we have to stop this. And that's when I fired this plastic surgeon altogether. And I said I can't deal with this anymore. We're going to deal with me as your doctor or you're going to have to find another doctor if you want to work with him."

Larry asked if Dr. Klein could tell us some more about the changes Michael made on his face. Dr. Klein: "Well, I mean, I didn't know a whole lot through the whole changing face schedule, because I'm telling you that when I met him, he had done a decent bit of surgery by then. I know..." Larry: "Was it done poorly?" Dr. Klein: "Well, it's not done poorly, but I think that there's a time, the magic is not knowing when to begin the big game. The secret is knowing when to end it. And I think that he believed that his face was a work of art, which is fine with me. But I think at one point that I wanted to stop the doctors from continuing it. Because it wasn't the doc, Michael, I think, that wanted all these things. It was the surgeon who kept doing it. So I got rid of the surgeon." Larry: "The surgeon got him to do it?" Dr. Klein: "No, he did some of it himself. But he didn't know, the surgeon did not know when to stop doing it. The judgment call there was..." Larry asked Dr. Klein if Michael was going too far. Dr. Klein said: "I stopped him from going to the surgeon because I said this isn't working anymore, you have to stop it. And what I spent the last part of the year doing is rebuilding a lot of things that I thought were done poorly. And to look at it, because I didn't think he, he had a... OK, to him, his face was a work of art. You want to talk about Andy Warhol's work of art. And there are women in Paris and elsewhere, and men, who do works of art. Some of them implant things under their skins through surgeries." Larry: "But there are plastic surgeon addicts, right, people who keep going?" Dr. Klein: "Yes. And there are also people who are..., it's called a dysmorphic disorder, that you don't like the way you look, which represents 18 percent of patients that see a doctor." Larry: "You can be beautiful, but look in the mirror and not think you're beautiful." Dr. Klein: "Oh, absolutely." Larry: "Do doctors take advantage of somebody then?" Dr. Klein: "Well, I don't take advantage of anyone because I think that..." Larry: "But do..., does some doctors?" Dr. Klein: "I think some doctors do, because I think there's so much distortion going around. I mean, you know, you have to understand, just go around and look at the lips that you see around this city. You know, when you go out for dinner and you see these women who create these lips. When I invented lip augmentation in '84, I had no idea what I was doing, in the sense that I had no idea it would become the number one use of soft tissue agents. And when I see these people walking around with lips that look more like something, you know, something that belongs below the waist." Larry agreed and said they look ridiculous. Dr. Klein: "It's ridiculous, but you know..." Larry: "OK." Dr. Klein: "You can't, here's the thing." Larry: "Why?"

Dr. Klein: "You have to restore a face. You don't want to renovate it. You don't want to make people look like they're..." Larry: "Why did he wear the mask?" Dr. Klein: "He wore the mask because it sort of became like the white glove. He would..."Larry: "Oh, it was a... It was a gimmick." Dr. Klein: "A gimmick. He had no reason other than to wear the mask than gimmickry." Larry: "He also had his children wear masks." Dr. Klein: "No, he didn't have them, that goes to the Bashir interview. We have to talk a little bit about that."

This conversation with Dr. Klein is important because when Dr. Klein answered the question about the clothing Michael's kids had to wear, Larry didn't really knew how to react. Dr. Klein was trying to explain Larry why Michael's kids had to wear masks. The reason was to cover their faces for the press. Dr. Klein expressed disgust over the swirling pedophile media coverage on Michael after the Bashir interview. A few days after Larry's Talk Show Larry King Live aired, CNN removed portions of the transcript, available at CNN.com. Dr. Klein told Larry that famed mentalist Uri Geller wanted and received money for Michael's interview in 2003. The following portion of text is not available anymore; Dr. Klein to Larry: "That Bashir, Martin Bashir did an interview on him, remember?" Larry: "Oh, yes." Dr. Klein: "OK. That..." Larry: "Right. Yes." Dr. Klein: "OK, Uri Geller sold Michael Jackson to Bashir for $200,000 (£122,000). That's how much he got paid to do that interview, Uri Geller. And in that interview, Michael was sort of assured that he'd paint him as a normal person. And they painted him as an absolute strange person." Larry: "Yes, they did." The transcript continues further in the conversation, starting here; Dr. Klein said to Larry King: "And I think in that interview, when he had the kids walking down the street with masks on, with like nylon masks on their face, the only time with masks they ever..., and they used to come to my house. And they used to come. They loved my dogs. I used to go over to their house. I've never seen the children wearing those strange masks they had them walking down the street with, ever." Larry: "Huh."

Dr. Klein explained in the conversation he was doing difficult restoration work on Michael's face. Larry King asked what was wrong with Michael's nose. Dr. Klein answered: "I originally didn't think there was much wrong with his nose." Larry: "Yes." Dr. Klein: "I thought he had a nice-looking nose. But in the beginning, it was never able to come off his body. But it got to the point where it was far too thin. It didn't look natural to me." Larry: "Now, you helped him rebuild it?" Dr. Klein: "I rebuilt it, yes." Larry: "How?" Dr. Klein: "Using fillers. I used Rezulin. I used hydronic acids because, and they worked very well. And it's not, it's an arduous procedure, because you don't want to put too much in. And you have to do it exactly, so you can flow the material so it's perfectly smooth. So we rebuilt them. And I'm telling you that he was beginning to look like the nose was normal again. And that's all I wanted, and regain the breathing, you know, passages of his nose, because there was a total collapse of the cartilage." Larry: "In the last photos that we've seen, his nose has been built up, right? He's looking better?" Dr. Klein: "Yes." Larry wanted to know if Michael was still working on restoring his face? Dr. Klein said: "No, because I think we got to the point where he was very happy with the way he looked and he filled in the cheeks a little bit and did a lot of little things. But I mean what I do to an individual patient is what I do. And what I do is just restoration work, because I don't think people should look, again, like anything has been altered.

Larry: "Well, you're -- you're not a plastic surgeon." Dr. Klein: "No, but..." Larry: "So are you extending yourself when you're doing a nose like that?" Dr. Klein told Larry he was the creator of this kind of cosmetic surgery. "I invented all this, I invented injectable aesthetics, I mean, for better or for worse, it's what I've been doing since 1979. So I'm not extending myself whatsoever. But if you ask a plastic surgeon, he'll say he invented everything, including the wheel."

About the fact that people have access to pills and drugs, Dr. Klein said: "The FDA is run, more or less, by the drug companies. When you look at toxins now, the various toxins you use that relax muscles, if you read the black box FAA warning, the warning in Canada is to the patients, they're given it to them. There is a warning in Germany, and also in England. But the warnings here are only to the doctors who don't know what they're doing to begin with. Because what doctor isn't injecting a toxin? So I think what we adequately have to do is teach doctors how to do it. The other thing is with these toxins, a lot of the science of research are done by doctors or even licensed Americans or foreign countries. How can you trust the data? Some of this data has been altered. So I'm in a war, yes. I'm working with a congressman and with a member of the House of Representatives, as well as the FBI and Justice Department to change this from happening because I think that the most important thing is patients."

Larry asked Dr. Klein if Michael was a bright man. Dr. Klein said: "Michael was probably one of the most talented people because there are producers who he gave ideas to, who told me if only they had listened to him. But he wasn't educated in the way that we're standardly educated." Larry also talked about Debbie Row:

"Was that a real love affair?" Dr. Klein: "I don't know what love is in that sense of the imagination. I think that she loves him very much. She admired him very much. But if you think they're riding off in a horse-drawn carriage, I mean we have to put -- what is a normal relationship? I think she cared for his welfare. Larry: "It was not a sexual relationship?" Dr. Klein: "I think they did have sex." Larry: "You do?" Dr. Klein: "Yes, I really do, and I can't guarantee that. I think they did have sex in their relationship." Larry: "You think Michael ever had sex to father the children?" Dr. Klein: "I don't know that answer... You can't guarantee that. You can only guarantee things you see. I don't want to make any suppositions about anything in this interview, because I want this to be as truthful as possible. I think they did have sex in the relationship. I don't know the answer, and I don't want to make any suppositions in this interview..."

Larry asked Dr. Klein point-blank if he was the donor of Michael's children. Dr. Klein could not look at Larry but he said: "I'm not going to answer the way you want me to answer it." Dr, Klein asked Larry: "Do you want to hear no? All that is important is how Michael loved these children. I once donated sperm to a bank. The best to my legal knowledge, I am not the father." Dr. Klein told Larry the authorities could take a DNA sample. "They can have my DNA at this point." And about Michael's children, "These are the brightest children I ever met." Dr. Klein complained the salacious coverage was over the top. Dr. Klein: "Now this is a little bigger because they're following me for a change but I think it's all, it's sensationalism, but it's happening to the world. We should more worry about what's happened at the FDA and drugs existing all over the playgrounds of high schools than what's happening to this, me." The doctor did not attend the memorial. He told Larry: "I couldn't, I watched it on television and it was still too emotional for me. Because I understand that's who he was. I thought it was a very beautiful service. I know you were there, but you know, services like that, my father was a rabbi and I do not do well at memorial services."

Dr. Cyril Wecht, a leading forensic pathologist, strongly believes the medic who provided Michael with drugs like Diprivan should be prosecuted. Dr. Wecht said: "They're drugs to be administered by an anesthesiologist or a trained anesthetist; it is to be given only in a hospital setting... also it must be given under highly aseptic technique because it is susceptible to bacterial contamination. For all of these reasons, if any doctor prescribed Propofol for Michael Jackson to take at home himself... in my opinion, that is gross wanton negligence and really approaches a question, legally, of manslaughter."

Weeks after Michael's death, his record sales continued to soar. The LA Times said Michael's sold nine million records around the world since his death. Billboard said that Michael sold 1.1 million for the week total, physical and digital album equivalents. The story said, "Michael sold 400,000 copies in the chart half-week immediately after his death, and then 800,000 last week, with a total since his death, three weeks ago, of about 2.3 million. Digital sales were high last week because retailers ran out of physical product. Now they are back in the pipeline."

Nielsen SoundScan said Jackson's albums sold 1.1 million copies over the last seven days and had combined to sell an impressive 2.3 million in the U.S. in the nearly three weeks since he died. Meanwhile, the New York Times reported similarly that Michael sold 1.1 million copies of his solo albums. They said: "Almost 1.9 million tracks, separate from albums, were sold as digital downloads. It makes it sound as if Michael sold another 200,000 albums' worth digitally." Ben Sisario of Nytimes.com wrote: "Sales were spurred by the Jackson memorial service in Los Angeles on July 7, which had a television audience of more than 31 million. Still, the numbers are extraordinary. In the two and a half weeks following Mr. Jackson's death on June 25 his fans snapped up 2.3 million albums, 17 percent more than in 2007 and 2008 combined. For the third week Mr. Jackson's *Number Ones* (Epic) was the best-selling album in the country, moving 349,000 copies. *Thriller* (Epic) sales rose 144 percent last week, to 264,000. But most Jackson titles are ineligible for the Billboard 200, the standard album chart, since they are more than 18 months old. Instead they dominate that magazine's catalog chart, where the Top 12 slots this week are all Jackson-related. (Last week Motown released a new collection of early Jackson tunes, *The Stripped Mixes*; it reached number 95 on the Billboard 200, with a little less than 5,000 in sales.) In the last few weeks the purchasing habits of Mr. Jackson's fans have shifted from downloads to the physical CD. In the week that ended June 28, 57 percent of Mr. Jackson's album sales were downloads, an extremely high proportion. The next week the ratio was 18 percent, and last week it fell to 10 percent; so far in 2009 downloads account for about 23 percent of album sales for all artists."

Michael's sister Janet was shocked at her brother's state after visiting his mansion in Las Vegas at the beginning of this year. Janet thought Michael was looking emaciated and found the barely-furnished home 'creepy'. She called on two of her Jackson brothers to come to the house and convince Michael he needed to get help for his huge drug problem. But Michael ordered his security to turn his brothers away at the door. The intervention never happened. Miko Brando was aware the family attempted an intervention at Michael's home just months before he died. The son of late actor Marlon Brando said to CNN: "I heard about it. But I wasn't there." About Michael's weight he told: "Michael was not unusually thin. Michael has always been thin. He has never been overweight. He always looked the same." Miko also rejected rumors he may be the real father of Michael's second son Prince Michael II. He said: "Absolutely not." About Michael's drug abuse he added: "It hurts me. It's ridiculous. Michael was just a wonderful, honest, nice friend, always there when you needed it."

Daily News reported that Martin Greenfield, 80, wasn't allowed to meet the King of Pop. Martin, a Brooklyn tailor-to-the-stars, has fitted Paul Newman, Frank Sinatra, Jerry Lewis, Patrick Ewing, Conan O'Brien and Bill Clinton. It didn't prepare him for working for Michael. "Michael doesn't do Brooklyn," handlers had explained. Martin Greenfield used Michael's stylist as a stand-in and he could only look at photographs of the star. The tailor delivered a blue Italian silk suit that Michael wore at a rehearsal two days before he died. Greenfield told Daily News: "There was nothing quite like making suits for Michael Jackson, and in the end, there was nothing sadder." Chelsea stylist Zaldy, who uses only his first name, showed up at Greenfield's Varet St. factory. He explained that there would be no Michael, no fittings, no similarly sized suits to work from, and not even measurements. Greenfield's son, Jay, asked him: "How can we make his costumes if we can't get his sizes?" Zaldy explained: "Simple. He is my size, and if it fits me, it will fit him." Workers of Greenfield made a muslin and the stylist flew to Los Angeles. He draped it over Michael and took photos. With the photos he returned to Brooklyn. The article stated that when the family was handed the pictures, Michael's head had been cut off. The family made a better-fitting muslin and the stylist shuttled to Los Angeles again. At the end Michael was happy with the results. He wore his clothes on his last rehearsals.

It's clear that Michael scored various drugs. He did not only asked for medication from his own doctors, but Michael knew also his way around various dental offices. In the Las Vegas Review-Journal it was reported that Michael had 'doctor shopping' down to a science. The doctor, who spoke on the condition of anonymity, said Michael called once and complained of a sore throat and cough. However, the doctor didn't believe him. He came to the conclusion that it was a ploy to score prescription drugs. The doctor: "It was all a lie. They just wanted drugs. They wanted me to call in all these pills under someone else's name." He also felt intimidated by Michael's handlers and started to shake. In November 2003 a friend of one of the doctor's patients called and said: "Michael is sick. Could you treat him?" When the doctor arrived in Michael's suite, the residence had been trashed. Michael who was in his suite in The Mirage in Vegas insisted on getting some drugs and the doctor didn't know what to say. He told Michael's man in charge, "I can't do that." The handler looked surprised and said: "What you mean, they always do that." The doctor felt the whole thing was staged. Michael was giving his daughter, Paris, 5 years old, a face, a gesture. She said, 'I love you, Daddy.' Michael also turned to his oldest son, Prince Michael, who was 6 years old. Also he said, 'I love you, Daddy.' The doctor said he was convinced the interaction was rehearsed for his benefit and shook his head in disbelief. "I'll see what I can do," the doctor said just before he left. He told Michael's handler, "came up to me and put a finger in my chest and said 'You *do* that.' I was waiting for someone to jump out of bushes and say 'You've been punked.' I felt I was on *Candid Camera*," the physician told Las Vegas Review-Journal. The doctor is convinced Michael had "classic signs of autism." The doctor also said that, "Doctor-shopping has become very common. It's Elvis Presley all over again."

Tito Jackson, 55, revealed in an interview to Britain's Daily Mirror, on June 15, that he and his siblings were so convinced that Michael was abusing prescription drugs, they once forced an intervention at Neverland Ranch. "We had to act," Tito said. "It was me, my sisters Janet, Rebbie and La Toya, and my brothers Jackie and Randy. We bust right into the house and he was surprised, to say the least. Not to mention firmly in denial. We went into one of his private rooms and had a discussion with him. Some of us were crying. We kept asking him if it was true what we had heard that he was using drugs. He kept denying it. He said we were overreacting." The family never saw Michael on drugs, not once." He didn't want his family to know anything about that part of him. He did almost everything in his power to make sure we didn't know. We didn't know what to believe. We didn't take what Michael said as the truth." The siblings' intervention was the third attempt to try and reach out to Michael. Neverland Ranch staff had already before barricaded the roads leading into the property. Guards had blocked the family's entrance and were preventing them from stepping foot on the estate. The family remained unconvinced by Michael's denials. Tito: "Before the intervention attempt, I would never go to him and say, 'Are you still doing it?' I would just say, 'Are you sure you're fine?' He'd say, 'I'm fine, TT'. He knew what I meant, he knew I was talking about drugs."

Tito wasn't sure whether it was "some kind of conspiracy." He and other family members were sure that the staff was operating under strict orders from his brother. "After that occasion we tried many times, but his team of people just shut us out, they would not let us close. They literally shut us out. I do know that Michael would say to them, 'I don't care who it is, don't let anybody on my property if they haven't called first.'" Tito isn't sure his brother is killed: "I don't know whether he was killed or not. But I would say that sometimes he had people around him that were not in his best interests. Whether his death was an accident or whether it was deliberate, something has gone on and we need to get to the bottom of it." About Michael's plastic surgery he told Daily Mirror: "Michael's plastic surgery started around 1979, when he went solo. It was just something that a lot of entertainers were doing at the time. He never told me why, but I think he thought it would improve his looks. It wasn't a big deal having lip jobs, nose jobs or butt implants, especially living in California. He was forever trying to improve his looks. In a way, it was sad." Tito told that Michael did not wanted to grow old: "He didn't want to turn into someone who couldn't make it up the stairs or couldn't make it to the bathroom. But I don't think losing his life at an early age was part of his plan, either."

Some people could not believe Oprah didn't say anything about Michael's death in public. Michael who once invited Oprah to his house decided to say nothing about Michael's passing. Gigi posted her emotional reaction on everythingoprah.com saying: "I am VERY upset at Oprah for her silence on Michael Jackson. It speaks VOLUMES. If President Obama, Former President Nelson Mandela, Elizabeth Taylor, Liza Minelli, Diana Ross, Quincy Jones, and on and on and on, can make the TIME and offer their PUBLIC condolences either in person or by formal letter (during the Memorial Service) to the family, friends, and fans of Michael, then why hasn't she? Those very people listed are people even SHE highly respects. MJ literally changed the world and broke down many cultural barriers, allowing people like HER (and ME-of color) to be on a talk show in the first place. I find her silence cruel. I love Oprah to death, but the more I ask various people (of the black community) what they think about her silence, I have been told (mainly by black women) that they feel betrayed, disappointed, and think that she is doing this because she still believes that he really was a child molester, even though he was proven innocent by 12 jurors. That case was a joke. There never was any actual evidence. It was all based on hearsay. I think MJ was a constant target for financial blackmail, and was too (emotionally speaking) child-like and naive to understand or believe that he was putting himself in a very bad situation by always trying to personally involve himself in various children's problems (terminally ill, mentally challenged, disabled, etc.), and surrounding himself with all kinds of people he didn't know that well. Never did a child initiate accusing him of anything or wanted to testify against him; it always seemed like an adult relative of that child was the one pursuing fame and a financial windfall."

A concerned Elizabeth posted 5 days later this message on the same site: "To the Oprah and Michael Jackson fans. We need to write to Oprah and tell how we feel that she has not mentioned Michael Jackson at all, and that we are disappointed, I think that if we send her about 50 or more letters or emails, I think she will respond. Look, Michael died on June 25th, it is now July 18th, it's been too long. It's time we speak! If she is a Christian, and can forgive or at least tell an innocent person from a guilty one then she should know whether or not Michael or would or wouldn't harm a child."

A clip of a previously unreleased Michael Jackson song had hit the net 3 weeks after his death. In the song "A Place With No Name," Michael sings about his desire to travel to a mysterious place: "Take me to a place without no name." It is not clear when the song was recorded. The original song "A Horse With No Name" reached Number 1 on The Billboard Hot 100 chart in 1972. Already years ago, America's manager reportedly approved Michael's "A Place With No Name." Jim Morey, America's current manager, who also represented Michael in the late '80s and early '90s, told TMZ: "The band was honored that Michael chose to do their song and they hope it becomes available for all Michael's fans to hear."

At his rented Los Angeles mansion, Michael had an elaborate security system installed. Many different cameras did record the goings on in and outside the property. A police source told the National Enquirer: "It was a very sophisticated and high-tech surveillance and security system. Not only were there cameras outside the house, but there were cameras inside as well, in private locations." Family and people close to the investigation hope Michael's death, possibly his murder, was captured on these cameras. But the video has not been recovered yet. A police source said: "There are also gaps in some security camera footage stored on computer hard drives. Police are combing through personal computers recovered from the house." A source also said that investigators were also seeking a black suitcase. The large suitcase probably would contain a secret stash of powerful drugs, syringes, an IV pole and intravenous bags. It did belong to Michael.

More and more people believed that Michael could have been murdered. Bryan Monroe, the last journalist to interview Michael Jackson said: "There indeed had been concern among several family members about the circumstances around Michael's death. Some folks have hesitated to go as far as saying it was murder." The probe into Michael's death might turn into a criminal case. A source close to the family, who did not want to be identified, told CNN in the week after Michael's death: "The family is aware of a potential criminal prosecution."

On July 13, 2009, London's newspaper Daily Mail interviewed La Toya Jackson. The article by Caroline Graham said: "In a moving and revealing interview, La Toya Jackson, who was closer to her vulnerable brother than anyone else and was asked to sign his death certificate, portrayed Michael as a lonely and isolated figure at the mercy of a money-motivated clique. She accused them of cutting him off from his family and friends and forcing him, largely against his will, to sign up for the grueling commitment of 50 concerts at London's O2 arena. She believes her brother was fed addictive drugs by handlers who wanted to control his moods."

"Michael was murdered," La Toya, 53, said. Throughout a four-hour interview, which took place in Los Angeles, California, Daily Mail reporter Caroline Graham said the sister of Michael was "very candid". According to a source close to La Toya's family and another source familiar with the interview arrangements for Daily Mail, La Toya got paid to talk. However the amount of money paid was not disclosed. La Toya told her brother Michael will never be buried at Neverland, his former home in Central California. She said: "After the second [child abuse] trial, he said to me, 'I will never come back to this place again. I hate it. This place helped destroy me.' Michael hated that place."

The behavior of doctor Conrad Murray at the hospital left La Toya deeply troubled. La Toya was demanding to see Michael's doctor, who is not certified as a cardiologist, to find out 'what the hell' happened, but the doctor didn't want to identify himself. It was Michael's daughter Paris who told La Toya that the man 'dressed in white' was Michael's doctor. "There's Dr. Murray," Paris said, pointing at him, according to La Toya. Paris continued: "He's the best cardiologist in the world. How could this happen to Daddy?" La Toya told Daily Mail she approached Dr. Murray at the hospital. She told the doctor: "I want to talk to you. I want to know what happened to my brother. He mumbled a bunch of nothing." She recalled he said something like, "Michael didn't make it, I'm sorry." La Toya said that her concerns were heightened when she heard the doctor later 'disappeared'. She said: "It wasn't right. It felt weird." Another doctor had told her Michael had fresh needle marks on his body. La Toya said about the star's medical records from a series of doctors, "It will all come out. You will be shocked." She continued: "He had needle marks on his neck and on his arms and more about those will emerge in the next few weeks. I can not discuss that any further as I may jeopardize the investigation. I can, however, say that I have not changed my mind about my feeling that Michael was murdered." About the results of a second autopsy, which she arranged, La Toya said to Daily Mail: "We want to sit down and compare the two reports before anything is made public. I have a strong idea of what the outcome will be but

I cannot say anything at this stage." La Toya told the paper the family had seen results from the private autopsy it ordered. La Toya wouldn't reveal the findings but said it did reveal that four fresh needle marks were found on Michael's neck.

La Toya revealed more important information about what happened in Michael's home, the day he died. According to Daily Mail, La Toya received a troubling call from Michael's mansion when she returned from the hospital to Katherine's home. La Toya explained: "It was Michael's long-term assistant Michael Amin, a devout Muslim known as Brother Michael." Michael Amin told La Toya that Michael's self-appointed business manager Dr. Tohme Tohme had fired all the staff at the Beverly Hills property. He had also fired all the staff at a second rented home in Las Vegas. She said: "That raised my suspicions." La Toya asked rhetorically to Caroline: "I want to know how Michael died, and then, at 11 p.m. on the day he dies, all the staff are fired?" Caroline wrote: "When she arrived at the house with her manager and close friend Jeffre Phillips, new security guards were in place." La Toya said: "I could smell and sense my brother everywhere. I could smell his favorite cologne, Black Orchid by Tom Ford. I went into his bedroom. There was a shirt discarded on the floor." She told Caroline her brother must have left his own room, walked all the way across a large hall and ended up in the doctor's bed. La Toya said with visible questions on her face: "Michael walked from his room to Dr. Murray's room. What happened in there we don't know. He ended up alone in the room with the doctor. No one was allowed upstairs apart from Dr. Murray and the children. Paris has since told me that even they were not allowed in that room when Dr. Murray was giving Michael his *oxygen*."

La Toya said that shortly after midday, the doctor ran downstairs and screamed at bodyguard Alberto Alvarez to call the emergency services. According to La Toya, Dr. Murray initially gave the star CPR on the soft surface of the bed before moving him to the ground, on the instruction of the 911 emergency operator who told him the procedure needed to be conducted on a hard surface. She said: "Why, if this man was a cardiologist, was my brother on the bed? Michael was dead in that room. I was told the doctor kept telling everyone he was alive, but Brother Michael saw him and said it was obvious he was dead. There were oxygen tanks along the wall next to the dresser. There was a metal stand with a cord hanging down. The police had already been in the house and had removed all the drugs and whatever bag was hanging there."

La Toya admitted to Daily Mail that Michael had a prescription drug problem which the family believes began after he damaged his back in an on-stage accident during his 1984 Victory tour. She insisted however that she believed Michael was 'clean' in preparation for the O2 shows. "He had just been to England on a cleanse and he was drinking juices and being pure. He had cleaned everything out of his system ready to do the concerts in London," she believed. Michael was not prepared to do 50 shows. La Toya told the reporter: "It's impossible even for a healthy person to do that many shows. Michael was fragile. He always wanted to believe the best of people. But he was meek. In the last few months, he became isolated. I believe the staff were given strict instructions that if any of the family called, not to tell him. And if any of the family came by, not to let them in." She said the people around her brother Michael, "were not interested in Michael the man. They were interested in Michael the cash cow.

Michael didn't keep a close eye on his finances. A lot of people made a lot of money out of Michael. The house he was renting at the end is a classic example. It would cost $25,000 (£15,000) a month to rent but he was charged $100,000 (£60,000) a month because he was Michael Jackson. As a family, we tried to get involved. We wanted to stage an intervention. But we couldn't get near Michael. I knew something terrible was going to happen. I believe he was cut off from the real world and the drugs were a way [for his hangers-on] to get in there. They got him hooked on drugs. He was pure and clean and then drugs came back into his system. I think it shocked his system so much it killed him." La Toya also told the family will file a civil lawsuit against anyone they believe responsible. They also push for police to serve criminal charges.

Michael's sister announced: "I am going to get down to the bottom of this. I am not going to stop until I find out who is responsible. Why did they keep the family away? It's not about money. I want justice for Michael. I won't rest until I find out what, and who, killed my brother. They worked him so hard. There was no breathing room. Every hour was packed with costume fittings, vocal lessons, rehearsals. Even Paris noticed. She told me, 'They worked Daddy too hard. They worked him so hard.' When someone is fragile you can't keep them going like that. A lot of people are responsible for this, directly or indirectly. They told him, 'The shows are booked, the tickets are sold.' His kids made him so happy but he didn't have any real friends. His problem was he didn't trust people. In the end, he died a lonely man surrounded by this shadowy entourage."

La Toya, who divorced from her former manager, Jack Gordon, 12 years ago, became close again to her brother and his children in recent years. She regularly saw them at her mother's house on Hayvenhurst Avenue in Encino. The Daily Mail said: "In person, La Toya bears a disarming likeness to her more famous sibling. She speaks in the same breathy high-pitch tone. A diminutive 5ft, she, like her brother, is clearly no stranger to the plastic surgeon's scalpel. But La Toya makes a compelling witness. Two years ago, she took part in a TV reality show Armed And Famous, in which she was given basic training to be a police officer, and continues to volunteer as a deputy. And although she famously fell out with the Jackson clan in the Eighties over a book in which she described Michael as a paedophile and denounced her father Joe for bullying them as children, for the past 15 years, she has helped keep the family together." La Toya told the newspaper she last saw Michael three weeks before he died. Katherine and Joe Jackson celebrated their 60th wedding anniversary at Michael's favorite Indian restaurant, Chakra, in Beverly Hills. She told the reporter: "He was surrounded by a bad circle. Michael was a very meek, quiet, loving person. People took advantage of that. People fought to be close to him, people who weren't always on his side. Less than a month ago, I said I thought Michael was going to die before the London shows because he was surrounded by people who didn't have his best interests at heart. Michael was worth more than a billion dollars. When anyone is worth that much money, there are always greedy people around them. I said to my family a month ago, 'He's never going to make it to London.' Michael's sister also revealed Michael himself 'never believed he would live to be an old man' and feared he would die in his fifties."

La Toya, who spoke to "put the truth out there" told that Michael was, "not found in bed, as has been widely reported, but instead was inside the nearby bedroom of his personal physician Dr Conrad Murray." She told "how an intravenous drip stand was beside the bed and oxygen canisters lined the walls", and La Toya told in heartbreaking detail how she "accompanied Michael's children, Prince Michael, 12, Paris, 11, and seven-year-old Blanket, to see their father's body." The article said, La Toya, "stood with Paris over an open casket as the child gently placed an inexpensive necklace around Jackson's wrist and tenderly garlanded his body with colored play stones."

Joe Jackson blasted doctors and other hangers-on for turning Michael into a Howard Hughes-style hermit. He said Michael did cut him and his mother out of his life towards the end. "His relationship was different because he was protected by the security guards. It was not only me but Katherine too. They treated him just like they did Howard Hughes. I knew the people weren't treating him right in the beginning but there was nothing I could do, he was his own man. All of them were cheating him. When he left rehearsals he was waving and all this stuff. Then he went upstairs and this doctor was there and he must have given him something to make him rest."

Investigators have questioned and searched the offices of many doctors who treated Michael over the last years. On July 22, federal agents and Los Angeles police raided Dr. Murray's office in Houston. Dr. Murray's lawyer admitted they were looking for "evidence of the offense of manslaughter." The Associated Press reported that the Los Angeles County Coroner had ruled Michael's death a homicide after an autopsy of Michael found lethal levels of the anesthetic Propofol in his body.

Dr. Conrad Murray told cops he gave Michael 50 milligrams of Propofol every night through an IV for 6 weeks for treating insomnia. Dr. Murray told cops he feared Michael was getting addicted and decided to reduce the dosage to 25 mg. Cops found Valium, Tamsulosin, Lorazepam, Temazepam, Clonazepam, Trazodone and Tizanidine, along with 8 bottles of Propofol in Michael's house after he died, but they still don't know where it was purchased. The various drugs were mostly prescribed by Dr. Murray, Dr. Arnold Klein and Dr. Allan Metzger.

The AFFIDAVIT FOR SEARCH WARRANT stated: "I, E. G. Chance, a peace officer and employed by the Houston Police Department, do solemnly swear that I have reason to believe and do believe that evidence of the crime of manslaughter is located at a "Self Storage" facility at 2100 W. 18th Street, Unit #337, in Houston, Harris County Texas, including but not limited to billing records, medication orders, transport receipts, billing receipts, medical records, and computerized medical records, said items being implements and instruments used in the commission of a crime and property or items constituting evidence of the offense of manslaughter that tend to show that Dr. Conrad Murray committed the said criminal offense. It is believed that said location is under the care, custody and control of Sue Lyon."

In short, the papers show in detail why the doctor received the SEARCH WARRANT AND AFFIDAVIT. Some further we read: "Peace Officer Orlando Martinez, swears under oath that the facts expressed by him/her in the attached and incorporated Affidavit are true and that based thereon he/she has probable cause to believe and does believe that the articles, property, and persons described below are lawfully seizable pursuant to Penal Code Section 1524 et seq. As indicated below, and are now located at the locations set forth below. Wherefore, Affiant requests that this Search Warrant be issued."

The SEARCH WARRANT AND AFFIDAVIT of the State of California, County of Los Angeles also stated: "On June 25, 2009, at approximately 1222 hours, Los Angeles Fire Department (LAFD) Rescue Ambulance (RA) 71 responded to an emergency call at 100 North Carolwood Drive, in the city of Los Angeles. The comments of the call stated a 50 year old male was not breathing, and cardiopulmonary resuscitation (CPR) was in progress. Upon their arrival, they were met by Dr. Conrad Murray, who identified himself as the patient's personal physician. Murray informed the paramedics that the patient, later identified as Michael Joseph Jackson, had stopped breathing and Murray had continuously administered CPR until the RA's arrival. Murray told the LAFD paramedics he had given Jackson Lorazepam (Ativan) before he stopped breathing. The paramedics began caring for Jackson and transported both Murray and Jackson to UCLA Medical Center. Upon arrival Murray met with Dr. R. Cooper, the physician in charge of the emergency department. Murray told Cooper he had given Jackson 2mg doses of Lorazepam (Ativan), during the course of the night. Cooper and her team attempted to revive Jackson with negative results."

Almost 3 ½ hours after Michael stopped breathing he was pronounced death. It further stated: "Cooper pronounced Jackson's death at 1426 hours. Murray refused to sign the death certificate, and the Los Angeles Coroner's Office was summoned to the hospital. Los Angeles Police Department (LAPD) Robbery Homicide Division (RHD) Detectives Smith, Serial No. 25301, and your affiant were assigned to assist the Coroner's Office conduct a death investigation. Upon arrival at UCLA Medical Center, neither the coroner's investigators nor detectives could locate Murray to re-interview him. Repeated attempts at contacting and locating Murray were unsuccessful.

"Coroner's investigators and RHD Detectives responded to 100 North Carolwood Drive to further their investigation. A search of the residence, specifically Jackson's bedside, revealed numerous bottles of medications prescribed by Dr. Murray to Jackson, including Diazepam (Valium), Tamsulosin (Flomax), Lorazepam (Ativan) and Temazepam (Restoril). Prescription pill bottles of Clonazepam (Klonepin) and Trazodone (Desyrl), prescribed to Jackson by Dr. Metzger and a prescription pill bottle of Tizanidine (Zanaflex), prescribed to Jackson by Dr. Klein were also found at Jackson's bedside. According to the Physician's Desk Reference (PDR), most of these drugs have an indicated or off label use in the treatment of insomnia.

"On June 27, 2009, Detective Smith and your affiant met with Murray and his attorneys for an interview. Murray stated that he was Jackson's personal physician. Murray had been treating Jackson for insomnia for approximately the past six weeks. He had been giving Jackson 50 mg of Propofol (Diprivan), diluted with Licodine (Xylocaine), every night via intravenous drip (IV) to assist Jackson in sleeping. Murray felt that Jackson may have been forming an addiction to Propofol (Diprivan), an tried to wean Jackson off of the drug. On June 22, 2009, two days prior to his death, he gave Jackson 25 mg Propofol (Diprivan), along with Lorazepam (Ativan) and Midazolam (Versed). Jackson was able to sleep with this mixture of medications. On June 23, 2009, he gave Jackson Lorazepam (Ativan) and Midazolam (Versed) only, withholding any Propofol (Diprivan), and Jackson was able to sleep. On June 25, 2009, at approximately 0130 hours, he again tried to induce sleep without the Propofol (Diprivan) and gave Jackson a 10 mg tab of Valium. Jackson was unable to sleep and at approximately 0200 hours, Murray injected Jackson with 2 mg Lorazepam (Ativan) after dilution, pushed slowly into his IV. Jackson was still unable to sleep. At approximately 0300 hours, Murray then administered 2 mg Midazolam (Versed) to Jackson after dilution, also pushed slowly into his IV. Jackson remained awake and at approximately 0500 hours, Murray administered another 2 mg Lorazepam (Ativan) after dilution, pushed slowly into his IV. Jackson remained awake and at approximately 0730 hours, Murray administered another 2 mg of Midazolam (Versed), after dilution, into his IV. Murray stated he was continuously at Jackson's bedside and was monitoring him with a pulse oximeter. According to Dr. Murray, the pulse oximeter was connected to Jackson's finger and measured his pulse and oxygen statistics.

"Jackson remained awake and at approximately 1040 hours, Murray finally administered 25 mg of Propofol (Diprivan), diluted with LIDOCAINE (Xylocaine), via IV drip to keep Jackson sedated, after repeated demands/requests from Jackson. Jackson finally went to sleep and Murray stated that he remained monitoring him. After approximately 10 minutes, Murray stated he left Jackson's side to go to the restroom and relieve himself. Murray stated he was out of the room for about 2 minutes maximum. Upon his return, Murray noticed that Jackson was no longer breathing. Murray began single man cardiopulmonary resuscitation (CPR) at once. Murray also administered .2 mg of Flumanezil (Anexate) to Jackson and called Jackson's personal assistant, Michael Amir Williams, with his cellular telephone for help. Murray reached Williams and requested that he send security detail's response, he left Jackson and ran out to the hall and downstairs to the kitchen. Murray asked the chef to send up Prince Michael, the eldest son, and returned to continue CPR. P. Jackson responded upstairs and summoned the security detail. Alberto Alvarez went to the aid of Murray and called 911 via his cellular telephone. Murray waited for the ambulance's arrival while conducting CPR, assumed care from the paramedics and accompanied them to the hospital. Murray observed the treatment to Jackson at UCLA Medical Center and assisted in notifying the family after Jackson's death was pronounced. Murray left the hospital after a while because he did not know that he was needed. Murray added that his doctor's bag was still at the residence and directed your affiant to its exact location inside of Jackson's residence.

"Murray told your affiant that he was not the first doctor to introduce Jackson to Propofol (Diprivan). Murray stated that Jackson was very familiar with the drug and referred to it as his "milk". Propofol (Diprivan) has a milk appearance. Jackson would also refer to the Licodaine (Xylocaine) as "anti-burn". According to the Physician's Desk (PDR), Propofol (Diprivan) creates a burning sensation at the injection site and Licodaine (Xylocaine) can be used to relieve the discomfort. Murray stated that he had repeatedly asked Jackson what other physician's were treating him and what was being described to him, but Jackson would not tell him. Jackson did mention that Doctor Arnold Klein and Doctor Alan Metzger had given him medicine and that it was not working. Jackson told Murray about two unknown doctors in Germany whom gave him the Propofol (Diprivan). At one time Murray noticed and inquired about injection marks on Jackson's hands and feet. Jackson stated that Doctor Cherilyn Lee had been given him a "coctail" to help him. Murray believed the cocktail to be a Propofol (Diprivan) mix. Murray also recalled how sometime between March and April of this year, Jackson called him in Las Vegas and asked him to call Doctor David Adams and arrange for Doctor Adams to give Jackson Propofol (Diprivan). Murray did as Jackson asked and arranged for Doctor Adams to treat Jackson. Murray was present at a third party cosmetologist's office were Doctor Adams sedated Jackson with Propofol (Diprivan). Murray stated this was around the time that Jackson requested him to be his personal physician on the European tour.

"Your affiant obtained Murray's cellular telephone records for the early morning hours of Jun 25, 2009. In his statement, Murray estimated the time that he noticed Jackson was not breathing to be at approximately 1100 hours. Murray's cellular telephone records show Murray on the telephone, with three separate callers for approximately 47 minutes starting at 1118 hours, until 1205 hours. Murray did not mention this to the interviewing detectives.

"Your affiant authored a search warrant for the doctor's bag and supplies and on June 29, 2009, the honorable Judge C. Olmedo issued the search warrant for Jackson's residence at 100 N. Carolwood Drive. Investigators served the warrant and recovered multiple bottles/vials of Licodaine (Xylocaine), several bottles/vials of Propofol (Diprivan), bottles/vials of Lorazepam (Ativan), bottles of Midazolam (Versed), and bottles/vials of Flumazenil (Anexate). None of these items were labeled as prescribed to any patient.

"Detectives contacted the Drug Enforcement Administration (DEA) to assist in tracking the medications found at Jackson's residence. DEA agents informed your affiant Propofol is difficult to track because the lot numbers are created in large amounts and shipped from manufacturer to distributor, distributor to surgery center, hospital etc. The hospital or surgery center records would be needed to examine how many units were received and how they are accounted for. DEA advised that all doctors or nurse practitioners who prescribe medicines in California are required to obtain a "DEA" number under which they are identified during their drug orders. DEA also checked all available computer systems to determine whether Dr. Murray purchasing, ordered or obtaining any Propofol (Diprivan) under his medical license or DEA number.

"The attorney for the Jackson family members, Blair Berk, contacted your affiant and gave him the name of Dr. Randy Rosen. Jackson's relatives stated that Jackson had told them Rosen had been treating him. Jackson's family and news reporters have documented that Jackson has used the aliases of Jack London, Mike Jackson, Mick Jackson, Frank Tyson, and Mic Jackson. They also mentioned that Jackson would have prescriptions written in the name of members of his entourage. Through interviews of Jackson's staff, employees and family, investigators determined that at the time of his death, Jackson's closest circle of associates included Michael Amir Williams Muhammad, Jimmy Nicholas, Blanca Nicholas, Roselyn Muhammad, Prince Jackson, Faheem Muhammad, and Kai Chase. On July 17, 2009, detectives received a call from an unknown female caller who stated that she had information on the aliases used by Jackson when he would visit Dr. Klein. She provided the names, Omar Arnold, Fernand Diaz, Peter Madonie, and Josephine Baker as names Jackson would use when seeing Dr. Klein. Detectives recovered a prescription at

Jackson's residence in the name of Omar Arnold prescribed by Dr. Klein.

"Los Angeles County Coroner's Investigator Fleak subpoenaed medical records from Dr. Conrad Murray, Dr. Arnold Klein, Dr. Allan Metzger, Dr. David Slavit, who completed an independent medical examination of Jackson for Anschuntz Entertainment Group (AEG), Dr. Randy Rosen and nurse practitioner Cherilyn Lee.

"Some doctors provided copies to the Coroner's Office. Dr. Murray's office provided records dating back to January 11, 2006, stating Jackson used the alias of Omar Arnold, Paul Farance and Paul Farnce. Dr. Klein's office only provided records dating back to March 2009, stating Jackson used the alias Omar Arnold, and indicating, "In furtherance of our telephonic discussions, we are submitting documents pertinent to Dr. Klein's recent treatment of Mr. Jackson." Dr. Tadrissi provided medical records were Jackson used the alias Bryan Singleton and Mike Jackson. Dr. Tadrissi's records also mention that he used Dr. Adams per Jackson's request and that Jackson was given conscious sedation per his own request. At the time of this warrant, Dr. Lee and Dr. Metzger's medical records have not been received by the Los Angeles County Coroner's Office.

"Detectives Smith and Meyers interviewed Cherilyn Lee. She first met Jackson in January 2009 when she was asked to come and look at Jackson's three children, Prince, Paris and Blanket, who were suffering from colds. She conducted a routine examination on all 3 children. Lee stated that Jackson was complaining of a low energy level. She returned the next day and completed a full blood screening. Two days later the blood came back normal-low blood sugar. Lee stated that she put Jackson on a good food diet with a protein drink. On Easter Sunday, Michael complained to Lee that he had problems sleeping. Michael mentioned the drug Propofol (Diprivan). Lee stated that she was not familiar with the drug. Jackson told her that his doctor told him that it was safe. He did not mention what doctor told him this. Lee researched the drug and learned that Propofol (Diprivan) was commonly used by anesthesiologists during surgery. She stated that the drug was not good for him and that he should not take it. Lee also told detectives that Michael asked her if she could get Propofol (Diprivan) or if she knew someone that could. Michael told Lee he would pay her or another doctor whatever they wanted for it. Lee said that she could not and would not get it for him."

A search warrant authorized seizure of documents at a storage locker of Dr. Murray in Houston. Law enforcement was searching for "items constituting evidence of the offense of manslaughter that tend to show that Dr. Conrad Murray committed the said criminal offense." People from Dr. Murray's office visited the storage locker six times. The last time they visited the locker was the morning of Jackson's death.

According to a report, Michael wore a prosthetic nose. It was missing from his surgically mangled face as he laid in an Los Angeles morgue. Michael wore the prosthetic to mask the effects of decades of plastic surgery. Rolling Stone magazine said, citing witnesses who saw Michael's body on the autopsy table, that there was left behind a small, dark hole surrounded by bits of cartilage. The story was also covered by FoxNews.com and NYPost.com. Michael was notoriously shy about his appearance and tried to cover his nose with makeup for years.

Almost a month after Michael died, his former business adviser Dr. Tohme Tohme (according to an article on MSNBC.com a financier with a murky past) said he was the person who recently turned over to executors $5.5 million (£3.4 million) of Michael's money. The money which had been "a secret between Michael and me," was not recovered. Dr. Tohme said: "I had the money and I gave it to them." Michael had told him, 'Don't tell anyone about this money.' But when he passed away Dr. Tohme told Michael's executors he had this money, and he gave it to them. Dr. Tohme responded to an inquiry from The Associated Press about documents in which administrators of the estate said they had recovered $5.5 million and substantial amounts of personal property from an unnamed former financial adviser. Dr. Tohme was called out by Joe Jackson on Larry King Live. Dr. Tohme was probably afraid of being sued. This is the portion of the transcripts dealing with Dr. Tohme; Joe Jackson to Larry: "Of course I do. I want to find out all I can about his situation there with certain people. For instance, Dr. Tohme..." Larry King said: "All right." Joe continued: "Dr. Tohme, he's no doctor. And he was fired by Michael and this is a terrible guy, he got about nine, eight or nine different aliases." Larry: "We're going to do a lot more on this. Thank you both very much." According to The Associated Press, Dr. Tohme said the money, which came from recording residuals, was earmarked by Michael for the purchase of what was to be his "dream home" in Las Vegas. Dr. Tohme said he was in negotiations for the home when Michael died. He also turned over a large number of items from Michael's Neverland estate that were once scheduled to be auctioned. Dr. Tohme said he had everything put into storage, when Michael decided to call off the auction. At the end of Michael's life Dr. Tohme would server as Michael's final business manager and spokesperson. He would not reveal any information about his life or career other than to confirm that he is a United States citizen, working in the world of finance. He said he was raised in Los Angeles. He said he was not affiliated with the Nation of Islam, and actually fired some representatives of the religious sect who had taken over handling affairs for Michael. Michael always told Dr. Tohme: "I want people to really know who I am after I'm gone." The two talked about the Michael's wish to create a special place "10 times bigger than Graceland" referring to Elvis Presley's home, where fans could come to view Michael's memorabilia and awards. Michael's spiritual guru June Gatlin revealed later her client was scared of his manager. Michael revealed (on taped conversations) he was even terrified of his chief aide, Dr. Tohme Tohme. The mysterious Dr. Tohme is believed to be the mastermind behind Michael's ill-fated comeback shows in London. Michael told June: "This guy, he just... has ways about him... There's a divide between me and my representatives and I don't talk to my lawyer, my accountant. I talk to him and he talks to them. I don't like it. I wanna get somebody in there with him that I know and can trust. I don't know what's in my accounts." June told NBC: "Michael said, 'He (Dr. Tohme) is mean, he's trying to keep me and separate me from everybody and everything that I love.' He was afraid of who this man is, afraid of whatever this man may be capable of doing... He had taken over Michael's complete life." Michael severed ties with his manager in May 2009 after learning Dr. Tohme had threatened the boss of a California auction house over memorabilia items that were set to go under the hammer. Michael sent a letter to all business associates, in which he insisted: "Dr. Tohme Tohme is no longer authorized to represent me."

Dr. Conrad Murray has already been named in court papers as the subject of a manslaughter investigation into Michael's sudden death. The probe into the *Bad* singer's death has focused on Michael's use of a powerful anesthetic, Propofol, also known as Diprivan, to sleep. The drug is extremely dangerous because of it's extreme variability. Any licensed physician can give the anesthetic Propofol, but the American Society of Anesthesiologists does not recommend that doctors not trained in anesthesiology do so. Too much Propofol can lead to a drop in blood pressure and trouble breathing. Enough can be fatal.

Uri Geller told Britain's ITV1: "I have never, ever seen him take anything, but I have seen the aftermath, and the aftermath sometimes, it was devastating." Uri: "I couldn't wake Michael up one day. I said Michael, what have you done, what have you taken? Michael open your eyes. Are you OK?" Uri knew that Michael could not survive as an addict and shouted at him: "Michael, stop it! Michael, you will die! You are killing yourself!"

An expert on Propofol, Dr. Omar Manejwala of the William J. Farley Center at Williamsburg Place in Virginia told reporters Sarah Netter and Sarah Amos of ABC News, that Propofol, known by its trade name Diprivan, is a particularly dangerous drug compared with other sedatives. He said: "I would say that people die much quicker from this agent than they would from other agents." A former nurse anesthetist, Thayne Flora told reporters of Good Morning America that she first tried Propofol in the early 1990s looking for relief from chronic headaches and family problems. But she found out she soon was addicted. She said: "You know, part of it is wanting to sleep and part of it is wanting to escape from pain, emotional, physical. And it just makes you go away for a while and you don't have to cope with those things anymore."

Edward Chernoff, Dr. Murray's lawyer, responded to a story published by The Associated Press about his client's alleged administration of Diprivan to Michael. "It's a waste of time responding to all these timed 'leaks' from 'anonymous' sources," Edward wrote. "I feel like a horse swatting flies. Everyone needs to take a breath and wait for these long delayed toxicology results. I have no doubt they want to make a case, for goodness sakes, it's Michael Jackson! But things tend to shake out when all the facts are made known, and I'm sure that will happen here as well." TMZ reported earlier in the investigation of Michael's death, that there was no EKG machine or pulse oximeter found in Michael's home. Machines like these are usually used to monitor the pulse of a patient being administered Propofol.

Officials carted away evidence from Dr. Murray's Houston office and a nearby storage locker in connection with their manslaughter probe. A Drug Enforcement Agency investigator said in a press conference, following the searches of the Las Vegas home and medical office of Michael's personal physician Dr. Conrad Murray on Tuesday, July 28, that agents were searching for specific documents as part of their inquiry into the pop singer's June 25 death. Dr. Murray was said to be fully aware of the searches. DEA spokesman Jose Martinez declined to say specifically what agents were looking for. DEA Assistant Special Agent in Charge Mike Flanagan said: "Search warrants on Dr. Conrad Murray's residence and office were executed around 9 a.m. PT. Murray was at that time at home." Mike Flanagan spoke also about the logistics of executing such searches and what materials investigators might target. According to video posted on TMZ.com, Flanagan said: "In a document search warrant, you end up with documents, pieces of paper, hard drives or mirrors of those hard drives, or the computer themselves. When you're going through documents, you're going through page by page by page. It's very, very tedious. And everybody in there has the expertise to do that — what they're looking for. That's very, very time-consuming."

Members of the Las Vegas and Los Angeles DEA and both cities' police departments were involved in the searches. "DEA agents, Las Vegas police and Los Angeles detectives entered Murray's home and office early on Tuesday morning, July 28," a spokesman for the U.S. Drug Enforcement Agency and Los Angeles police said. Murray has not been detained by authorities. "This doctor is in serious trouble," criminal defense attorney Roy Black told Good Morning America in an interview. Black believes when Dr. Murray is charged it will be up to his defense to prove why he prescribed and administered a drug that is meant for use in the operating room. Black: "Propofol should not be used for insomnia." The probe into the star's death increasingly appeared to focus on whether Dr. Murray gave Michael drugs before he died. The net is tightening on Michael's doctor, who remains secluded in his Las Vegas home. People were claiming Michael used to rely on Propofol like an alarm clock. He was instructing doctors to stop the IV when he wanted to wake up. People believed Michael may have been using Propofol for the last two years. The mystery surrounding the death of pop icon Michael could hopefully soon be solved.

In an exclusive interview with the NNPA News Service, L. Londell McMillan, Michael's family attorney told: "Katherine Jackson, who is represented by myself and my team, have been in negotiations and discussions with Debbie Rowe and her lawyers." McMillan, who represented stars such as Lil Kim, Stevie Wonder, Prince, and Kanye West served as attorney for Michael for three years. Katherine Jackson had hired McMillan, a high-profile celebrity attorney to handle her legal affairs. During a critical hearing in Los Angeles they were hoping to find answers to lingering issues. McMillan said: "Mrs. Jackson and Ms. Rowe have both been conducting themselves in a very amicable, courteous manner, to do whatever is going to be done in the best interests of the children." He further said: "There have been quite a bit of back and forth and differences of opinion with respects to how Michael Jackson's business will be handled and who will control, administer and handle his business assets. And that is how the difficulty has created much concern and debate." McMillan also believes that Michael's mother should be allowed to be involved in the decisions of business affairs of the estate. Based on 2002, when that will was drafted, and June 25th of 2009, when Mr. Jackson passed away, there's been considerable amount of evidence that Mr. Jackson would not and does not want this particular estate served by individuals that were listed in 2002 without his mother having a seat at that table." He continued: "For the life of me, we are having difficulties understanding why Mr. Branca and Mr. McClain continue to object to Michael Jackson's mother serving on the trustee team with her advisers to make sure that Michael Jackson's legacy is going to be administered and controlled in a way that she knows and those that were close to Michael toward the end of his days knows what he would have wanted." He said: "To have his estate go into the hands of people from 2002 that he's ceased doing business with, and that he later had disputes with, presents challenges and problems, and it also puts a legacy issue in question. And that is what we are seeking to resolve." The interview was published in an article, written by NNPA National Correspondent Pharoh Martin on Blackpressusa.com. McMillan also said in the interview: "Michael did not have his family play a major role in his business, other than his mom. His mother is one that is a trustee and has been a trustee in his businesses and she should be a trustee in his post-death business. She's the one person that he's trusted more than anybody else in his life." McMillan is concerned that if Michael's mother is not in control of her son's legacy, the legacy will go into the wrong hands. McMillan closed the conversation, saying: "Elvis Presley's family has a seat at the table. The Beatles' family has a seat at the table. Michael Jackson's mother should have a seat at the table." Katherine Jackson's lawyer Londell McMillan also said that Michael's will may not be valid because it wasn't notarized. But, a will does not have to be notarized to be valid in California. Most formal wills are not notarized.

L.A. County Assistant Chief Coroner Ed Winter arrived at the Beverly Hills medical office of Dr. Lawrence Koplin. It seems like every doctor that ever dealt with Michael has something to hide. Celebrity deaths by drug overdose are nothing new. Dr. David Kloth, past president of American Society of Interventionism Pain Physicians and current president of Connecticut Pain Society told Newsweek: "Propofol is a medication that was invented 20 to 25 years ago for anesthesia. It's what we call a sedative hypnotic. It puts you to sleep; it makes you forget things." The drug Michael often took works quickly and leaves very little lingering effects when used correctly. Dr. Kloth: "It wears off very quickly. If someone's on a continuous drip, and you turn it off, in five or 10 minutes, they're wide awake." But Propofol wouldn't have helped his exhaustion. Dr. Kloth told reporters: "It does not cause stage 4 REM sleep. Michael Jackson was unfortunately either misinformed or misunderstood. He would actually wake unrested, because the brain did not enter the appropriate stage of sleep." Cardiac anesthesiologist Dr. Kenneth Elmassian who works at Michigan Regional Medical Center told Newsweek: "The fact that the drug was administered outside a hospital or health-care facility is 'mind-boggling'. You can't go to a pharmacist, hand a prescription over and get the drug." Dr. Kloth: "My prediction is that Michael Jackson will be deemed a polysubstance overdose. It is probably possible and probably likely that he took other medications that evening." If it turns out Michael was improperly supervised while on Propofol, Dr. Kloth thinks charges of manslaughter are not inappropriate: "You have given him the bullet, which he shot himself with. You gave him the loaded gun and said: pull the trigger."

According to Associated Press Dr. Arnold (Arnie) Klein threw things into turmoil at the day's start of Monday's pivotal hearing on Michael Jackson's affairs, this time concerning the worked out child-custody arrangements between Katherine Jackson and Michael's ex-wife Debbie Row. While Los Angeles Superior Court Judge Mitchell Beckloff did approve Katherine Jackson's permanent guardianship petition for Prince Michael, Paris Michael, and Prince Michael II, as well as a bid by Debbie Rowe to have regular visitation with her two children with Michael, the Beverly Hills dermatologist, raised what were described as "nonspecific objections" to the custody arrangements. Dr. Klein's lawyer said the objections were based on the doctor's long-term relationship with Michael and his three children.

Mark Vincent Kaplan, Dr. Klein's attorney, said: "Legally, he is not a presumed parent." Mark Vincent explained that as a friend, Dr. Klein had serious concerns about the children's education and other parenting issues. The judge dismissed the concerns and said Dr. Klein did not have a legal basis to object to the arrangement agreed to by attorneys for Katherine Jackson and Debbie Rowe. The judge also said Dr. Klein could raise another objection later if he wished.

Katherine, who was reportedly being supported by Michael at the time of his death, was also granted a financial allowance for six months retroactive to the day her son died. The amount was not specified in court. The judge told Debbie Rowe that she will have unspecified visitation rights and continue getting the same amount of spousal support she has been getting based on an agreement reached with Michael several years ago.

According to reporter Jill Kaufman, it is no wonder the administrators of Michael's estate are planning to roll out tons of merchandise to cash in. Jill wrote on MTV.com: "The details of the multiple deals were redacted in the 500-plus-page court filing that was made public on Tuesday at a hearing in which Jackson's mother withdrew her bid to become one of the administrators of his estate." The article further read: "Among the known deals is the $60 million (£ 36.6 million) pact with Columbia Pictures to make a feature-length movie out of the more than 100 hours of high-definition footage of rehearsals for Jackson's planned *This Is It* 50-date residency at the O2 arena in London. Jackson's estate would receive 90 percent of the profit from the film, with the remainder going to concert promoter AEG Live. There are also plans for a soundtrack, a director's-cut DVD, two special editions of the film after its theatrical run and a stipulation that Branca and McClain can produce at least one tribute concert as long as the broadcast doesn't interfere with the film rollout." There are also plans to produce a wide variety of Jackson-related memorabilia. These include photo books, buttons, live recordings on USB drives, online games, trading cards, lithographs and even denim and high-end clothing. According to the administrators of Michael's estate, there are also proposals for accessories for VR worlds like Second Life and Stardoll, embossed wine decanters, wallpaper and screensavers for cell phones, theme packs for the XBox, tattoos, a traveling *MJ Exhibition* of memorabilia from the late singer to be shown at museums and more.

Actor Rupert Everett thinks it's 'fortuitous' that Michael died. He said: "Michael can finally be at peace now he is dead." He told the Daily Mirror: "He was a freak. He looked like a character from Shrek. He was a black to white minstrel. He personified the pain and anxiety of a black man in a slave country. We all watched as he changed from black to white. He was living performance art. Rupert is convinced the star was unable to lead a normal life because he was hounded by photographers." He said about the concerts in London: "It wouldn't have mattered how good or bad he was. He wouldn't have managed to do all of them and the press would have destroyed him."

The exact location of Michael's body at Forest Lawn Memorial Park is to be kept secret from fans. "The fear is that thousands of Jackson fans will descend on the cemetery and create a security issue or maybe even damage or deface the grave," a source who works at Forest Lawn Memorial Park said. It was originally thought that Michael would be buried near the grave of his grandmother Martha Bridges, who died in 1990. According to The Mirror, Michael's family could move the body of Michael if its security is put in jeopardy. A cemetery source said: "Michael has already been laid to rest, but other than the Jackson family and the management at Forest Lawn, no one knows the exact spot. Staff at the cemetery have been fed several different locations, it's as if they are hoping to confuse everyone so it can't leak out."

Former child actor Mark Lester, 51, told reporters that he may be the father of Michael's daughter Paris. The Jackson family spokesman Brian Oxman told morning show GMTV he denied those claims. He said that Michael may have given Lester, his good friend, the impression that he was the father but that was not in fact the case. Brian said that he heard from Michael that he was the father of these children, and he said he believed Michael. "Mark Lester is a very straight shooter, an honest man and when he describes the process by which he was asked to make a donation of sperm, I believe every word he says. Michael Jackson always told me he was the biological father, so you have on one hand Mark saying he might be, and Michael saying he might be - so you have the question, who the daddy is. Mark always told the truth and I believe he is telling us straight right now. There was nobody who was closer to Michael Jackson and his family than Mark Lester and his children. He was the godfather and his children played with Prince, Paris and Blanket. Michael promised him it would always be that kind of relationship, so I understand he is very upset."

Brian Oxman fears Mark will struggle to convince a judge to order a paternity test to prove he fathered Michael's daughter because California law forbids it. Californian laws protect children from questioning their parentage if they are born to a married couple. Any paternity issues need to be addressed within two years of birth. Brian told

GMTV: "If there were a request for a paternity test the judge would have to waive the law in the state of California, which says that a child born to a man and a woman who are married is conclusively presumed to be the child of that married couple - unless the paternity test is requested within two years of the birth of the child." He also said: "So the result would be on the late side but it's up to a judge to make that decision. So in the Michael Jackson case I say, 'Anything is possible'. I think this is one of the most extraordinary cases I've seen." Lester has already offered to take a paternity test to discover if he really is biologically related to Michael's daughter. The Oliver! star told the News Of The World on August 9, that he had donated sperm to Michael as a "gift" in 1996 and further revealed that he felt a "definite bonding" with Michael's daughter Paris. He is godfather to Michael's three children Prince Michael, 12, Paris, 11, and seven-year-old Prince Michael II, aka Blanket. But lawyers for the Jackson camp slammed the claims. Attorney Londell McMillan said: "These are just merely claims with no legal standing whatsoever." Michael's former friend Uri Geller insisted that Lester was telling the truth and vowed to continue supporting him. Earlier, the famous TV psychic claimed that he had predicted Michael's death after noticing the "devastating" effects of his alleged drug habit. Uri said: "As a close friend of Mark, I respect his own situation to reveal this information at this time. I knew it all along simply because Michael told me. Mark has his own reasons. I really have to respect them." A family insider of Michael said: "They twisted his words around. He's not claiming to be the father of Paris Jackson." Lester admitted he only came forward with the revelations because he feels Katherine, Michael's mother, has cut him out of the kids' lives since their father died.

According to TMZ, there is an all-star tribute in the make. The remake of the late pop singer's *Will You Be There* will reportedly feature vocals from Usher, Wyclef Jean, Jermaine Jackson, Whitney Houston, Lionel Richie and Dionne Warwick. John Mayer was said to be participating in the remake, but his spokesperson told MTV News that TMZ's report was false. This effort is reportedly being led by Shawn King, wife of TV talker Larry King. She will also lend her vocals to the song. Larry told TMZ his wife is not yet sure if Jennifer Hudson could participate in the tribute because she has just given birth to her first child. Proceeds from the song shall be split 50/50 between the Larry King Cardiac Foundation and an unspecified charity close to Michael. The New York Post reported that Shawn King, Whitney Houston, Madonna and President Barack Obama will not participate in a global tribute by Michael's brother Jermaine. According to The Associated Press, the tribute is being planned for September 26 on a crown-shaped stage at the Schoenbrunn Palace in Vienna, Austria.

The lineup for the three-hour show will reportedly feature around 10 major entertainers who will perform 15 to 20 of Jackson's hits. Jermaine Jackson said the site was chosen because his brother "loved castles". The show will be called *Michael Jackson: The Tribute*. Jermaine Jackson and his mother have asked Michael's former manager, Ron Weisner, to produce the show. Ron told TMZ he expects 100,000 people to attend and said the tribute will become a TV show. Katherine who loved the idea of a tribute said in a written statement: "I am overwhelmed by the worldwide sympathy that my beloved son Michael has received over the past month. It is a difficult time for my family and I, as you probably understand. When Jermaine told me about the *Save The World*

Awards in Austria, at which he received a special honor on behalf of Michael, and about his plan to hold a tribute on September 26th for his brother in Vienna, I immediately found this a wonderful idea because of Michael's influence and impact around the world. An event of this dimension not only keeps Michael's spirit alive, more than that: It gives millions of fans the opportunity to experience his music and celebrate the life of my son. I am sure Michael would love it. It makes me very happy to know that this special event will be seen around the world and give all his fans a chance to be with Michael and his timeless music once again. I fully support Jermaine's endeavors to spread Michael's important message of making a better world for us all."

The promoter of this concert Georg Kindel of World Awards Media GmbH told AP that the tribute concert would be broadcast live to 1 billion people. He also said negotiations were ongoing with networks over rights to broadcast what's being billed as Michael's main global tribute. Jermaine was assembling the lineup of about 10 "of the biggest artists of our time". Georg told a reporter of The Associated Press: "It will be a very special evening for the millions of fans around the globe." He wouldn't divulge the cast. Austrian media have reported that Whitney Houston, Lionel Richie and also U2 may perform. He added: "I don't even know myself, who will take the stage! It will be about Michael Jackson the man and the humanitarian. Everyone was expecting it would be staged maybe in London or New York or Los Angeles." He further revealed that a "significant portion" of the proceeds will benefit several charities, including the Larry King Cardiac Foundation, which helps patients who can't afford heart surgery. The tribute was originally planned for London's Wembley Stadium on Aug. 29, which would have been Jackson's 51st birthday. Jermaine Jackson decided instead on Vienna. Georg Kindel told The Associated Press: "Jermaine said he visited the beautiful place in Vienna and was really fascinated. Jermaine said: 'This is a really royal and ideal place for such a tribute to Michael.'" He said that the place where the big memorial was held last month was different from the majestic yellow palace, its sprawling and sculpted gardens. "You can't compare it with a real historic palace which was built hundreds of years ago. This is not Disneyland. There's a zoo, there are parks... I think (Michael Jackson) would like the site. It's a little bit like Neverland, but much bigger," he said in his office in Vienna.

A weary-looking Dr. Conrad Murray, the former personal physician to Michael who was under investigation for his part in the King of Pop's death posted a one-minute video to YouTube with a message for his friends, patients and other supporters, saying "I have done all I could do". The doctor who had claimed he was delayed in making an emergency call because phones in the house did not work, referred to his two interviews with Los Angeles police detectives. It was the first time Dr. Murray had spoken publicly since Michael died, June 25. A solemn-sounding Dr. Murray, suspected of giving Michael the dangerous sedative Propofol, said as he looked into the camera: "I told the truth and I have faith the truth will prevail. Because of all that is going on, I am afraid to return phone calls or use my e-mail. I recorded this video to let all of you know that I have been receiving your messages... Your messages give me strength and courage and keep me going. They mean the world to me." Miranda Sevcik, the spokeswoman for Dr. Murray's lawyer said the video was recorded at a private residence in Houston. She said that after Michael died, Dr. Murray received death threats and hired a body guard. He was forced into seclusion at his Las Vegas home and had received many calls from patients, former patients and strangers offering him support. Dr. Murray had not worked since Michael's death and had closed his Las Vegas practice. He was already in dire financial shape when he signed on with Michael at $150,000 (£91,500) a month, owing at least $780,000 (£476,000) in judgments and outstanding payments. The spokeswoman said the only reason, the doctor made the video was to address supporters. He had told her he missed being able to work. She added: "He says he wants to get back to work, he really does genuinely care about the people he works with. He has to just wait, he's in limbo." But according to Gregory D. Lee, a retired supervisory agent with the Drug Enforcement Agency, Dr. Murray only wanted to improve his image. "This doctor has been demonized. This is an attempt to humanize him and possibly sway any potential jury pool out there," Lee said.

As officers from the Drug Enforcement Administration (DEA) have continued to dig deeper into Dr. Murray's history, trying to solve the mystery surrounding Michael's death. Dr. Murray's attorney Ed Chernoff insisted his client had no idea about what Michael was addicted to or what he was taking for his habits. He told the Los Angeles Times: "When he accepted the job, he was not aware of any specific requirements regarding medications that Michael Jackson was taking or any addictions that he was suffering from." CNN reported that the medic did not conduct drug tests on Michael and only knew of drugs he had been prescribed from the singer himself. Attorney Ed Chernoff added Dr. Murray only "realized that Michael Jackson had some very unusual problems" after he moved into the singer's Holmby Hills, California mansion in May. Dr. Murray has admitted he put the legend on a drip containing the drug Propofol. He also told cops, he set it up to give 25 milligrams to help Michael sleep. The News of the World reported that Dr. Murray's legal team will claim Michael reset the machine controlling the drip, increasing the dosage which led to the heart attack that killed him.

Michael's 51st birthday has sparked several celebrations across the world. Cities around the world celebrated the King of Pop with gatherings honoring Michael's musical legacy. On August 29, thousands of Mexicans claimed they broke the record for most people dancing to *Thriller*, on what would have been Michael Jackson's 51st birthday. Organizer Javier Hildago shouted to thousands of people wearing white gloves, black fedoras and aviator shades: "We did it!" He claimed 12,937 people danced in front of Mexico City's Monument of the Revolution, led by a Michael Jackson impersonator wearing a red-and-gold sequined jacket. The Guinness Book of World Records will decide in a week if the record is broken. The current record was set in May by a group of 242 College of William & Mary students. According to Guinness they performed the routine in Williamsburg, Virginia. In Mexico, the impersonator Hector Jackson said: "More people responded than we even imagined! Mexico gave the best tribute in the world to Michael Jackson."

Rock Daily previously reported, "Michael was originally supposed to be laid to rest at the Forest Lawn Great Mausoleum in Glendale, California on August 29th, but instead the burial was ultimately pushed to Thursday, September 3rd." The worldwide celebrations were slightly clouded by news Friday that Michael's death had been ruled a homicide.

In Hongkong hundreds of young people were on the streets doing their *Thriller* dance wearing baseball caps, miniskirts and T-shirts. In Trafalgar Square in London, a group of people wearing white 'suits' and hundreds of followers were trying to do the *Thriller* moves. The event that started at noon was called, *Thriller Zombie Dance Event*. Originally promoted as an attempt to set a new record for the most people doing the *Thriller* dance simultaneously, it has since changed to simply a celebration.

    In Hannover, Germany, a group of people wearing white sport shoes, were dancing on the streets on Michael's hit *Beat It* and so were thousands of people in Paris, France. They danced inside the Central Station of Paris. In Bucharest, people danced in the middle of the streets on *Beat It*. In East Germany, people were dancing in front of the Hauptbahnhof on *Beat It* and so were hundreds of people in Munchen, Germany. But also in Hamburg, people were dancing on *Beat It* in the middle of the streets. Young kids, some not even older then 10 years old, were watching and trying to copy what others were doing. In Bremen, Germany, one dancer started off by himself and was followed by many others when *Beat It* started.

    In Tubingen, Germany, people had been dancing on July 24, on the Neckarbrucke, on *Beat It*, wearing mostly white shirts and blue jeans. Hundreds of exciting and screaming fans enjoyed a show in Moscow, Russia. Again, a huge crowd of people started crawling on the street before they all stood up and danced together on *Thriller*. Some really looked creepy wearing old clothes, make-up and black hats. Hundreds of screaming and shouting people were watching the show.

    A dance tribute in Stockholm took already place on July 8. When Michael's music started, people looked up to see were the music came from. They couldn't believe their eyes when they saw over two hundred people dancing on *Beat It*. The same song *Beat It* was played at 11 o'clock in the evening. In the middle of the streets, more then hundred people stopped the traffic to dance.

People had danced in Paris at the Opera, at Les Halles, at Gare De Lyon, at Trocadero, and under the Eiffel Tower. People had danced in TaiChung, and on Ximen Plaza in Taipei, Taiwan, they danced on the Museum Square, the Dam Square and Leidseplein in Amsterdam, The Netherlands (even without any music they performed the *Thriller* dance). In Hollywood people gathered for a *Beat It* dance, and Spike Lee hosted a special Brooklyn style bash called Spike Lee & The Great Borough of Brooklyn, The Source, for Michael. His celebration was going to be held originally in Fort Greene Park, but was moved to Prospect Park, which was better suited to accommodate the anticipated crowd of 10,000. The Reverend Al Sharpton offered the prayer and DJ Spinna provided the music. Spike said he hoped to make the "joyous, festive and celebratory" Prospect Park Party an annual event. Reporter Jennifer Armstrong wrote for Popwatch: "Fans have clearly gotten to acceptance, and perhaps to a sixth stage of grief, partying. It felt like a truly joyous (and endearingly amateurish) celebration of Michael Jackson's enormous influence, with none of the disbelief and sadness and even soul-searching (what did his bizarre life say about us as a society?) that weighed on earlier commemorations. Toddlers decorated a black umbrella with puffy paint that spelled out 'MJ Forever.' Electric Slide pockets erupted spontaneously throughout the crowd. Naturally, people sold things — homemade T-shirts, framed pictures, sunglasses with Jackson's birth and death years etched onto the side (why not?). And naturally, people dressed in, shall we say, homage to the star. (Sparkly socks? Nice. Guy in full

Jackson regalia, including black suit, white glove, penny loafers, fedora, curls, white pancake makeup, and fake entourage with umbrella-holder? A little much.) Despite the oddities, however, the crowd remained almost eerily peaceful and patient and friendly, content simply to listen to Jackson tunes, dance together, and occasionally participate in sing-alongs and call-and-response as led by Lee and organizers from a bare-bones stage set-up. Aside from the self-appointed souvenir hawkers, there were no food and drink booths, no official vendors. 'There's nothing here except peace and love,' a fellow fan, Manhattanite Erin Carlson, marveled. And she was right, as hippie-ish as it sounds. It was nice to know that Jackson's music is still bringing folks together, spreading joy despite the dark, sad parts of his life. Even on a rainy day in Brooklyn."

According to the BBC, Michael's childhood home of Gary, Indiana, held a street party, while fans flocked to Michael's Neverland Ranch and his star on the Hollywood Walk of Fame in California.

Erich Bergen, from the Las Vegas production *Jersey Boys* and freelance journalist Steve Friess teamed to produce *Las Vegas Celebrates the Music of Michael Jackson* in The Pearl Concert Theater in the Palms. Erich Bergen told ReviewJournal.com: "If we can concentrate for at least two hours on the art that he did, I think we'll be better off." Tickets were available from $29 up to $504. ReviewJournal.com reported that Vincent Paterson, who "played the white gangster in the *Beat It* video" and directed the video for *Smooth Criminal* was expected to attend the show.

The Black Entertainment Television network had produced several documentary pieces on Michael that had run throughout the weekend of his 51st birthday. The one-hour special included interviews with Liz Taylor, Quincy Jones, Michael's sister Janet and brother and Jermaine, and Brooke Shields. The special chronicles his career as a young performer both as a member of The Jackson 5 and as a solo artist. Another -two-hour- documentary, called *Michael Jackson History: The King of Pop*, showcased rare footage from a 1980s interview that had not been seen for 25 years. The segment included interviews with Latoya and Jermaine Jackson, Quincy Jones, and thoughts from Princess Diana and former President Nelson Mandela. A program called, Our Icon, went behind the scenes of a 2007 cover shoot for Ebony Magazine. It featured a star-studded tribute from several insiders, including *This Is It* Music Tour Director Michael Bearden, Brian McKnight, Questlove, and Ebony Magazine staff.

On Nokia Theatre Times Square, New York, frontman of A Tribe Called Quest paid tribute at 10 p.m. to Michael at an event. The event featured Grammy award-winning producer and artist Mark Ronson, and DJ Spinna. Michael's former labels Motown and Sony had supplied Q-Tip with rare video footage to play at the celebration. Q-Tip said in a statement: "Michael Jackson was a huge influence on my music and was an inspiration to me and so many others. I want to bring people together to celebrate the man, his music and his legacy that will undoubtedly live on forever!" The Grammy award-winning rap star already dedicated his weekly "Open" party at Santos Party House to Michael, the weekend he died. Sean 'Diddy' Combs told MTV: "The hottest DJ in the game right now is Q-Tip. That right there is a DJ playing, taking you on a mind-traveling experience."

The annual *Thrill The World* extravaganza coordinates a global *Thriller* dance in October. Last year, the festivities drew participation from 4,179 people at 72 events in 71 cities. This years' event will be held on Saturday, October 24, the weekend prior to Halloween.

According to a new press report Janet Jackson, the iconic sister of Michael was going to pay tribute to her brother on September 30 at the Music of Black Origin Awards. The event organizers have asked the singer to appear at the show in Glasgow, Scotland. The Daily Star quoted a spokesperson for the MOBOs as saying: "Janet is a music icon in her own right and a previous MOBO presenter. We loved her past involvement with the show and MOBO will continue to support her music and champion her career. Michael Jackson was a key catalyst and influence on the culture, lifestyle and music that MOBO supports and represents. His sound, style and dance moves have inspired subsequent generations of pop, soul, R&B and hip-hop artists. Artists such as Usher, Ne-Yo and Justin Timberlake often cite Michael Jackson as their inspiration and it is key that we commemorate his life, achievements and legacy."

Sony Pictures confirmed Oct. 30 as the release date for Michael's *This Is It* movie, which documents the King of Pop's final concert rehearsal. *This Is It* will offer certain sequences in 3-D, along with interviews with friends and creative collaborators. The Estate of Michael Jackson supports the film which is produced from hundreds of hours of rehearsal and behind-the-scenes footage captured in high definition. Rob Stringer, Chairman of Columbia/Epic Label Group, said in a statement: "Michael lives on through his songs, his creative genius, his body of work and his passion for his art. He was a perfectionist on stage and through this unique film, audiences will be able to see, many for the first time, how much Michael poured into making his performances as special as they were perfect." The statement further said: "*This Is It* will offer Jackson fans and music lovers worldwide a rare, behind-the-scenes look at the performer, his career, and the stage spectacular that would have been. The film will provide moviegoers with an unforgettable front row experience compiled from extensive footage that shows Jackson's meticulous preparation for his 2009 London shows." Most of the footage was shot in June, 2009 at Staples Center in Los Angeles, California. Sony spent $60 million (£36.6 million) dollars acquiring the rights to the last footage of Michael Jackson. According to press reports, Sony is putting tickets on sale a month early, looking to generate a sense of scarcity and excitement. Sony pushed the film's start date forward two days. The film will open on Wednesday October 28. A&E was reportedly moving forward with a one-hour reality show about the Jackson brothers. The show could be used as a pilot to launch a series. The brothers already filmed a pilot before Michael died.

Michael Jackson was buried on September 3, instead of August 29 as originally planned. The family released a statement: "The burial will be at Holly Terrace in The Great Mausoleum at Glendale Forest Lawn Memorial Park in Glendale, Calif., and will be limited to family and close friends."

Katherine Jackson had filed legal papers and asked the judge in the Jackson probate case to have the estate pay for the burial. But it had been confirmed that lawyers for the estate will neither support nor oppose the motion. They said it was up to the judge to make a decision.

According to TMZ: "If Dr. Murray is charged with a crime, there's a statement in the affidavit that could be evidence of a consciousness of guilt. The document also states both 'UCLA doctors and L.A. Fire Department Paramedics stated that Dr. Murray had only disclosed that he had given the medication Lorazepam [Ativan] to Jackson prior to his medical emergency.' Dr. Murray did not disclose that he had given Jackson Propofol." Michael's death certificate had been amended, listing his fatal injury as "intravenous injection by another." Michael's main cause of death was "acute Propofol intoxication." The presence of multiple anxiety and insomnia medications in his system was a contributing factor. A police affidavit showed that Dr. Murray told cops he injected Michael with Propofol right before he died.

The report said: "Other conditions contributing to death: 'Benzodiazepine effect'." The manner of death was ruled: 'HOMICIDE'. The full autopsy report was not released by the Coroner. Instead there was a press notice: "The drugs Propofol and Lorazepam (Ativan) were found to be the primary drugs responsible for Mr. Jackson's death. Other drugs detected were: Midazolam (Versed), Diazepam (Valium), Lidocaine (topical anesthetic) and Ephedrine (used to treat hypotension associated with anesthesia)." The family of Michael released a statement: "The Jackson family again wishes to commend the actions of the Coroner, the LAPD and other law enforcement agencies, and looks forward to the day that justice can be served."

TMZ also reported: "Michael Jackson's family will be rolling to his funeral tonight in style -- because they've got themselves a fleet of Rolls Royce Phantoms for the event. United Royal Coach confirms they'll be picking up immediate family members at the Jackson Encino compound this afternoon -- and will deliver 'em to Forest Lawn in five stretch Phantoms. We're told Katherine and Joe will ride in the first vehicle. Since the family members are regular customers, they even got 'em at a reduced rate, which no doubt helped lower the already "extraordinary" burial costs." TMZ also reported: "The Jackson family has an after-party scheduled to begin right after Michael Jackson's funeral tonight, a party they're calling a 'Celebration of Life'." The article said: "The family will go straight from the Forest Lawn cemetery in Glendale to a place called Villa Sorriso Ristorante, an Italian joint in Pasadena. The restaurant's Executive Director of Operations has confirmed that Randy Jackson made the reservation several days ago and "bought out the facility for the night". The exec also tells us several members of the Jackson family have been regulars at the place for years. We're told the restaurant is expecting more than 150 people to attend."

Michael was interred in the cemetery's Great Mausoleum, alongside stage and screen luminaries from the past century. Forest Lawn is the final resting place of many of the biggest Hollywood names, including Humphrey Bogart, Theda Barret, W.C. Fields and Walt Disney.

Janet Jackson had written on Twitter, just before her brother was buried: "Hangin' out with my babies Rocky n Bullwinkle while writing songs for the new project. I'm really looking forward to chairing the amfAR Milano event this September! I want u guys to check them out n support them any way u can. There's more to come and it's important that u guys get EVERYTHING 1st! I love you!!!" She also left a little note for her brother Michael: "I love you, Mike, and I miss you. Dunk."

Acknowledgments

I would like to thank many people for their help to get this book published in such a short time. First, thanks to my family members and especially my father Cor, my mother Roos, my brother Ton, and my sisters Annemieke and Irene for all their help and support while writing this book. A deep appreciation from the bottom of my heart to UP Publishing, Dan Poynter and Danny O. Snow for their endless patience, inspiration, their trust, their professional support and critics. I would also like to thank deeply Debra Shaw, Uncle Henk, Ans en Ton Neus, Michelle Janssen, Marcel Gonzalez-Ortiz, Peter Aardoom, Angelique Stekelmans, Bianca Papen, Henk and Gré de Boer, Kim Kuijpers, Dennis van Doorn, Bart Brom, Hester Goldberg, Cynthia de Graaff, Joost Claes, Henny Ferket, Family Poelen, Reinder Smid, Josephine Oudijn, and of course Uri Geller for their inspiration and believe in this adventure, and all others that are not named here but have supported me throughout the years. Without the *loving* hearts of others, this book would have not been what it is today.

Jos Borsboom
09/09/2009

About the Author

Jos Borsboom (born November 14, 1968) worked internationally as a fashion photographer, film director and film producer for more then 20 years and is well acquainted with the ups and downs of the entertainment business. He was born and raised in The Netherlands and lived in Italy, France, Germany, Spain and the U.S..